FRAN PORTER was born in England and has lived in Northern Ireland for the past twenty years. She has a BA in theology, and an MSc and PhD in Women's Studies. She lives in Belfast, and works as a freelance researcher and teacher.

Changing Women, Changing Worlds

Evangelical Women in Church, Community and Politics

FRAN PORTER

THE
BLACKSTAFF
PRESS

BELFAST

This project was funded by the Joseph Rowntree Charitable Trust and this publication received grant support from the International Fund for Ireland – Community Bridges Programme, which aims to support groups and organisations that promote greater dialogue and understanding and tackle issues of division between people from different cultures and religious traditions within Ireland.

INTERNATIONAL FUND FOR IRELAND

First published in 2002 by
Blackstaff Press Limited
Wildflower Way, Apollo Road
Belfast BT12 6TA, Northern Ireland
and the Centre for Contemporary Christianity in Ireland
Howard House, 1 Brunswick Street
Belfast BT2 7GE, Northern Ireland

Typeset by Techniset Typesetters, Newton-le-Willows, Merseyside

Printed in Ireland by Betaprint

A CIP catalogue for this book is available from the British Library

ISBN 08564-717-8

www.blackstaffpress.com
www.econi.org

The Centre for Contemporary Christianity in Ireland
is a ministry of ECONI

Jesus said,
'Let anyone with ears to hear listen!'

Contents

Acknowledgements

This book is about the participation of evangelical women in church, community and politics. It comes out of a project conducted under the auspices of the Centre for Contemporary Christianity in Ireland as part of its ongoing work to research and reflect on the ways evangelicals engage with the society in which they live.

Evangelical women's involvement in church and society raises a number of questions faced by many women in their lives and work, and also some aspects that relate more specifically to evangelical faith and practice. This book explores these questions of participation, inclusion, difference, authority, domesticity, and priority. Using the stories and words of women involved in church, community and politics, and those of male church leaders, it examines these questions and considers their implications for women themselves, for men, churches, evangelicalism and civic society. I hope it will be of interest and value not only for the evangelical community both in Northern Ireland and elsewhere, but for all who seek a better understanding of the gender relations operating in society and church.

Based on extensive interviews with women active in church, community and politics and with male church leaders, my thanks are due, first and foremost, to the seventy women and ten men who spent time with me talking about their lives and work and their thoughts on these questions. It is not an unknown experience to talk occasionally to individuals about things that matter as much as this. However, it is an extraordinary one to be able to do so with so many people and especially with women who are so acutely situated in the matter of their own selves. The time spent in this endeavour was personally energising for me and invaluable for the project as our conversations served to affirm again and again the need to focus on the question of women.

As an empirically based project, my aim was to incorporate the voices of the interviewees by way of illustration and argument. What may be stated analytically can be brought to life vividly by the experiences and words of actual people in a way that is more accessible to a reader. While not all who took part may agree with my analysis, I have endeavoured to be true to the context and intent of their stories and viewpoints as originally given to me. As researcher, I have worked not simply with the sound of one voice, but a whole chorus of voices and stories that build together into the overall picture I present here.

My thanks are due to many others who contributed to the various stages of the project. The Joseph Rowntree Charitable Trust provided not only the financial resources to carry out the research, but also gave encouragement and support. In this regard thanks from myself and the Centre are due particularly to Stephen Pittam for his valuable endorsement of our endeavour. We would also like to thank the International Fund for Ireland – Community Bridges Programme for helping to fund the final publication.

David Porter, Cecelia Clegg and Lis Porter played an invaluable role in forming the project concept and helping me to write the project proposal. The project was further aided by an advisory group made up of Cecelia Clegg, William Crawley, David Livingstone, Heather Morris and Carmel Roulston.

During the life of the project I had the companionship of two research assistants who were responsible for the transcription work involved. At the beginning of the project Caroline Chambers gave her friendship, intelligently engaging with the issues while carrying out the transcription work and providing administrative support. In the latter stages of the project Sarah Parkinson, who also had excellent transcribing skills, immersed herself in the intense experience of living with a constant stream of voices and stories in order to keep the project to its timetable.

It was my pleasure to get to know the staff and volunteers at ECONI during my time as project consultant to the Centre for Contemporary Christianity in Ireland. In particular I would like to thank David Porter, Derek Poole, and Alwyn Thomson for initiating the project, fostering its development, and providing help and reference at various stages. Lynda Gould's companionship and help and her enthusiasm for and affirmation of the project was more important to me than perhaps she realises. I also want to record my gratitude to Claire Martin for her graciousness and technical expertise and to Jacqui Livingstone whose efficiency and professionalism never diminished the warmth of her welcome.

For skilfully steering the book to published form I am grateful to the staff at Blackstaff Press.

And finally, as ever, my thanks and love to David, who has always understood that I too am unable to stand outside the question of women.

FRAN PORTER
BELFAST, APRIL 2002

Foreword

In a country where the Christian faith has had such enormous influence, it is vital that we reflect on how that faith is to be lived today. For Christian witness and response does not stand still. In each era and generation we fight new battles for the truth which is in Christ, and that very task draws us into new biblical insights. The important thing, however, is to fight the battles of today. Whenever we are tempted to regurgitate yesterday's issues, and remain trapped in yesterday's dilemmas, we nudge the church ever more firmly into the museum culture. The depressing thing about the museum culture is that it does not greatly affect the mindset and attitudes of our day. Those outside the faith will not stay awake at night worrying about the message we proclaim. For a museum is simply full of relics and bygone customs – interesting certainly, and producing nostalgia and even affection in some. But once it occupies this status, the church is increasingly seen as largely irrelevant to the issues and concerns which occupy real people in the twenty-first century.

Within the culture outside the church, the issue about women's inclusion in the full life of the community has long been settled, in the area of work and leadership at least. In education, girls outstrip boys in every subject in the secondary school curriculum. The theoretical arguments have been long concluded, and there is little real debate about the relative ability of each sex in the professions or business arena. This is not to say that the practical outworking has all been achieved; for some time we will be seeing women still having to struggle and maybe resort to the courts to obtain what is legally theirs. In many other areas, however, women experience much less real freedom, as many of our contemporary writers tell us. The incidence of violence towards women is as high as it ever has been, with sexual violence forming a significant proportion of that. The issue of body-image also affects many young women, with eating disorders now reaching epidemic proportions. These do not indicate a culture which has yet found a healthy response to issues of gender and sexuality.

Into this context, the church could be making a wonderful contribution: demonstrating how the Gospel of Jesus Christ is in every sense *Good News* for women. It could be living out the picture of unity and inclusion which St Paul speaks of in his letters to the early Christians. It could be modelling the mutual respect, mutual gifting, and mutual service which women and men in the New Testament church offered to God. Sadly, the opposite is often the case. Far too many churches seem committed to restricting women rather than releasing them into a fully Christian lifestyle. Rather than searching the Scriptures together to make sure that what the church practises is truly biblical, there is all too often a refusal to face the issues head-on, and a hope that they will simply go away.

Fran Porter's book, *Changing Women, Changing Worlds*, is a timely reminder that the church's decline is wrapped up with the way it connects or fails to connect with the lives of so many of the population. The study itself is well researched and well presented. But the author goes the extra mile. In deciding to incorporate interviews with seventy women and ten men, she gives us an insight into the impact that these questions have on ordinary Christians and the way they live. The book is thoughtful, analytic, balanced, detailed, sensitive and faithful. Fran does not overstate her case nor labour its urgency, although it is indeed urgent. Nor does she censor those comments from women who are feeling profoundly depressed about the church. When one of her interviewees comments, the 'male dominated elderly world of the church is not going anywhere very fast ... It's not living out gospel values, it isn't being a good example of anything to people outside of the church, it's not making us effective and it isn't cutting ice at local level', the author simply reports it, and leaves it with us.

My hope is that this book will be read carefully and its arguments and findings will be carefully considered. I hope that it will find a warm response from the Christian community in Northern Ireland and be received not only as a challenge for the present but encouragement for the future. It is my belief that if we take seriously what Fran Porter has shown us, we will all be more effective in our outreach to others and better equipped to serve Christ in our generation.

ELAINE STORKEY
CAMBRIDGE, MARCH 2002

1

The Question of Women

Women are highly involved in churches in Northern Ireland. Not only do more women than men actually attend church services, but they sustain much of the ongoing work of congregational life. Women also make up the majority of those involved in the community activism that has been a feature of Northern Ireland society over the past three decades. And women participate in political life, their contribution having been given more focus in the peace process of recent years.

All of this activism has been occurring at a time of enormous social change in the lives of women over the past fifty years. Many women are no longer occupied solely with the domestic world of home and family. Changes in educational, employment and economic opportunities, an emphasis on equality for women in social and public institutions, and a recognition of the need for legislation to safeguard women's rights, however imperfectly realised, both reflect and contribute to women's greater involvement in the world outside of the home.

Given this background of women's high community and church participation in a context of social change, what is the contribution of evangelical women to civic life in Northern Ireland? How are they now involved not only in their churches, but in the wider society? What are the issues they face in taking greater participation in public processes? How as Christians do they make sense of the changes in the society in which they live? And what are the implications of all of this for evangelicalism? These questions are the concerns of this book.

Such issues are of great interest to many people, but to raise them also causes disquiet. The way evangelicals relate to society is intrinsically bound up with matters of faith. And in an age increasingly finding it difficult to relate to Christianity, to raise the subject of women can appear threatening to evangelicalism. Indeed for some, the social changes of recent decades are 'the sort of thing that has changed the world, and ... turned everything upside down – all the values that we've always respected'.[1] It is useful, therefore, to begin by looking at the way evangelicalism approaches the question of women and to consider the specific concerns that the subject raises. This provides a background to looking at the six specific questions around women's participation covered in the following chapters.

Evangelicalism and Women

For the most part, evangelicalism tends not to give overt attention to gender. While there is some focus in local churches on women as wives and mothers, most evangelical writing does not place a consideration of gender centre stage. When the subject of women does occur, this is frequently by treating the matter as an 'issue' facing Christians. When women are given a focus, there is an emphasis on biblical interpretation and a concern about evangelical unity. Before exploring each of these ways that evangelicalism approaches the subject of women, it is important to say a word about the term 'gender'.

A WORD ABOUT GENDER

Why have a book about women and then talk about gender? To talk about gender is to acknowledge that humanity is both female and male, to recognise that cultural expectations about the attributes and behaviours of women and men affect the way we experience the world in which we live, and to give attention to this reality. Used this way gender is differentiated from sex, which refers to biological distinction between women and men. Gender speaks of the way any given society believes women and men ought to be and should behave, that is, what is properly feminine and masculine. In many ways and in general usage the terms sex and gender are interchangeable because so much that descriptively may be to do with a person's biological sex is also to do with gender, that is, expectations about being female or male.

Lack of attention to gender usually has meant that much of women's lives and experiences have been ignored or become invisible because, in practice, a person whose sex is not specified has been presumed to be male. The use of 'he' in the generic form is an example of how the male is taken to be representative of women and men, as is the phrase 'the man in the street'. To talk of 'male church leaders' when speaking of the men interviewed in this book may be an unusual experience for men in church leadership who are used to being referred to simply as 'church leaders' in a male-dominated arena. However, in the context of this book it is important to distinguish between the comments of church leaders who are female and those who are male. Such matters are addressed throughout the book. For now the point is that speaking about gender is a way of giving focus to women's lives. While it is becoming more common today to have gender raised as relevant when thinking specifically about men, it more frequently occurs in relation to women. This is because, when gender is not given a focus, it is usually women who are invisible and suffer the resulting discrimination or exclusion. In other words, 'in general (as the record of history makes clear) women as a group suffer devaluation and injustice in gender relations more than men do'.[2]

This book focuses on women and in doing so explores their gendered reality. Consequently it is about the way women and men relate together on a personal and familial level and through social structures and institutions. Hence, it concerns not only women, but also men. Simply to talk about gender is not to presume a particular understanding of how gender is constructed and operates. Indeed it is the subject of much discussion, disagreement and controversy, as will be evident in this book. However, to talk of gender is to affirm that not paying due attention to the reality that humanity is female and male does a disservice to our understanding of ourselves and the way we function in our churches and wider society.

WOMEN AS A NON-QUESTION

In general, evangelical literature (about evangelicalism, evangelical theology, life as an evangelical, contemporary challenges to evangelicalism) is characterised by an absence of gender awareness. This omission is evident not only of gender as a hermeneutical perspective and analytical tool,[3] but also in the lack of content concerning issues to do with women and church leadership. For example, Stanley Grenz's revisioning of theology 'to articulate the biblical, evangelical vision in a manner that both upholds the heritage we embrace and speaks to the setting in which we seek to live as God's people'[4] makes no reference to gender or feminist contributions.[5] David Smith's exploration of the social impact of British evangelicalism concludes with a consideration of its future possibilities by outlining some of the important voices to be heard within the contemporary evangelical movement, but does not include women's or feminist voices.[6] The book that resulted from a North American Consultation on Evangelical Affirmations, an event focused on crucial issues facing evangelicals, does not include a contribution specifically related to women.[7] The Consultation Affirmations recorded in the book include a commitment to social justice and a need to respond to the victims of gender (and other forms of) discrimination. It does not, however, enlarge on this in the rest of the volume.

In other words, generally when evangelicalism addresses its own identity, shares its vision, and seeks to be relevant to society, it does not consider the significance of gender, the lived realities of being female and male, in these enterprises.

WOMEN AS AN 'ISSUE'

Part of the explanation for this absence of gender awareness is found in the way the subject of women is usually categorised within evangelicalism in that literature which does have specific content relating to women. This inclusion is usually through an issue-based approach in which women, their role and possible leadership are treated as one of the issues which contemporary evangelicalism faces (along with subjects such as spiritual gifts, the holy spirit, baptism, ecumenism, denominational identity, and social and political action). In this issue-based approach there is a tendency to categorise the 'issue' of women's role as being outside of the centre of evangelical gospel understanding, as secondary, *adiaphora* (matters indifferent),[8] marginalia[9] and is one reason why it is not included in many works concerned with evangelicalism, its definition, defence or unity.

Within the issue-based approach to considering women there is a tendency to set the issue in a negative context. The subject of women is dealt with as a 'contentious issue',[10] as one of the 'fracture points' within evangelicalism and a threat to evangelical unity,[11] and as an example of an issue on which evangelicals express dogmatism, a factor of 'the dark side of evangelicalism'.[12] This contributes to a usually unspoken understanding that to raise the question of women's place within evangelicalism is to be troublesome. This can be further reduced to the idea that women themselves are the problem. Indeed, one article on the ordination of women has a subsection entitled 'The Problem of Women's Leadership'.[13]

THE PLACE OF THE BIBLE

Within the literature that does consider women's role within evangelicalism there is a strong emphasis on understanding this primarily as an issue of biblical interpretation. The specific arguments of this debate are dealt with in chapter five. The concern at this point is with the way the Bible is used within evangelicalism to approach the subject of women.

David Bebbington places the differences in the 1970s over the ordination of women as part of the debate within evangelicalism concerning hermeneutics[14] that arose at the time.[15] Oliver Barclay also links the discussion on women's ministry to hermeneutics, and his comments also illustrate how a subject concerning women often is set in a negative context: 'Hermeneutics was unfortunately used by some to avoid what had been taken as the plain teaching of the Bible on women's ministry, homosexual practice and other issues ... Hermeneutics thus became a tool for mischief as well as for good.'[16]

This emphasis on biblical interpretation, however, conceals two important factors in any discussion concerning women. First, in placing the emphasis on hermeneutics, writers can set this *against* other considerations: 'The modern consensus is that the acceptance of women in ministry is a matter of both common sense and justice... Despite the pressure to restrict the debate to these terms, for evangelicals the central issue is biblical teaching, and in particular the significance of the Pauline letters.'[17] Apart from the unfortunate implication (presumably not intended) in the above quotation that a notion of justice is not a core concern of the Bible, the emphasis on hermeneutics sets any discussion in a framework primarily concerned with authority rather than a more positive and holistic consideration of women as people.[18] This is perhaps a logical consequence to viewing issues around women as controversy; in such a context some adjudication is required. While clearly within evangelicalism biblical authority is a defining factor and need not be understood negatively *per se*, the point here is that the framework of any discussion will influence and/or reflect the direction of any debate, but this is rarely acknowledged.

Another example of the significance of framework is evident in John Stott's discussion of the matter of women and church leadership.[19] He places his chapter on 'Women, Men and God' in his book's section on sexual issues (along with 'marriage and divorce', 'abortion and euthanasia', 'same-sex partnerships') rather than in the section on social issues in which he considers, among other things, economics and race. John Stott does discuss social changes and acknowledges the legitimacy of feminism's call for justice for women. However, his placing the discussion as a sexual rather than a social issue reflects the focus of his biblical interpretation which concerns a particular understanding of masculinity and femininity and not structural factors that affect relationships between people as in the case of his consideration of industrial relations and poverty.

The second factor hidden in the emphasis on hermeneutics is that, while biblical interpretation is presented as being the determining component of evangelicalism's view of women, this is in reality a partial truth. It conceals the fact that opinions concerning women are never, and never have been, purely a question of biblical interpretation. Speaking of attitudes towards women within nineteenth-century evangelicalism Jocelyn Murray comments:

If the opposition to women had been confined to the possibility of their ordination to the priesthood or to the formal ministry of a denomination, we might assert only that opposition arose out of biblical interpretation and ecclesiastical tradition. But the continuing opposition to *any* widening of women's roles brings us back to our contention that the concept of the 'ideal Christian woman', engaged humbly in restricted feminine service, also intervened.[20]

Wilard Swartley's *Slavery, Sabbath, War and Women* specifically explores how commentators' predispositions affect their biblical interpretation regarding each of these issues.[21] It is not, of course, possible to come to the biblical text with no *a priori* positions. Nor is it necessarily problematic to come with existing agendas. But in evangelical literature these pre-existing positions are frequently not acknowledged and, therefore, their influence on the debate or exegesis is usually denied under the guise of hermeneutics. When this happens, any debate potentially may fail to address issues appropriately.

EMPHASIS ON EVANGELICAL UNITY

Placing any discussion on women within evangelicalism as a secondary issue related to differing biblical interpretations is clearly understood to be a means of maintaining evangelical unity.[22] Secondary matters 'leave primary Christian truths intact... On these we must insist.'[23] Hence, despite the divisive and controversial nature of disagreements concerning women, some consider that 'nothing that divides evangelicals is at all significant in comparison with the cross that unites them'.[24] Where diverse understanding 'is clearly biblically grounded, evangelicals will have to learn to live with such disagreements'.[25] Appeals to 'give due respect to fellow evangelicals who have drawn from the Scriptures conclusions different to our own'[26] are expressed alongside the hope that evangelicals 'through prayer, study and discussion [will] grow in our understanding and so in our agreement'.[27] However laudable this approach is generally for an evangelical spirituality, and regardless of how unrealised it may be in practice, mainstream evangelical opinion here clearly sets 'the woman question' as something outside its core identity.

While each of the factors considered above is relevant to the way evangelicalism has (or has not) broached the question of women, there is an additional extremely influential factor involved that requires consideration, namely, the impact of feminism on the debate.

EVANGELICALISM AND FEMINISM

It is the expression of feminist concerns that has caused the church in recent years to address the question of women. This has either been directly through Christian individuals who share feminist concerns, or indirectly as a result of social changes in regard to women. Within evangelical literature that does look at this subject a number of authors identify (either directly or by implication) feminism as all or part of the source of challenge to much evangelical understanding concerning women, for which a response is appropriate or necessary.[28]

The dominant attitude towards feminism is a negative one. Indeed, feminism has taken on a symbolic value in that it has come to represent in the minds of many Christians the dangers of a secular age which has no place for God's law. In particular, there are specific fears for the family and for the authority of the Bible. In Northern Ireland, all of this is compounded by the particular context of community conflict.

PERCEPTIONS OF FEMINISM

Feminism has an image problem! Perceived largely as negative and troublesome, many people do not want to associate themselves with the term. Take, for example, these comments from women interviewed for this book:

> I wouldn't like to see people calling me a feminist because ... to me the perception of feminism is women in dungarees trying to assert their rights, you know, and all this sort of thing.

> Well, just that word feminism, to me it's quite a militant term and I don't like it, you know. What else can I say about it? No, I just don't like it.

> Feminism, it's a term that sometimes I draw back from because I have this image of it as being militant feminism, which isn't a fair image at all, you know, but it's just one that I have.

> Well, feminism stirs up negative things in me I would have to say. Whether this is what it is or not, I don't know.

> The image of feminism is aggressive ... I mean ... when you say the word at first I think, you know, burning bras, and chanting.

> There's always that little frightening thing about people when you talk about feminists and I think there's always that feeling of not being comfortable, you know, with aggressive women.

> My immediate thoughts are the kind of women's lib thing ... it's the whole kind of hard-nosed, almost lesbian, you know, in-your-face woman thing, and I don't like it.

> I can't think of feminism without thinking about the spiritual dimension and I do also believe that it is a tool in the hands of the enemy. It is a destructive tool in the hands of the enemy.

> I wouldn't like to be called a feminist! Because I think of people that are called feminists – I suppose it would be someone who's anti-men.

> I have become increasingly concerned about being, either labelling myself or other people calling me a feminist simply because, whether intentionally or not, it has become equivalent to hating men.

> I certainly wouldn't like someone to describe me as a feminist. I just don't like the word, but yet I would very much adhere to a lot of the principles behind it.

As a few of these quotations indicate, even when women support what they understand feminist ideas to be, they distance themselves from the term itself because the negative perception of feminism is so pervasive. This negative perception includes viewing feminism and feminists as aggressive, extreme, anti-male and men-hating, and even a tool of the devil. The term is used as a negative judgement on women's sexual identity, either in terms of their femininity or their sexual preference. In short, feminism has become a term of abuse, a put-down, almost a weapon against women:

> It's very much a kind of a, you know, a derogatory term to describe somebody as a feminist, you know, she's a real, she's a real feminist, like. You know, as if she's really assertive or aggressive or something.

> I'm afraid of it as a term, I'm afraid of ever being labelled it because I have been labelled it and it's been a derogatory term ... I'm very scared of it because of what other people [take][29] it to mean.

In terms of its ideology, that is, what feminism actually stands for, the most common understanding is that feminism is concerned in some way with women's equality or women's rights. Some women support the original cause of equality as espoused by feminism but consider this has 'gone too far', either in terms of the methods employed or the kind of equality being envisaged. Other women think that feminism has lost sight of its original vision of equality and has come to mean something else, such as female superiority. The important point to note here is that a distancing from the term feminist is not the same as a distancing from the idea of sex equality *per se*. Rather, it is more often concerned with what equality means in practice, how it is achieved, and what it implies for our understanding of male and female identity:

> But there's a lot of stuff that would, I suppose, broadly speaking be feminism that I wouldn't label as feminism. You know, so I believe in the fight for equal pay, I believe in the fight for equal rights, I believe in all of that. But I wouldn't necessarily label that as feminism.

> I suppose if I'm really honest, the first thing that comes to mind [about feminism] are people in strange outfits being very radical and jumping up and down. I would say, I would always have said and I still would say I'm not a feminist and yet my attitudes probably would be quite feminist or perceived by people as feminist. I think, I suppose I struggle with it, you know, you always have this picture of people burning bras. But I suppose I believe in equality of women. Feminism seems to take it further, it seems to take it to the point of women being superior to men and I think I would have a lot of trouble with that. So I would say I'm more into equality of women and men rather than a feminist.

This negative assessment of feminism is not the total picture from the women (or men) who were interviewed. Some expressed a growing appreciation of some aspects of feminism and others did identify themselves with it, sometimes by redefining their understanding of what feminism should be, or was for them. It was the very few who applied the term to themselves without qualification:

> I have no, I call myself, I have no problem with the word. To me it is just women claiming what is rightfully theirs. It's being, just standing up and saying I have a right to be treated with equal dignity and respect as any person on this planet and my life, it is of as much value as any other. To me that's what feminism is, nothing else and I have no qualms about calling myself a feminist. It's not a dirty word. I'm proud to be called that. To associate myself with that word, no problem.

However, the negative perception is the dominant image of feminism. Even as women spoke of feminist issues in which they were interested, they had to deal with feminism's bad image. This meant that in addition to giving consideration to the issue at hand, they had to give time and energy to the context in which their concerns would be received, carefully qualifying, rewording and explaining what they did not, as much as what they did mean. In part this is because feminism has become imbued with a symbolic value over and above its actual content and the truth or otherwise of the perceptions associated with it.

SYMBOLIC VALUE OF FEMINISM

Feminism has become so associated with a liberal social agenda that supporting feminism has become synonymous with supporting that modernistic agenda, and to oppose feminism is to oppose the secular drift of society.

Mark Chaves has shown how the meaning of women's ordination in church institutions in the United States of America has changed because of the symbolic importance now attached to women's ordination.[30] He observes that there is a difference between the formal regulations that a denomination has regarding women's ordination and the actual practice of women's involvement. On the one hand, those institutions that do ordain women do not necessarily do so in great numbers. And on the other hand, in churches where women do not have access to ordination, the women nevertheless often are very involved in many ways in the life of the church. He also notes that just because a denomination ordains women, it does not mean that women necessarily experience equality of opportunity, pay or conditions as ordained persons. In other words, the possibility of formal access to ordination in a denomination is not the same thing as actualising that experience in full for women. Rather, formal rules about women's ordination have a different meaning.

This different meaning is about the symbolic value of ordaining women. It has come to signal an acceptance of the principle of gender equality advocated in the wider society.[31] Hence, 'Denominations not yet ordaining women after the policy comes to mean "gender equality" resist something more than actual females in pulpits and at altars. They resist modernity. More accurately, they resist a part of modernity in which the liberal agenda of elevating individual rights is of paramount importance.'[32]

This opposition to modernity can be a mark of a denomination's identity in relation to other church institutions and wider society. The Free Presbyterian Church of Ulster and the Evangelical Presbyterian Church in Ireland exclude women from leadership on the basis of their understanding of biblical tradition. Both institutions note their stance in contrast to the pressure of modernisation or liberalism of other churches around them.[33]

Other issues, for example homosexuality and abortion, also contain this symbolic value of an attitude toward modernity. For evangelicalism, however, feminism or the position of women has a particular significance because of the role gender played in the development of fundamentalism (which has common roots with the contemporary evangelical movement) and evangelicalism.[34]

Margaret Bendroth's exploration of fundamentalism places attitudes about gender as key to understanding the development of fundamentalism and its relationship to the wider society. The historical movement of fundamentalism emerged in the late nineteenth century in North America and was a coalition of conservative, mainly Calvinist, Protestants who were predominantly white and middle-class. These fundamentalists were committed to a defence of orthodox Christianity in the face of the increasingly liberalising influences within Protestantism and the secular trends in a society that had once been defined by Christian values.

The end of the nineteenth century had seen considerable social change. A combination of women suffragettes and social reformers had led to women having a sphere of influence outside of their traditional area of the home. Victorian ideals of women as safeguards of family decency crossed over into the public sphere, with women perceived as 'homemakers for the entire nation, responsible for both private and public standards of morality'.[35] This was at a time when middle-class men were adjusting to an increasingly professionalised business arena that curtailed opportunities for personal initiative. In a context of majority female-populated Protestant churches, early fundamentalist leaders saw their home, public and church lives as feminised with the inherent danger of creating a passive type of manhood. All of this was viewed as part of the liberalising trend that was leading to watered-down doctrine and wrong practice. The response developed was a masculine spirituality that was brave, victorious and challenging.[36]

While not anti-feminist *per se*, as time went on, fundamentalism took on a distinctly anti-feminist stance. The journey was not without contradiction. Women continued to be part of the movement and indeed the movement needed the women to do its work. So what Margaret Bendroth describes as an 'uneasy truce between two incompatible elements in fundamentalism itself',[37] that is, between more open practice for women and fundamentalist theology, did not survive in the years after the First World War. Controversy that arose over the doctrines of biblical inerrancy and dispensational premillennialism led to a fundamentalist position of seeing both of these as incompatible with women's emancipation. Fundamentalist men developed a theological rationale for opposing women's leadership in both home and church. As well as being doctrinally correct, this position was seen as the 'inherently more masculine choice'.[38]

The evangelicalism that emerged after the Second World War began to engage more with wider society both intellectually and socially, but continued to adopt conservative gender norms, advocating women's homemaker role particularly in the 1950s. The second wave of feminism (from the 1960s on) saw the re-emergence of traditional biblical arguments about women although without the masculine rhetoric of the earlier decades. Yet it is the theological and gender assumptions that are deeply rooted in the past that continue to affect contemporary evangelicalism's handling of gender.

Callum Brown has shown how a similar feminisation of piety to that experienced in North America existed in Britain from 1800 up until the 1950s and indeed was very much a part of evangelicalism.

> It was modern evangelicalism that raised the piety of women, the 'angel in the house', to reign over the moral weakness and innate temptations of masculinity. Reversing pre-industrial society's privileging of male piety, this evangelical gendered framework for religion dominated public discourse and rhetoric, not just in the nineteenth century, but for the first six decades of the twentieth century as well.[39]

One response to this negative construction of masculinity was the rise of 'muscular Christianity' from the mid-nineteenth century. This was an attempt to 'redefine manhood by marrying physicality to spirituality'[40] and emphasised militaristic[41] and sporting activities.

Callum Brown traces the social rather than the theological significance of this gendered religiosity. He demonstrates how evangelical female piety and social attitudes towards femininity were intertwined until the late 1930s. After this time talk of women's religious influence on men's morality was replaced in public rhetoric by an ideology of domestic bliss in which women were to create a contented domesticity for their men. Rooted in an evangelical vision of the 'good woman',[42] this traditional gender role continued in British society largely unchallenged until the cultural revolution of the 1960s, of which the rise of second-wave feminism was a part. In Callum Brown's view, it was 'the simultaneous de-pietisation of femininity and the de-feminisation of piety'[43] that produced the secularisation experienced in Britain from this period.[44] Hence, while on the surface evangelicalism rarely acknowledges the significance of gender in its history, the gendered realities of women and men have been very much a part of its story in the past two centuries, and feminism in particular is associated with a threat to the faith itself.

Feminism, then, has a symbolic value. It is about the stand a church denomination, Christian coalition, or even individual takes against an increasingly modernistic age in which Christian faith is under threat. This symbolic value can be a barrier even to thinking about the position of women. However, for evangelicalism, attitudes toward gender are deeply embedded in its origins and are an integral part of its history. Two specific fears are raised in contemporary evangelicalism: fear for the family, and fear for the authority of the orthodox position.

FEAR FOR THE FAMILY

The perception of feminism as an extreme position to adopt[45] has meant that it has become associated with a threat to the family. This was demonstrated in an advertisement placed by the group 'Christians Against the Agreement'[46] in the run-up to the referendum vote in May 1998. In a text entitled 'The Sin of Voting "Yes"' they stated, 'The Bible strongly denounces attacks on the family unit, but the "Agreement" aims to destroy the family by promoting the causes of sexual perversion and feminism.'[47] And James Dobson of Focus on the Family described the 1995 UN World Conference on Women with over 40,000 delegates as 'the greatest threat to the family in my life-time'.[48]

Feminism has attacked the family for the abuses of power within it, particularly domestic violence. The Battered Women's Movement grew out of the Women's Movement and revealed and named the violent abuse of women (and children) in the home. There is now a level of public acknowledgement of the nature and extent of this violence with some social and legislative provision to address it. Many evangelicals acknowledge the value of feminism in this regard. As one woman put it, 'I think, as a movement, we owe a lot to the feminist movement for bringing to our attention the exploitation of women and children.' However, not all evangelicals share this woman's assessment:

> The feminists' occasional insights, like their criticism of male neglect of the home and masculine tendencies toward violence and oppression and their emphasis on the special contributions of feminine moral viewpoints, are not grounded in a worldview founded on truth. Thus, these illuminations are negated by faulty analyses and misdirected applications. In fact, their disregard for the real needs of most women and children far surpasses that of the old male order that they seek to replace. Their willingness to impose their will through almost any means at their disposal involves an embrace of power that is a match for most of the 'male oppressors'.[49]

The understanding of feminism as anti-family is in part, but not exclusively, connected to women's increasing participation in paid employment outside of the home. Traditionally women are responsible for family households, not necessarily financially, but in terms of the day-to-day domestic responsibilities. They are primary carers of children and other dependants, not only in terms of practicalities, but also in terms of emotional development and concerns. With women working outside of the home, the anxiety is that these responsibilities are being neglected. This belief about women's role is a contemporary expression of the domestic ideology discussed above in which women are viewed as belonging to the private world of the home, the domain of domesticity, care and nurture.

In fact, some women have always worked outside the home. Sometimes this has been because of a lack of male employment opportunities. Frequently it has been to supplement the main income of the household. But it is also more and more out of personal choice of women themselves (and, of course, these are not mutually exclusive options). It is this sense of personal choice by women that is frequently attacked because it is contrasted to serving the needs of the family. It is considered selfish on the part of women to place their own needs or desires above those of their family. For Christians this stance is connected to their beliefs about Christian self-denial.[50] This dilemma that women face is explored in chapter six. For now the point is that feminism is associated with fears for family stability and 'family values'.

Of course, women's increased economic opportunities and resulting potential economic independence does affect the dynamics within a family unit and the options open to women. Identity, for women and men, which is based on or endorsed by certain roles and responsibilities, is vulnerable if those roles and responsibilities change.

Feminism is also frequently blamed for the increased divorce rates and growth of lone parent families. It is seen as promoting sexual promiscuity and moral decline in the rest of society. If the family is the building block to a stable society, then any changes to this arrangement have implications not only for individual families, but for society as a whole. In this view, feminism and families are incompatible.

FEAR FOR THE FAITH

For evangelicals, the social changes of which feminism is a part are seen as a threat to biblical authority, which is at the heart of evangelical identity. Indeed, feminism is seen as directly opposing the source of authority within evangelical faith. This sense is captured by one of the men interviewed for this book. While his views on feminism had changed in recent years, he spoke of a time when 'Feminism was an ugly word to me, okay. Feminism spoke of revolution. Feminism spoke of anti-authority, anti-establishment, anti-institution.'

This threat is not perceived as peripheral, but focuses on a central tenet of evangelical faith and identity. To challenge traditional and hereto accepted biblical interpretation is seen as a challenge to the faith itself. To support a particular stance on women is to support a belief in the authority of the Bible. There is now considerable biblical exegesis about women's participation in church and society that, from the standpoint of a belief in the authority of Scripture, offers alternative readings, some of which will be examined in chapter five. However, this is still unsettling for some. After all, if the biblical interpretation concerning women on which evangelicalism has relied for so many years is perhaps in some way in error, then can any certainty be found?

Here the perceived battle between secular society and divine authority is exemplified. As Mark Chaves comments:

> In an era and a culture in which formal gender equality enjoys widespread legitimacy – one indicator of which is the fact that even contemporary opponents of women's ordination do not often oppose the fundamental justice of gender equality – it hardly would be possible to sustain formal

gender *in*equality without drawing on a source of authority that is alternative to Enlightenment principles of basic human rights.[51]

And it is just this claim to authority that is challenged by the social changes in regard to women.[52]

Taking a traditional stance on women's participation in the church can be seen as part of a person's evangelical credentials. One woman spoke of the peer pressure that she observed operating on ordained men in regard to their inclusion of women in non-ordained leadership or teaching roles: 'The fear that some of our ministers have [is because] of what their colleagues will think. And how ... they'll be judged, and particularly how they'll be judged in regard to their so-called evangelicalism. That's the big fear that if they're seen [to include women] somehow they have abandoned their reformed evangelicalism.'

A few women's initial description of evangelicalism was to define it on the basis of the position on women, for example, 'I would have seen evangelical [as] ... Bible-based teaching churches and possibly where women wouldn't have had a lot of roles.' This understanding was also echoed by one of the men interviewed: 'From my own perspective one of the interesting things is by and large the more evangelical the church, the more opposition traditionally there has been to the involvement of women in leadership, probably because of their understanding of the Pauline texts.'

This is not the whole picture of evangelicalism in Northern Ireland in regard to women. It does, however, indicate the core concern that the subject evokes for many, namely, the foundation of their faith itself.

NORTHERN IRELAND

Evangelicalism's encounter with feminism in Northern Ireland is affected by the particular context of civil strife. There are two points relevant here. The first is the association of feminism with nationalism.

The women's movement in Northern Ireland has not been as robust as its counterpart in Great Britain. While second-wave feminism was developing in Britain in the 1960s and 1970s, energies in Northern Ireland were taken up with the political crisis. The emerging women's movement in Northern Ireland was hindered by ongoing sectarian conflict with its violence and divisive nature. Particular high-profile events such as hunger strikes, alongside ongoing sectarian issues, produced conflicting nationalist loyalties that prevented a united women's movement. Women have been able to form alliances to work on various socio-economic issues of mutual concern and in doing so have made a significant impact for local communities, in welfare provision, and on legislation.[53] Nevertheless, their ability to address political structures and constitutional issues on the whole has been hindered because of the competing loyalties of a conflict where 'differences have been viewed at the grassroots level and by the main parties as necessarily threatening'.[54] A recent and notable exception to this is the formation of the Northern Ireland Women's Coalition (NIWC) in 1996, which includes both unionist and nationalist women, and their involvement in peace negotiations and the devolved Northern Ireland Assembly.[55]

The association of feminism with nationalism comes from the fact that the Northern Ireland Women's Rights Movement (formed in 1975) emerged out of the Civil Rights Movement, which involved mainly nationalists and was working class. Many nationalist women gained their first experience of political activism in addressing the issues of unemployment, housing and low wages facing their community. One woman expressed her understanding of this: 'I mean when you look back in the history of the women's movement here in Northern Ireland particularly, I mean most of the women who came out in leadership came out through the troubles, simply because on the nationalist side most of the men were lifted, and women had to learn to be leaders, and have learned very fast. And that's probably something that the Protestant community never really faced in that sense. So women were always kept in their place.' It is this background which has fostered the association of feminism with republicanism and which may have kept many unionist women alienated from activism in the women's movement. As one woman interviewed expressed it, 'I suppose I always felt that Catholic women were more into feminism.'[56]

The second aspect in thinking about how feminism has impacted on the specific context of Northern Ireland concerns the link between internal conflict and heightened traditionalism in the role of women. Rosemary Ridd comments:

> It is a curious paradox that conflict, however much it may be outwardly directed towards bringing about change in society, can be at the same time

an inherently conservative agent. The sense of insecurity that accompanies such disturbances reflects strongly upon women, particularly where they are represented as the custodians of a society's cultural values which, like its art treasures, are in constant need of protection and especially when that society comes under attack.[57]

Certainly in Northern Ireland the women's movement has been concerned with matters pertaining to supporting family life without a robust challenge to traditional gender divisions. The dominant strand of feminism in Northern Ireland is 'of the welfare type laced with liberal feminism, that is, there was a concern with welfare issues which women were seen to be better placed to deal with because of their caring role, whether arising from a basis in socialisation or biology'.[58] Indeed, the term 'family feminist' has been used to describe the nature of many women's activism in Northern Ireland, no doubt in an attempt to place a distance from the perception of feminism as anti-family discussed above.[59]

The particular path that the women's movement has taken in Northern Ireland does not alter the overall perception of feminism. Indeed, the 'negative image of feminism and the attribution of a "lack of femininity" to feminists … is more acute in Northern Ireland'.[60] Nor is there any reduction in feminism's felt threat to evangelicalism. In this context, the question of women continues to evoke a sense of fear and uncertainty.

Exploring the Question of Women

If evangelicals tend to avoid giving too much consideration to the question of women, partly because the subject is linked to negative perceptions about feminism, why do so now? After all, there can often be disagreement and division, even conflict, when women's position in the church is considered. It can be thought by some that to raise the subject does more harm than good. For others, however, it is a question long overdue for exploration. Whichever approach is adopted, issues surrounding women's involvement in church, community and politics are implicit in the realities of many women's lives.

EVANGELICAL WOMEN: BETWEEN CULTURE AND THEOLOGY

Regardless of the perception of feminism, and the accuracy or otherwise of that perception,[61] the position of women within church and society is a current concern. Fairly common phrases such as, 'I'm not a feminist, but ... ' indicate that while feminism itself may be disowned, the matters raised by the women's movement are not. As some of the women interviewed put it:

> I don't call myself a feminist, but I utterly believe in the equality of women and men.

> Well, I certainly wouldn't be a women's lib type person by any means, but I look around me, I look around my own church and I see the number of women who have so many gifts and so many talents and really until let's say probably over the past maybe three or four years there maybe wasn't the same opportunity to use those.

> I'm not a feminist ... But I suppose I believe in equality of women.

> When I say I'm not a feminist, what I mean by that is I will not tackle injustices by shouting from the rooftops: 'I'm a woman and I've a right to be here' ... If I'm going to be discriminated against because I'm female, well then I want to find constructive ways of addressing that, not aggressive, shouting for my rights ways of addressing that.

> I would say I'm not a feminist. But I'm very much committed to ... women's involvement and women's abilities and women as much as men being involved in reaching their potential.

> I don't like the concept of feminism. I am certainly for equal rights, and equal opportunities and all of those things for everybody across the board, but I never like it to be in your face, and that's the way I perceive feminism to be.

> I wouldn't see myself as a feminist and what I would associate feminist to be. But I do think there's room for discussing it, and the role of women as well.

> [Feminism is] another word ... that I find it hard to identify with, you know ... I mean I think women are equal. I don't think women should see themselves, or be treated, as lesser individuals.

Irrespective of the name given to it, there is a concern over the way women are viewed and treated. There is awareness that women's participation in church and society is not all that it either could or should be. And there is expectation of equality in areas such as education, employment, and law. All of this reflects the social culture that has developed in the past thirty years. For what not all women recognise, although some women do, is that the equality in society which they expect to receive and sometimes actually experience is largely the result of feminist endeavours.[62]

As already discussed, questions around women raised by contemporary culture are often avoided because of their association with negative perceptions of feminism. As Mary Stewart Van Leeuwen points out, 'feminism is a term that many people use imprecisely and very emotionally. And to an extent this is understandable: when new social movements threaten old categorical certainties, it is tempting to dismiss them with a sweeping, pejorative label whose negativity, it is hoped, will persuade movement members to revert to the status quo or at least keep quiet.'[63] Such 'unreflective name-calling',[64] however, does not change the realities of the contemporary culture. Engagement rather than avoidance was endorsed by one male church leader interviewed: 'I think if somebody complains to me about something in the church, say, you know, "I really don't like the worship here", I have a choice. Either I say, "oh you're out of order, you're silly", or I ignore what you have to say. My attitude is if somebody makes a criticism there's usually a grain of truth in it. Usually somewhere there's – anybody who's being negative – there's something that's causing hurt and something that needs to be addressed. Likewise I think feminism, even in its extreme forms, which would make me very uncomfortable from a Christian point of view, they're still actually saying something the church needs to address, and therefore I think whatever happens, any movement that comes along the church needs to say, "well, what can we learn from this?" and that's the way I look at it.'

The notion of women having all kinds of legal, economic and social entitlements on a par with men in society has become part of public rhetoric, regardless of how unrealised it may be in practice. In their belief in various forms of equality for women, evangelical women in Northern Ireland are reflecting the ethos of the culture in which they live. It is a product, in part, of second-wave feminism and the movement for women's liberation, that is, eradicating the inequality which women experience on the basis of their sex. The negotiation of Christian faith with this culture is something evangelical women are facing, whether consciously or not, through their participation in the church, the community and the political world. For evangelicals this faith involves not only various theological positions (about gender relations and Christians' relationship to society), but also a sub-culture of its own.[65]

And for women in Northern Ireland, an additional backdrop is the cultural patterns evident in a society experiencing civil conflict, patterns which have tended to foster conservative gender roles for women. Evangelical women are, therefore, participating in church and civic society and making sense of their lives negotiating between culture and theology, or perhaps more accurately, between cultures and theologies.

The following chapters explore the different areas of this ongoing negotiation. Despite the expectation of equality of opportunity women are still under-represented in certain jobs, responsibilities and roles in church, community and politics. Chapter two outlines the current situation of women's involvement in each of these domains and considers the various mechanisms that facilitate women's greater participation in those areas traditionally populated by men. However, while such participation may be achieved, the actual experience for women is not always one of full inclusion. Drawing on women's experiences in their new and more traditional spheres of activity, chapter three considers a variety of both good and difficult experiences told by the women interviewed. The chapter identifies elements that enable and elements that hinder women's inclusion in church and civic life.

One of the pressing questions surrounding women's participation in church and society concerns whether their contribution is different to or the same as that of men. This question is rooted in deeply held beliefs about the nature of women and men, which in turn are intrinsic to our sense of personal identity. Chapter four explores the significance the notion of difference has in women's church, community and political participation; it examines what can happen when we use differences in status and power between women and men to form our sense of identity.

For Christians, and especially for evangelical Christians, integral to any discussion of women's participation, particularly in relation to the church, is the matter of biblical interpretation. Women's increasing participation in all areas of church and civic life is bringing them into positions of responsibility and authority previously held mainly by men. Entering into these new roles means women (and men) are having to examine their understanding of authority and its gendered application. Chapter five investigates this subject and in particular the theological notion of 'headship' with its contemporary understanding and practice, exploring the relevant biblical material.

The domestic ideology already discussed is very much a factor in women's church, community and political participation. Traditionally in Northern Ireland domestic care responsibilities for homes, children, husbands and other family members rests in the main with women. Related to the question of women's nature raised in chapter four, the matter of domestic responsibilities is woven into the fabric of women's lives. Chapter six explores the practical and personal realities of this for women, including some women's responses that challenge a narrow understanding of female identity.

In the midst of the pressing political focus of Northern Ireland's divided society on the one hand and the general concerns of Christian churches about maintaining their life and witness on the other, the needs, aspirations and gifting of women have often taken second place. Drawing together the themes in the previous pages, chapter seven considers the importance of focusing on asking the question of women for women themselves, for men, churches, evangelicalism and civic society.

INTRODUCING THE INTERVIEWEES

Appearing throughout this book are the words of evangelical women involved in church, community and politics and those of men who are evangelical church leaders. Before introducing those who were interviewed, a word about evangelicalism in Northern Ireland.

Evangelicalism is a significant part of the religious profile of Northern Ireland and is found throughout Protestant denominations. The 1993 Belfast Churchgoers Survey[66] identified conservatives (those who retain a strong commitment to the central importance of a conversion experience and a firm belief in biblical inerrancy) as making up 27 per cent of Anglicans; 38 per cent of the Presbyterian Church in Ireland; 43 per cent of the Methodist Church in Ireland;[67] 79 per cent of Congregationalists; and between 83 and 94 per cent of Baptistic, Pentecostal/Charismatic, and other Presbyterian Churches. Overall, 50 per cent of all Protestant church-goers in the survey were conservative with a further 25 per cent identified as liberal-conservatives, that is, those who espouse either one or other of the two central tenets noted above.[68] The survey also notes that Protestant churchgoers, whether evangelical or not, tend to be conservative in their theological convictions.[69] An exploration of evangelical women, therefore, involves most Protestant denominations in Northern Ireland.[70]

In order to find out about the experiences and thoughts of women themselves and male church leaders about the participation of women in church, community and politics, 70 women and 10 men from evangelical Protestantism were interviewed for this book.

While each woman interviewed was initially identified because of her church, community or political participation, in reality many had diverse experience both within and across these boundaries, providing a rich resource of experience and reflection.

Of the 70 women, 35 were identified because of their church participation. This group included women who were employed and those who acted in a voluntary capacity in churches (at congregational and denominational levels) and para-church organisations. Some of the women were ordained or held equivalent formal leadership positions within churches. Others participated in the formal leadership structures of the churches in a lay capacity.[71] Some specialised in work with women or children and young people or had other responsibilities in the ongoing life of the church.

The women involved in para-church organisations were also involved in their local congregations as were the women contacted because of their community or political participation. In fact, therefore, nearly all of the seventy women interviewed spoke of their experiences in churches in Northern Ireland and were actively involved in a variety of ways at the time of interviewing. Most of these activities consisted of: work with children and young people (through crèche, Sunday school, children's church, Bible class, uniformed organisations, and youth groups); women's organisations; lay leadership; and involvement in home and Bible study groups, prayer initiatives and the music and worship of the church. Other activities were each mentioned by one or two women: preaching, visiting, and hospitality; work with students, younger adults and older people; outreach initiatives through local projects, missionary support work, and involvement in summer schemes both at home and overseas; committee work for the denomination; and work with church magazines and publicity.

Twenty-five women were identified from the community, charitable and voluntary sector in Northern Ireland. Some of these were involved in initiatives that had formal church connections; others had none. Some worked in community centres and in community development, some specialised in youth work, some concentrated on working with families, while others focused on training or health issues. Many of these women were in senior positions within their organisations, carrying responsibilities for personnel, finance, and the ongoing development of their particular projects, and for many there was a cross-community dimension to their work.

In addition to these 25 women active in the community sector, 26 of the women interviewed from the church and political sectors also had some kind of wider community involvement. Again involving church and non-church initiatives, some of the activities were similar to those in which the community-identified women were engaged. In addition, there were two other areas of activity: responding to the needs of victims of the conflict in Northern Ireland and involvement with schools, particularly through serving on school boards.

The third group of women interviewed were those engaged in the public world. Ten women were contacted because of their political involvement and among the women in the church and community groups there was a further three women active in politics. All were members of political parties, some holding party office, some experienced in electoral politics and involved in government. Between them these women had connections with a number of different political parties. Seven of them support the 1998 Belfast Agreement and six do not.[72]

These 70 women came from across Protestant denominations, were aged between 24 and 77, and came from throughout Northern Ireland, sometimes living and working and worshipping in different areas. Forty-three either were married or had been (and were now widowed or divorced); 27 had never married. Thirty-three women did not have children. Of the 37 women who had children, these ranged from being pre-schoolers to having left home.

Many of the women were in paid employment in their various sectors. Some, however, were employed in other occupations and there was opportunity in the interviews to talk about their experiences as women in the workforce, often contrasting and comparing this to their participation in church, community or politics.

The picture provided by these seventy women is, therefore, varied, rich and extensive. The interviews were carried out on a confidential basis. The women talked not only about their current occupations but also of past experiences. Sometimes they told what had happened to their women friends and colleagues. They narrated their stories and shared their thoughts. Sometimes they spoke of very private things, and revealed their joys, fears, hopes, dreams, and pain. The aim of this book is to convey something of this rich account of women's reality, focusing on the common themes that are pertinent to exploring evangelical women's church and wider civic participation.

Ten men were also interviewed for this project. All were evangelical church leaders with knowledge and experience not only of their own current congregation, but also of their denomination as a whole. There were three each from the Presbyterian Church in Ireland and the Church of Ireland, two from the Methodist Church in Ireland, and one each from the Association of Baptist Churches and the Life Link network.[73] Further details of the demographics of all eighty interviewees and the interview process are given in appendix one. The interview schedules used for the different groups of women and the men are found in appendix two.

In order to maintain the confidentiality of the women and men interviewed, in the following pages the specific details of the church, community group or political party involved are usually absent. There are some specific references when the examples are taken from material already in the public domain. Occasionally more details are given in respect of the interviewees, but only if to do so does not enable identification. This approach is fitting because the intention is not to be an exploration of any particular church denomination or congregation, community group or voluntary sector organisation, or political party or form of government. Rather it is to consider the common issues facing evangelical Protestant women in particular, in their participation in church, community and politics. While these issues have a variety of nuances depending on each particular context, there nevertheless remains a core group of questions that are involved in evangelical women's negotiation of the culture and theology that affects their lives. There are, of course, implications for individual religious institutions, community groups and political bodies from exploring these questions. The aim in this book is to make visible and foster understanding of the questions of participation, inclusion, difference, authority, domesticity and priority that concern women in their church, community and political involvement.

2

The Participation Question

Writing about gender, religion and politics in Northern Ireland, Rosemary Sales states:

> The sexual division of labour in the Church – with male clergy and a predominantly female membership, whose role is largely confined to domestic tasks – is a metaphor for gender relations in the wider sphere of social and political life.[1]

The sexual[2] division of labour describes the way in which certain jobs, roles, and functions in the family, social institutions, the workplace, and public life are divided among women and men so that either one or other sex predominates in any particular situation. For example, in the Northern Ireland workforce, 99 per cent of secretaries, typists and receptionists are women as are 87 per cent of cleaners, caretakers and road-sweepers. While 79 per cent of nurses are women, 81 per cent of those employed as scientists, engineers and technologists are men.[3] It is this sexual division that has been increasingly challenged, although certainly not dismantled, in the second half of the twentieth century. As the following chapters demonstrate, intrinsic to the sexual division of labour are beliefs about women's (and indeed men's) nature and our sense of personal identity. It is not simply who does what, but why and how. Issues concerning the sexual division of domestic labour are explored in chapter six. This chapter takes a look at this sexual division of labour in the world of church, community and politics and then considers the possible means that enable women to cross over into areas that are currently male dominated.

Where are the Women?

In the church, community and political sectors women are present and active in great numbers but rarely, with some exceptions in the community sector, in positions of authority, decision-making, visibility or public representation.

The situation in many churches is summarised in the words of one community activist talking about her church: 'I think the structures of the church, the appearance of who's in authority in the church, are totally different to what the realities are of the work ... that goes on within the churches. I mean I think there are [just] two women elders in our church. And certainly none of the instigation or anything creative ideas-wise, movement forward-wise, has come from the [elders] full stop. Anything that has come has come from outside and often from women. Most of the stuff is run by women. I mean I think Sunday school is entirely run by women. The only thing that isn't run by women I think is the men's fellowship, which obviously would be difficult to be run by women ... And I wonder if you pulled all those women out, what would happen to the church, you know, really.' The picture is of lay women being the majority in attendance[4] and sustaining much of the overall ministry and activity of an individual congregation by their practical support and presence. As one male church leader put it, 'The people who are most supportive and involved and committed in my experience are in the main women in the congregation.'

Women are not, however, involved in terms of equal or even notable numbers within denominational church structures at congregational leadership level (either in terms of government or public worship). As a consequence of this they are also under-represented at denominational levels. In a number of denominations women are absent altogether from church government. For some denominations and individual congregations this sexual division is based on their theological understanding and strictly maintained by the ruling body of the institution or congregation. On the whole these churches would not see this situation as devaluing or undermining women or suggesting their inferiority to men. Rather this sexual division is a divinely ordained ordering of gender relations in the church. This immensely important area of debate around the biblical case for and against women's participation in leadership of the church is considered in chapter five.

In denominations that do have formal access for women in leadership positions the numbers of women involved remain low. The three main Protestant churches are the Presbyterian Church in Ireland, the Church of Ireland, and the Methodist Church in Ireland. In their church structures, each of which incorporates both clergy and laity in decision-making and leadership, women now have full theoretical access to these positions, most recently to the ordained ministry (since the 1970s in the Presbyterian and Methodist Churches and since 1990 in the Anglican Church). However, there are in reality few women who occupy lay leadership positions and fewer still who are ordained.

In 1999 less than 9 per cent of ordained persons were women in each of these denominations.[5] At the 1999 General Synod of the Church of Ireland, the church's main ruling body, out of the five dioceses involving Northern Ireland only 13 per cent of the lay representatives were women (for the whole of Ireland the figure was 19 per cent).[6] Speaking in the context of women predominating in what he described as the spiritual leadership of the parish in leading house groups, prayer groups and congregational worship, one male Church of Ireland leader made the point that, 'The amazing thing is when it comes to church government ... in terms of select vestry, women struggle to get elected ... When it comes to the bodies that diocesan synod elect, like diocesan council, you almost have to fight to get women on ... In terms of the power structures ... women are not to the fore.'

Since the 1920s women have been eligible for ordination as ruling elders in the Presbyterian Church in Ireland. This gives them access to the decision-making structures of the church, although in practice they are a minority and many kirk sessions remain exclusively male.[7] Hence,

Presbytery Meetings and the General Assembly, the church's decision-making body, are predominantly male, something recognised by one of the Church's male leaders: 'Basically I would say that the Presbyterian Church as a denomination, in terms of how it functions, makes its decisions and organises its life, it's not a female-friendly denomination. I mean there are women in the eldership, there are women in the ministry, they are a quite small proportion.'

Women are present in various ways on church committees. For example, in 1998/99 nearly one third of the lay officers of the boards, committees, funds and institutions of the Methodist Church in Ireland were women as were the lay members appointed to the General Committee of the Conference. However, the Methodist Church in Ireland's own report on the role of women in their denomination evaluates the position of women in this manner: 'Women form up to 70 per cent of many of our congregations, yet they tend to be excluded from power and policy-making in the Church structures. The exercise of power and decision-making tends to be predominantly male.'[8]

Overall, the majority of women's involvement in the churches is concerned with a variety of 'low status' tasks that are more often considered women's domain. Much of this is the 'housework' role and responsibility for children that women typically occupy outside of the churches, and much of it is unseen.

 A similar picture emerges in terms of the political world. Women's participation in electoral politics in Northern Ireland remains low. The 2001 general election saw 3 women among the 18 MPs at Westminster (17 per cent), after 27 years of no female representation.[9] All 3 MEPs are male, and only 14 out of 108 (13 per cent) Members (MLAs) appointed in the 1998 Northern Ireland Assembly[10] elections are women. In July 1999 there were 86 women out of a total of 582 (14.6 per cent) councillors in local government.

These figures contrast with 118 (18 per cent) of all Westminster MPs being women in 2001 (in 1997 there were 120, the largest number of women MPs in the parliament's history); 37 and 40 per cent of women in the Scottish and Welsh Assemblies respectively; and 30 per cent female membership in the European Parliament. In May 1999, 23 per cent of local government councillors in Scotland were women, as were 20 per cent in Wales. The figure for the whole of Great Britain was 26 per cent. There were 12 per cent of women TDs in the Republic of Ireland's June 1997 general election.[11]

The situation is only marginally better when considering the numbers of women candidates for these positions. In the 1997 Westminster elections, while a record 20 per cent of the total who ran for seats in Northern Ireland were women, notably 14 out of the 25 were not seeking seats for the mainstream parties.[12] In the history of direct elections to the European parliament since 1977 only 6 women have (unsuccessfully) run as candidates (5 of these as recent as 1994). There were 49 women out of a total of 296 candidates (16.5 per cent) for the 1998 Northern Ireland Assembly elections[13] and in the 1997 local government elections 16.8 per cent of candidates were female.[14]

The main political parties in Northern Ireland state they have a female membership ranging from one third to one half[15] and in the case of the Democratic Unionist Party (DUP), 60 per cent. These proportions, however, are not reflected in women's participation within the hierarchies and decision-making processes of the parties. Only Sinn Féin and the Social Democratic and Labour Party (SDLP) have formalised quotas of 40 per cent women on their national executives and these are the only parties to have adopted a positive discrimination approach in regard to women on these bodies. In 1995 the Ulster Unionist Party (UUP) had 15 per cent female membership on the Ulster Unionist Council's executive committee and the Alliance Party of Northern Ireland (APNI) one third of women on its lead policy-making body. In 1999 both the DUP and the Ulster Democratic Party (UDP) had no women within their formal leadership structures, the Progressive Unionist Party (PUP) having one woman out of twelve members on its executive body. Only two of the major parties have had a woman as party chair – APNI and SDLP.[16] Hence the comment that, 'the only glimmer of light comes not from any tier of elected office but rather through the appointments route'.[17]

In Northern Ireland public bodies have had an increasingly important role in the affairs of the province, particularly since the introduction of direct rule in 1972. At the end of March 1999 there were 141 public bodies with 3,031 members, 34 per cent of whom were women. Seventeen of these bodies have no female members.[18] Despite the improvement on previous years that these figures represent, women are less likely to be appointed to the more senior positions and are under-represented in bodies relating to sectors of high female employment. Most of the 18 per cent of boards chaired by women in 1996 were concerned with matters usually understood as 'women's issues' and a survey of the nine months from July 1996 to March 1997 showed that 'female appointees are clustered in the lower pay bands or appointed to bodies where members receive no remuneration'.[19] In the Civic Forum set up in 2000 as part of the Belfast Agreement, 21 out of 58 members appointed are women (36 per cent).[20] The policing board for the Police Service of Northern Ireland established in 2001 has 19 members, 2 of whom are women.[21]

The Northern Ireland Assembly is the arena of politics that has received most attention over the past four years in Northern Ireland. Commenting on the low level of women MLAs elected, Yvonne Galligan and Rick Wilford state that the 'extensive powers that were to be devolved to the new Assembly again testified to the veracity of the adage "where power is, women aren't"'.[22]

The situation in the community sector paints a somewhat different picture. For while largely absent from formal electoral political office, women in Northern Ireland are very active within their own neighbourhoods, not only in churches, but in community organisations and in children's and women's groups. Conservative estimates are that there are more than 1,000 groups working for women or being run by women in Northern Ireland, which is one group for every 750 women here.[23] In this civic space 'between the traditional public and private spheres and the economic and political areas of society',[24] women are actively engaged in improving their own situation or that of their community.

That the community sector is populated by women was reflected in many of the comments in interviews with women working in this sector. In considering the gender composition of their group or organisation they often expressed the desire that more men would be involved. As one woman expressed it, community work is seen as women's work: 'I think that sometimes the kind of work I'm doing in the community is thought of almost like, you know, well that's for women, and we have found it very difficult to get men in the community actually involved in the community centre other than if they're employed [in it], you know. And in a sense I think it's kind of seen almost as kind of soft work or the kind of caring work that women do.' That community work is an example of gender-segregated employment is demonstrated in the lower salary scales that the sector offers its paid employees. As another woman active in the voluntary sector commented, 'If they paid more, men would see it as being prestigious enough to apply for a job. Yep. That's it, I think, in a nutshell.'

There is some evidence of a gender hierarchy within parts of this sector. One woman described women as 'the backbone' of community groups with an 'absolutely vital' role and yet as frequently absent from positions of leadership: 'When I see, now not only in my community, but when I go out to communities and … it's a mixed group of men and women, who are the leaders in that group? And it's always, always – I have to say I'm going right through them all in my head at the minute – there's always the man as the chairperson, and the treasurer is usually a man too, but the secretary, because it means that she's sitting writing frantically, writing notes, is a woman. And anyone that has any say or that has any authority within the rural groups is a man. And if there's a man in the group he'll be definitely assigned to being the leader of that group.'

This is a similar phenomenon to what happens in other sectors. For example, nursing and primary school teaching are female-dominated professions, but the men in those professions are dominant or overly represented at senior levels. The need for women's participation at senior management levels was expressed by another community activist: 'I definitely would like to see more women in management positions in the community sector as opposed to in the more kind of servicing, facilitating, behind the scenes kind of things. And I would certainly like to see the women who are already in those positions being given more recognition and more profile … [in] the media and the power structures.' Hence, in this woman's assessment, even when women and men hold similar positions, there is a difference, an inequality, in their experience in these positions.

A sexual division of labour exists in each of the three sectors being considered. The question of women's participation across this traditional division raises many issues to do with the nature, responsibilities, authority, and family and social relationships, of both women and men. These matters are considered in the rest of the book. The purpose in this chapter is to consider the means whereby women might cross the sexual division of labour and participate in all areas of church, community and political life.

It is important at this point to be clear that talking about women crossing the sexual division of labour that currently exists is not a rejection or devaluation of the work that women typically do. There is a social value system that places higher worth on the work that men typically do, as is illustrated in the gender pay differentials of a sex-segregated workforce. One might even say that the workers themselves are held in different regard, for it is a fine line between devaluing the work that women do and devaluing women themselves. However, acknowledging the existence of a sexual division of labour and considering the means for women to cross it is not about endorsing such a gendered value system. This needs to be said because the subtle way that gendered thinking is embedded in society means that crossing the sexual division of labour often is mistakenly taken as a negative judgement on women's traditional sphere of activity. Exploring women's participation in, for example, church leadership or public office, is not to disregard or devalue their involvement in the more traditional activities with which women are associated. It is, however, to challenge that these are the only spheres in which women can or should participate. And indeed, as the coming chapters illustrate, this in turn helps stimulate a discussion about gender itself, its construction and associated values.

Crossing the Sexual Division of Labour

How may women's greater participation in church and civic life best be facilitated given the sexual division of labour that currently exists in the world of church and politics and in certain ways in the community? Broadly speaking there are three main approaches: meritocracy, equal opportunities and affirmative action. The merit view considers that women now have access to participation across the traditional divide on the same basis as men, generally making no allowances for the existence of systemic factors that mitigate against women's inclusion. A belief in equal opportunities claims that women are disadvantaged in the current organisation and culture of the various sectors, and seeks measures to address this disadvantage through encouragement, education and structural support. The stance of affirmative action ensures that equal opportunities are realised through setting numerical objectives, establishing quotas or utilising systems that ensure women's participation. Behind each of these approaches are different explanations for women's limited participation across the sexual division of labour, which in turn reflect diverse understandings of gender and society.

MERITOCRACY

Those who advocate women's participation on the basis of merit view women as now having equal access to involvement in areas previously populated either exclusively or dominantly by men. If women want to, and if they are able, then they can participate fully in all areas of church, community and political life. In other words, there is a level playing field, and women are at no particular disadvantage relative to men. As one woman put it, 'I do feel women in Ireland have generally as much place as they want. I mean there's no job not open to us.'

There are women in each of the three sectors who hold this view. One ordained minister spoke of her church's openness to women: 'We're not too bad in that there are certainly openings for [women] and women's ordination is encouraged. Not necessarily promoted as something, you know, that we're out to recruit women into this, but any woman who goes forward for selection for ordination I feel gets a fair shot at it, you know.'

A woman involved in politics spoke warmly of her party's support for her and explained the lack of women in prominent or public roles in her party as the choice of individual women who prioritised family responsibilities: 'I've had nothing but encouragement. In our party the majority of members are women, and women are actively encouraged at every level. The problem with that is ... I suppose generally speaking the vast bulk of our members would be Christians, and ... they would tend to believe that they should spend the time bringing up their children and perhaps then, you know, they don't want to go for half measures with either home life or a political career. And so while they're never held back in any shape or form it is their choice not to become active, because [politics] takes over your life to a large extent. And I admire those women for saying no ... but they tend to step back, and it's their own choice ... It's really their own choice, because the party encourages people, very much so, encourages women.'

A para-church worker expressed a view shared by a number of women that a general apathy toward certain kinds of activism was more influential than a person's gender: 'I'm not really coming to this as someone who sees problems with women getting involved. I think there's a lack of interest in my kind of job, in the church in general, male and female.'

The merit view does not assume that there are no issues for women in participating across the sexual division. However, it does consider that through choice and perseverance women can participate fully. A woman active in the community spoke of the determination women needed: 'Women using their tenacity to stick with the job, rather than being put out by saying there's too many men in that or the men won't recognise me, and then women just walking away from the role. I think the tenacious aspect needs to be used in order to keep us going. I think we give up too easily. I wouldn't want to knock a man off his post just to get a woman in. Or I wouldn't want there to be more women on the committee because it previously had been male-orientated. I just feel that if women are good at what they're doing, they will be recognised as such and a space will be made. Now that's within the remit that I'm working. I'm sure that you will interview other people in much more powerful positions, where they really have to be very forceful in order to get their voice heard. I can't speak of those situations. I can only speak of what I'm doing here. I feel that ability is recognised and women just need to stay in there and continue doing their job well and recognise their own abilities and stay with it.'

Certainly among a number of younger women there was an expectation that they now had equal access to various positions. A politically active woman was aware of divergent attitudes across the generations: 'I think there's an attitude difference between, I suppose, young women like myself who are in their sort of mid- to late twenties, don't have children to a large extent, and in many ways didn't sort of fight the whole sort of sexism thing in the sixties. And where older women I talk to in politics are very for things like quotas and, you know, positive discrimination type thing, I'm very opposed to anything on those lines at all. I believe purely on everybody being there on merit.' This expectation of equality is mirrored in a survey of students in Great Britain which found that there is a low level of awareness of the gender pay gap, that is, women earning less than men for equivalent jobs.[25] In particular, younger women were the group most likely to be shocked, angry or disappointed when learning of the existence of the gender pay gap.[26]

Opposition to the notion of any kind of pro-activity, apart from general encouragement, to aid women in crossing the sexual division of labour is because such mechanisms are seen as contrary to the idea of merit. In other words, it is a choice between women participating on the basis of their own merit or on the basis of certain privilege given to them because they are women. In this view merit and such privilege cannot go hand in hand, but rather are mutually exclusive. This view trusts that decisions about who to appoint, for example, as church leader, community chair or political candidate are made on the basis of merit of the person being considered, and that no discrimination exists in the mindsets or practices of those responsible for making these decisions. While frequently those who advocate a meritocracy recognise that women could not always participate on the basis of their own abilities, they do not consider that this situation is pertinent any longer. And they strongly oppose the idea that women participate on the basis of anything other than their own merit.

The notion of merit seems just and a neutral concept. Why should a woman participate if she is not able, does not have the skills or experience, and indeed if someone else, in particular a man, is more qualified for the particular appointment or role in question? Viewed from one angle this appears to be an eminently fair and reasonable way of looking at things. However, it could be that the notion of merit itself is not free from gendered application and understanding.

One woman reflected on a conversation she had with someone over the absence of women from the highest ranks of a particular profession in Northern Ireland, an absence which was perpetuated by the fact that there were no women considered suitable to fill these positions. When she asked whether every man ever appointed to these positions had always merited that appointment, the response was 'absolutely not'. She therefore questions whether the notion of merit is not itself being introduced only because women's participation is the focus: 'Okay now, I'm committed to merit, to people earning the position they have. However ... I think it's interesting that the issue of merit wasn't a big issue. It wasn't a big issue until women came on the scene ... A lot of the time [the idea of merit] is propounded as the moral high ground, when in fact it was never an issue for anybody before. They were never thinking about that.' Given this background to its introduction, the suspicion is that the principle of merit is still something applied more to women than to men. This suggestion of the insufficiency of meritocracy as a means for women to participate in all areas of church and civic life looks for other approaches to facilitating women's involvement.

EQUAL OPPORTUNITIES

Advocating an equal opportunities approach to women's participation across the sexual division of labour considers that the playing field is not in fact level, that women are at a disadvantage, and hence that measures are required to facilitate women's participation. As Eilish Rooney argues:

> If there really was a 'level playing-field' in politics – as politicians of all hues frequently demand – then elected, representative assemblies could be expected to reflect the socio-economic and gender composition of the people who elect them. Just as, if there was true 'parity of esteem' in the workplace, then women, as well as Catholics, would be present in all ranks in proportionate numbers. If there was a fair distribution of rights and responsibilities in the home, then care of children, the elderly and the sick would be carried out equally by men and women. None of these situations obtains.[27]

Ensuring that there is equality of opportunity to participate is not the same thing as treating everyone equally. After all, 'equal treatment only works when it is applied to people in similar situations'.[28] People in unequal situations require different treatment and attention if all are to have the same opportunities. Measures to facilitate women's participation across the sexual division of labour may be grouped under the three general headings of active encouragement, specific education and structural support.

Active encouragement

Active encouragement recognises and highlights women's absence in certain areas of church, community and political life and then seeks to redress this in promoting women's involvement in these areas. This is different to a general acceptance of permission for women's participation. It is active not passive and requires time and energy.

An example would be the Methodist Church in Ireland's own report on the role of women in its denomination. This contains a number of recommendations to do with the education of its members, training of ministers, working with congregations, monitoring of gender representation, and the provision of structural support, all of which are designed to foster women's participation within the Church.[29] Reports of this kind are part of an active focus on and endorsement of women's participation.

They do, however, need implementation. As a Methodist woman commented on this report, 'The Methodist Church actually produced a very good document quite recently about the women's role in churches. And I was very heartened by that, but what has happened to that, where is it? It's sitting on my bookshelf and I reckon it's probably gathering dust in a lot of bookshelves because since its publication, I haven't heard it mentioned within the wider church.'

Active encouragement is an ongoing process. Speaking of her own investment in nurturing both women and men but particularly women, one para-church worker said, 'It all goes back to helping people start to think about who they are and people are coming out of cultures of church where you just don't do that ... I just think we don't have enough people around who help people see what skills they actually have ... [But then] it's not enough just to say to somebody, here's the skills, now go and use them. You have to support and nurture, you know, just build a relationship of trust.' A woman who is on the lay leadership team of her congregation expressed a similar idea: 'I've tried to take people under my wing and model something for them, to give them an opportunity. I think it's about recognising potential leadership and nurturing that in people, male and female.' This is similar to the idea of mentoring that one of the politically active women talked about, recognising that in the world of politics this would initially need to be done by men. The inevitability of men as first mentors for women would also apply in many areas of church life throughout Northern Ireland.

The need for women to be encouraged was a common theme among the interviewees, for example, 'I think women need to know that their views are important. And they need to be encouraged to be involved, and not "let's sit". And they need to be encouraged to speak out, even if it's difficult. And I think within, well [my] denomination, they need to be encouraged to be involved in committees and things.' As a young community worker put it, 'I think a lot of women need to know what they're good at.' A community trainer emphasised how this endorsement needs to come from a variety of sources: '[Women need to be] encouraged more, valued more by the church, by the community, and by the family. Being valued by the family. By husbands.'

Part of this process of active encouragement is changing women's own expectations of themselves. That this needs to happen suggests that women's 'choice' whether to participate or not is not always such a free and independent act, but rather the result of accepting a particular understanding of themselves. One woman commented, 'Women have grown to accept the stereotypes that society places upon them, or maybe that their home has placed upon them, or whatever.' She went on to say that challenging these stereotypes needs to go hand in hand with providing the actual opportunities for women to use the talents that they have, but she recognised, as do other women, that some women do not avail themselves of opportunities that already exist.

This lack of confidence in women has concrete outcomes as one interviewee illustrated: 'A lot of women, although they may see themselves as equal and whatever, do lack the self-confidence to get involved. I mean ... if there's an advertisement which says you need ten things for this job, and you have five of them and a man has five of them, the woman will think "oh, I've only five of that, I'll not go," but the man will say "well, five, I can go," you know ... would go and bluff the other five, you know ... So although we have been brought up with equality and what have you I think there is a realisation – well, there should be a realisation – that it's still not here, that utopia is a long way off.'

When thinking of women from evangelicalism, an element of the active encouragement for involvement in civic life needs to be an endorsement of the value of community and political involvement. The existence within evangelicalism of a suspicion of social concern and a disenchantment with Northern Ireland politics, compound other issues women face in thinking of involvement in society outside of church. Among the interviewees there were as many women who stated that their church (either its leadership or some of its membership) did not support, or in some cases did not even know of, their activities, as there were women who expressed receiving help and recognition. In some instances this lack may be attributed to a general disinterest or failure to relate to people in their individual situations. In others, however, the absence of support appears attributable to a lack of valuing what the women were doing, either because of their role or because they were women.

Specific education

The second group of measures involved in equal opportunities concerns education and training initiatives. Education in general is a means to opportunity in life. It can provide personal empowerment, employment possibilities, and potential financial security. In terms of 'levelling the playing field so that everybody gets a fair chance', one woman said, 'There's a certain degree of it needs to be dealt with early on, in that if you don't give the people the right education and opportunity you can be discriminating against them from the very beginning.'

In particular, knowledge and training gained through certain professions gives people greater access to involvement in politics. Preparation for political life frequently comes from experience in certain high-status and well-paid professions, 'brokerage jobs', which provide the security, flexibility and expertise that is valuable in the political world.

> Women in Northern Ireland are disadvantaged on such eligibility measures. Two-thirds of all women leave education with no formal qualifications, and the same proportion is clustered into three occupational sectors: clerical; catering, cleaning and other personal services; and health, education and welfare, within which they generally experience low pay and low status, while much smaller numbers of women are employed in high status, brokerage occupations.[30]

The profile of the Northern Ireland Women's Coalition (NIWC) candidates in the 1996 election to the Northern Ireland Forum for Political Dialogue reflects the educational and qualification levels more usual for politicians: 70 per cent were graduates or held a professional qualification, 53 per cent were adult returners to education, and 70 per cent were in full-time employment.[31]

Another factor in women's under-involvement in electoral politics is the lack of knowledge generally available about political life, both in terms of procedures and party systems. This would also be true in regard to public bodies.[32] A similar situation holds for some men beginning political life. The difference for women is that they are frequently excluded from the 'boys' network' which acts as an informal introduction to political processes. Women's lives have not generally equipped them for electoral and party politics. The fact that for many the route to political involvement has been through family connections and tradition[33] suggests a kind of 'insider' knowledge that provides an advantage of political 'know-how'. For the women involved in the NIWC, acquiring political skills was very much part of their participation in the political world. In the words of Kate Fearon, 'The bottom line was that the NIWC was a political education project on a huge scale.'[34] There are non-party initiatives aimed at providing women with the confidence and skills they need for political participation[35] and some individual parties provide training and development courses aimed at encouraging women to run for both party and public office.[36]

Part of what is required for women's participation across the sexual division of labour is a demystifying of political and community processes, professions, and church organisations. One woman employed in what has until recently been very much a male-dominated profession spoke of her education work with young people, particularly females, introducing them to non-traditional spheres: 'I like working with, sort of, young people in schools and things, I enjoy that ... It's not about, for me anyway, encouraging girls to go into science and technology careers, it's just about demystifying it so that if they want to they can. I'd hate to think there were people out there who wanted to do it and felt they couldn't because they were a girl.'

The same idea was expressed by another woman of her experience in community work: 'I remember saying to a woman, "Come on to a committee," and she said, "No I couldn't go onto that committee." "Why?" "Well, I wouldn't – they would talk about a whole lot of things I wouldn't understand." I says, "How do you know that?" "Well, I'm sure they do." And it's about [how] men build that little mystery round what they're doing, you know, this would be too much for women, you know, they wouldn't have the brains to understand it... It's all about demystifying the whole thing because men like to put that shroud round, that you really wouldn't understand, you're stupid, you know. And it's all about trying to crack through it. And then you find – I can do this standing on my head, you know. But ... there is that fear. Very, very much. And I'm sure it must be the same for a woman going into the ministry, or a woman going into any position of power, it must be the same for her, because you're going – how does it work, what do you actually have to do, what do you actually have to say? So it's all about that learning process for women.'

The community sector has been one area that has emphasised women's training and education. This emphasis is equally valid within church structures. In church contexts the language used is often that of gifting. Indeed, it could be that the idea of gifting is a form of meritocracy – gifting determines the person most suitable for the particular role or job in question.

An emphasis on people's gifting has been one means of enabling women to participate in more areas of church life. A male church leader had concentrated on the idea of gifting in involving more women in church life: 'My view is that ministry should be done on the basis of gifts, and that if somebody has a gift they need to know what that gift is and they need to use it. Now women have as many gifts as men have. Some are similar and some are different there, but, I'm talking about spiritual gifts particularly, and what needs to be done is that people need to accept ministry on the basis of gifts. And that's how you decide who is on a team and who isn't, on the basis of their gifts. Not on the basis of anything else really. Gender becomes secondary to that too, you know, it's on the basis of their gifts. So in [our denomination] as a whole if we could have more teams of people in gift-based ministry you would find that women would come to the fore and that's what I long to see happening. And I think it will happen.'

Another man thought this gift-based approach to ministry had to be taught from church leaders and modelled in practice, which in turn would encourage women's participation: 'Somehow in the church I think we have to teach the equality of gender, the mutuality of gender, the collegiate nature of the church, and it needs to filter down from the top ... When women come into church they hear women preaching from time to time, they see women leading worship, leading in prayer, doing all the things that men do, and I think it empowers some women to feel, you know, these are my gifts.'

Of course to ensure that such leadership is possible, there are training implications for everyone involved in a denomination. In the words of a woman with both church and para-church experience, 'You need enlightened leadership, really. And again where does that come from? Enlightened individuals, enlightened training at, you know, the core of the denominations, wherever they get their training. You have to go right back there which I suppose means that if you can get enlightened lecturers in there you'd be well on the way.'

Structural support

The third group of equal opportunities measures that facilitate women's participation across the sexual division of labour consists of forms of structural support. Such support includes consideration of childcare, attention to terms and conditions of employment, and removing discriminatory practices.

Questions around women's relationship to domestic responsibilities are explored in chapter six. The matter of childcare is raised here as a major factor affecting the nature of women's participation in church, community and political life. The reality that, in the main, women are primary carers means they do not have equal opportunities without structural support of some kind. The task of childcare affects not only the amount of responsibility that a woman has, but also the extent of control that she has over her use of time. The sexual division of domestic labour wherein women care for children and other adults (either as dependants or servicing their domestic requirements) does not fit easily into political, much church and some community business, which is not arranged around these realities for women 'who cannot clock on and off from their caring responsibilities'.[37] Hence, Ruth Lister speaks of 'the sexual division of labour and time'.[38]

This was recognised by many of the women interviewed: 'I would love to see more women being involved, but you see, realistically, I recognise that as a single person, I have the time and the flexibility. So for example, [my para-church organisation], we meet late afternoon. We try to get more women onto [the committees], but they're home feeding their children or whatever, or their husband, and it's just not really feasible.'

A politically active single woman considered that having a family and engaging in politics are incompatible activities for a woman: 'It's all very well. A lot of people say, "oh there should be more women in politics". But a man can just, you know, step out and do it and come home and his tea's ready and maybe his wife's done his ironing for him and all the rest of it. Whereas with women you've got to do that as well unless you've got a husband who is domesticated.'

Part of the answer to this is to provide childcare. As Eilish Rooney and Margaret Woods note, women devote a considerable amount of time to women's community groups[39] and 'the domestic responsibilities reason given by councillors and party representatives to explain why women are not involved in electoral politics would not apply to this kind of activity'.[40] However, the 'local group is a woman and child friendly place'.[41] Not all areas of community activism are as open in this regard as a community worker observed: 'Well I mean the women in management, some of it is cultural stuff like, you know, work culture.

You know, the timings of meetings, the childcare arrangements, because inevitably in the real world it is women who will take responsibility for childcare.'

The paucity of childcare in Northern Ireland[42] further exacerbates the situation regarding women's employment and education opportunities (part of the usual requirements that enable greater participation), as well as their availability for wider church or civic involvement.[43] One woman suggested churches could provide childcare to enable women to participate throughout denominational structures at decision-making committee levels. Another woman thought that denominations could look at the way training for ordained ministry is conducted. At present this requires attendance at a college, which, for both men and women, often means significant time away from the family home: 'If it's a young woman with a family it's bad when the husband is away and it's been very tricky for a lot of families, but I think it would be even worse when the mother's out of the house ... I would see that as being something that maybe would deter a lot of younger women with young families from offering themselves for ordination.'

A number of women suggested that the times at which various meetings are held could be examined so that women would be enabled to participate. Often in terms of church involvement this was viewed as not only benefiting women, but as a general facilitation of lay people's participation: 'I think the structure of how we do things would need to change here because so many of its committees meet through the day which means people who are on regular jobs outside of the church can't be on those committees, can't participate ... So the structure of how the institution is organised would need to change. And that would help not just women, but it would help to get more lay people involved as well, which would be enormously useful too.' A woman commented on how her political party had organised a weekday event specifically looking at women's participation in the party but that its timing excluded women who were in paid employment during the day. When she raised this it was clear the expectation was that if women were really interested they would take a day off work in order to attend.

Clearly different sectors and the various roles within each require different solutions. However, the need to give attention to the question of when meetings are arranged is something, in the words of one woman, 'every organisation should look seriously at'.

Another measure of structural support to ensure equal opportunities for women concerns the terms and conditions of employment for various roles and offices. In this regard a number of politically active women commented on the hours of the Westminster parliament where debates can go on into the night and even into the early hours of the following morning: 'How anybody can be in parliament is really, really difficult, where debates can go on endlessly, to midnight and beyond. I mean, I think it must be a severe strain on family life and marriage as well ... I think it's wrong. I mean political life is important. How we order our affairs and manage our education and roads and all those ordinary things, are hugely important. But it should not be at the expense of the family life.'

Issues around the number of hours worked and the expectation of availability at all times was something raised by women employed by churches. One woman reflected that the absence of recognised boundaries or a discussed understanding of expectations meant that whenever attending to a family matter clashed with the needs of the church she had to justify her non-availability to the church: 'I would much rather that I didn't have to fight for terms and conditions, that it was a given and I think it ought to be a given, but it isn't. And I hate, I really hate having to go to my boss and say, I cannot do this, you know, because it makes me feel that it's my problem ... I feel like I'm always having to ask for things that should be a given, that they are in most other professions.' This woman considered that this applied as much to men with families and to single people who were also entitled to agreed terms and conditions, but that in her experience men employed by churches did not raise these issues. Hence, 'I think there's an abuse of women and men in church life and in culture, but it's a case of I draw boundaries because I have to. But I really wish that some men would. And maybe some of them are, but the ones I know aren't.'

Also included in structural support are mechanisms designed to prevent sexual discrimination. A woman in politics stated, 'We have a fairly careful procedure about the kind of questions that you are and are not allowed to ask at selection meetings. There are certain things you can do to protect people from the kind of spurious questions like "What will you do with your children if you get elected?" And, you know, the man who was pretending – I actually saw this happen once at another party, and they asked the girl "What will you do with your children if you get elected?'' And she had one child, and the guy who was speaking before her asking to be selected as a candidate had four children, and no one asked him what he would do with his children. And I just thought it was bizarre in the extreme. And so those kind of things you can do something about, to remove the kind of barriers that are there.'

Commenting on her employment in a predominantly male-populated profession another woman active in the para-church sector in a voluntary capacity reflected on the changes in procedures that had taken place since the 1970s when 'I was asked questions in my interview which would be ruled out of court now in terms of how I would react in situations because I was a woman.' She went on to observe that in regard to the prevention of sexual discrimination, 'we've got legislation in organisations, secular organisations, that actually make sure that structures and practices are operating along those lines, but we haven't got that in the church'.

Some people may be of the view that equal opportunities is appropriate within secular organisations rather than within religious institutions. The extent of the influence of community, public and employment practices on church organisations is a recurring theme in this book. From her experience in both church and community one woman commented, 'What I would like to see would be ... Christians articulating something of the equal opportunities agenda, and that that could be brought more into mainstream church life!'

The belief in equal opportunities is not always endorsed without reservation. The woman quoted above who spoke approvingly of removing barriers of sexual discrimination in terms of the selection process for electoral candidates also favoured a general encouragement of women, good education, and the demystifying of processes and professions. However, she was uneasy about too much focus on gender. 'I would like to see people completely blind to the whole gender issue, selecting people on the basis of what they can bring to the job.' She was concerned about the effect of too much attention to gender and wondered about the implication of having questions that can and cannot be asked. 'The kind of message you send out if you say, "you can't ask that", are you drawing attention? I mean some of the things you do to help can actually make things worse. If you draw attention to the fact that you cannot ask candidates about their family arrangements and whatever, they will – people will then think, "ooh, ooh, is that because there's a woman standing, or is that because they don't know what they're going to do?" And you can raise those sorts of issues in their mind that were never there. So you have to be very careful.'

Those who do embrace equal opportunities see it as compatible with the idea of merit – that in removing the disadvantages which women experience, they may participate on an equal basis of their own merit. There is, however, a third approach to facilitating women's participation across the sexual division of labour that advocates additional measures.

AFFIRMATIVE ACTION

Affirmative action is also sometimes known as positive action or positive discrimination. This takes the notion of equal opportunities further and establishes criteria not simply to promote, but to guarantee women's participation across the sexual division of labour. It can be viewed either as a means to fast-track women's participation, which otherwise would take longer to realise, or as necessary because equal opportunities in and of themselves are not sufficient to ensure women's involvement. Most frequently associated with the application of numerical quotas of women to be appointed to a particular committee, a political party's electoral candidates and so forth, affirmative action is the stance most vehemently opposed by most of the interviewees who discussed it. And even the few who believe that some kind of affirmative action is necessary at the present time, tend to do so only reluctantly.

Affirmative action is most obviously associated with politics. In March 2001 in the build-up to the general election, the Equal Opportunities Commission called for new legislation which would permit the use of positive action by parties in order to ensure more women candidates.[44] The Commission took this position following research comparing levels of women's political representation in seven countries (including the UK), concluding that 'the single most influential factor, more than social and cultural issues such as women's professional standing, is the use of measures such as twinning,[45] zipping[46] and quotas'.[47] In the 1999 elections for the Scottish Parliament and Welsh Assembly the Labour Party adopted twinning of candidates. This resulted in equal numbers of their female and male candidates being elected in Scotland and two more Labour women than men being elected in Wales.[48] As already noted above, in Northern Ireland only two parties (Sinn Féin and the SDLP) have formal quotas of women on their national executives. Yvonne Galligan and Rick Wilford state that, 'Unless and until there is a paradigmatic shift to gender facilitation among the parties, most women will remain perched at the margins of both polity and society.'[49]

This view was not supported, however, by any of the political activists, from different parties and different positions on the Belfast Agreement, who discussed the idea of affirmative action: 'I would be totally against having quotas of women, totally. It's like saying you want quotas of Catholics or Protestants. You want quotas of comprehensive school kids in Oxford. You can't do this. How would you feel if you were a man and a woman is put in the position ahead of you simply because we need another woman, you're better qualified, you're better suited to the job, you're better in every direction, but you happen to be the wrong gender ... You can't start having tilted playing fields just to accommodate genders or colours ... It's soon going to be the case that if you happen to be Protestant Anglo-Saxon male you're not going to have a hope.'

Other political activists also linked opposition to affirmative action for women to resisting such measures on behalf of any group in society: 'We don't assess our Assembly team and say, well, how many Protestants do we have, how many Catholics do we have, how many atheists do we have, have we got a balance? Because we simply don't believe it's relevant to the job that they do. Equally I don't believe that their gender is relevant. I would like to see people completely blind to the whole gender issue, selecting people on the basis of what they can bring to the job. I'm not particularly interested whether those are white people, black people, Protestant people, Catholic people, men, women – just that they're the right person for that job.' As with some equal opportunity measures, affirmative action is clearly placed as incongruent with the notion of merit: 'The more you make an issue out of gender I think the more of an issue it becomes. I'm not interested in advancing anywhere on the basis of, you know, she's a girl. I never want that to happen. I feel the same about religion, about, you know, about disability, you know, all of those things. It should always come down to a merit principle.'

Affirmative action is opposed also because it is seen as ineffective, as not working. In some cases this is because it can lead to the wrong person being appointed. As a church worker put it, 'I don't know that going down the line of having a quota of women on things is the right way forward. It's the same as having a quota of young people on things, because inevitably you end up with the wrong people anyway, they just happened to be a woman.' Even if the women appointed are able for the job, they can experience enormous difficulties. One woman spoke of a situation where women in that position were not taken seriously: 'I've always been opposed, and again I've got myself into trouble ... for this, but I've always been opposed to protected seats, you know – quotas. I've always been opposed to that. Because I've found that in a situation where you had a quota, basically those people were ignored, because the rest of the body of people thought they weren't there as of right.'

This idea that quotas are self-defeating was also echoed by one of the women in politics in terms of creating disadvantage for women who gained positions through the use of quotas: 'If you put more people into a position based on what they are, being male or female, rather than their ability, you undermine their credibility in the job. And for that reason I would be against, for example, having the kind of positive discrimination that they used in the Labour Party, where they twinned constituencies, and quite openly said "a woman will have this constituency, a man will have this constituency". In reality it put a lot of women in parliament, and they're almost all invisible. Now there are a lot of invisible men in parliament too, but I wonder – I think the women who have done the best job for the Labour Party are the ones who would have won their selection anyway. Similarly with the Conservatives the women that you know, that you see, that you hear – they would have won their selection meetings.'

An example of how a woman's credibility can be undermined by the notion of position by virtue of gender was expressed by a young para-church worker. She had been asked to speak at a particular Christian event and had a conversation with a man who had in the past participated in this event, but had not been invited to do so this particular time. He 'knew that I had. And we had a conversation about [the event], and he said that he'd heard that the committee were wanting to bring on as many women as possible to fill the quota for that year ... Now I don't know whether that's true, but that was his perception, and he said, you know, they have been basically looking around for women speakers to fill that number, and it doesn't necessarily mean that they're good speakers or that they are better than men, but they have to fill those seats. And that comment instantly made me think, you know, you're implying to me that I'm not as good a speaker as you, you know, and that really you should have been included, but because I'm a woman I'm being the token woman in that place. And that's one of the very few times I've ever felt a bit of tension and I've felt that I've been insulted as a woman ... I did actually feel devalued.'

Despite that experience, this woman supported the idea of quotas: 'I think statistically there are far fewer women speakers in the world, Christian speakers, than men. Statistically. And if you look at the number who speak at festivals and events and – or ministers of churches, for example, there are more men than women I would say. Maybe I'm wrong. So therefore if an organisation [is] going to look for their top ten list of good speakers they'll automatically go for men rather than women. But I think it's really important that they decide no, we won't do that, because it will be far easier for us to lay our hands on ten good men than ten good women because we're more aware of where they are or we'll have heard more about them or whatever. So I think it is good that they set aside a pool, a number, just as I think they should do for disabled speakers because I think they need – that community needs to represented ... So I think it's a good thing.'

In fact the few women who supported, albeit mainly somewhat tentatively, the idea of affirmative action, were nearly all active in church life. In the words of one woman lay leader, 'I do think it's a major mistake if a church becomes so female led that men are then squeezed out of opportunities and leading, and equally if it's so male led that women are squeezed out. And it is a balance, as everything else, and I think so often historically women have been squeezed out that there maybe does need to be a bit of positive discrimination. But it's got to be carefully balanced so that it doesn't go the other way ... We want to have the best people preaching and teaching. And sometimes that means maybe a bit of positive discrimination towards the young people and women, and that's good and right. But I don't want to start to give away the leadership in the church to women for the right, for the sake of being women if there isn't gifting there, and if there isn't maturity there and if there isn't an anointing there.'

One community worker had similar thoughts in terms of women in management positions within the community sector: 'Sometimes I wonder about recruitment, you know, about active discrimination in terms of, you know, quotas and things to get women into positions because they must be there, it's just that they're not coming through for promotions and things.'

The strong distaste that a number of women have against affirmative action is rooted in the notion that it is both contrary to individual merit and unjust. An alternative view was given by the woman quoted above who wondered about the gendered application of the notion of merit: 'It's my view that to have excluded people means that you have to make some recompense and that this is not a moral affront to the notion of merit, and therefore for a term of time we may need to positively discriminate in order to redeem the situation and to bring it back to a norm or an ideal, or a more perfect kind of balance. Now I think that the issue of women in society is that important, that we have to go that far, but I don't think society at large thinks that. I think it's that important within churches and I don't think anybody's saying it ... And this in fact is as morally imperative as retaining the merit thing. I think it's that important.'

Each of the stances to facilitating women's participation across the sexual division of labour raises questions. For some a focus on women's involvement, whether through affirmative action or some kind of equal opportunity measure, threatens the notion of women earning their place because of their ability. Clearly, and indeed justly, their own demonstrable achievement in any given area is important to these women. Others see a need for some kind of equal opportunities measure – in the words of one woman, 'the middle part between doing nothing and [positive] discrimination' – in order to enable women's ability to lead to their participation. This view sees the disadvantage that women experience and seeks to redress that, and in doing so challenges the existing status quo. The greatest critique of the current situation, however, comes from the notion of affirmative action, which effectively 'legislates' for women's participation across the sexual division, because other approaches have proved either ineffective or slow in making an impact.

The various measures to facilitate women's participation across the sexual division of labour are not necessarily mutually exclusive. It is possible to actively encourage women and offer appropriate education and training for them to participate on, for example, a management board, and also to have a quota of places on that board reserved for women. This does not inevitably have to mean that women not qualified to participate will be appointed. On the contrary, it offers the possibility that able women will now become involved. It does not, unfortunately, mean that the perception of women's position as unmerited will necessarily change and this can, of course, affect the actual experience of the women concerned.

The women who strongly supported the idea of meritocracy on its own as being the way forward for women to participate in all areas of church, community and political life were, on the whole, women who had never considered themselves particularly discriminated against because they were women. Their own stories support the idea that gender is not a factor in a woman's participation across the sexual division of labour. However, as the following chapter demonstrates, the experiences of other women tell different stories and these must be considered in evaluating the extent to which women are not only free to participate, but are also fully included in the church, community and public life.

3

The Question of Inclusion

'The passing of a resolution and the living of it out and the working of
it out are two very different things.' These words spoken by a
female interviewee of the decision by the Presbyterian Church in
Ireland to ordain women are also relevant to a variety of areas in which
women may now be involved in church, community and politics.
Permission for women to participate and the achievement of particular
positions or appointments, is not always in and of itself the same thing as
full inclusion.

Of course, in the world of church and civic society there is much scope
for disagreement, personality clashes and principled differences (as well as
accommodation, co-operation and harmonious partnership!). Experiences
of hostility, exclusion, mistreatment and misunderstanding are not
reserved for matters around gender. The women interviewed, and some
of the men, spoke of a number of different kinds of conflict experienced in
the course of their lives and work. This chapter, however, addresses the

various kinds of antagonism experienced by women *because they are women*. While such conflict does not always manifest itself in isolation from other areas of disagreement, it is evident that forms of sexism[1] are often intrinsic to women's experiences in church, community and politics.

While it was a minority of women who stated they had never experienced any kind of conflict because they were women, and most women could articulate at least one experience of overt or hidden sexist treatment, for many women such negative experiences were not the dominant factor in their activism. A few were reluctant to talk about negative experiences because on the whole they had been well received and it seemed almost petty to talk of the occasional incident of difficulty. For others, while the opposition they experienced had been obvious, it came from particular individuals and at the same time these women had received support and encouragement either from other individuals or the congregation, group or body with which they were involved. Hence, for some of them, the negative experience had been reduced in its impact. There were others, however, for whom experiences of opposition and conflict had infiltrated their lives in inescapable ways, often with ongoing and unavoidable repercussions.

This chapter explores the different kinds of conflict which women can experience as they participate in church, community and politics. This conflict includes overt opposition and indirect forms of prejudice as well as structural factors and mindsets. It also involves women's experience on both sides of the sexual division of labour. While individual women have different stories to tell, the overall picture suggests that church and society in Northern Ireland still have much to learn about becoming inclusive of women.[2]

Before exploring the different kinds of conflict that women describe it is useful to consider women's reflections on good experiences of inclusion.

Experiences of Inclusion

One reason why some women felt acceptance and inclusion in their activism was because of the fact that they were in positions which women were expected to occupy, often working in areas populated by women, that is, focused around women and children. That is not to imply that women only experience opposition from men. Such is not the case, although men are more usually in positions of power and influence from which they can make life difficult for women. Nor should it be assumed that in these female-populated spheres women are immune from conflict that occurs *because they are women*. However, when women are active in areas considered to be women's domain, areas which often involve a majority of women, they may not encounter the overt kind of prejudice that other women experience, operating as they do to a large extent organisationally and even physically separate from men.

For other women, their sense of inclusion (despite some incidents of opposition) came from encouragement, personal endorsement and support from those who had appointed them, worked with them, or whom they now served in their particular capacity. In such cases there was sometimes a reluctance to focus on gender, because it seemed a non-issue. As one church worker put it, 'I don't want to look for problems that aren't there.'[3]

For those who did comment on reasons for women's good experiences of inclusion, three factors were identified: following in other women's footsteps; good processes; and an emphasis on gifting.

The main factor identified in women's good experiences of acceptance and inclusion was not being the first woman in the particular role. Notably women in positions of church leadership commented on how this had helped them, for example, 'The path has probably been made a lot easier for me on all three occasions because there was a girl before me [each time].' Following in another woman's shoes gets over the novelty factor in having a woman in a leadership role.[4] Reflecting on her church where they have experienced women preaching, one female church leader said, 'People were used to women in the pulpit and a lot of the difficulty is just simply being used to the idea. I mean women doctors, it took some time to get used to the idea.' As a political activist commented on her church experience, 'I think the ordination of women within our church was a bit of a shock for a lot of people to see. I mean, I'm quite content with it myself, probably because I've had some very good experiences from female preachers and what have you, you know.'

An ordained woman who was the first woman appointed to her congregation was also aware of the impact of a first experience of a woman in leadership: 'I know there were reservations and people would have told me that themselves, you know, "I wasn't keen but now that you've arrived I think it's a great thing." ... I mean there will always be the one or two who will hang on to [their view] ... there'd be one or two strong evangelicals in [the church], who don't really understand why I think I can be ordained and a woman, but they like me and they're willing to put up with it. But I wouldn't necessarily have changed their views. And there would be others whose views I would have changed. But ... I think there are very few who now wouldn't want another woman minister.'

This value of having female predecessors does not apply only to women in church. One para-church volunteer spoke of her professional life in which she had experienced both sexism and encouragement from her superiors: 'My immediate boss actually was very sexist in the way he, you know, he related to me. But the head of department was fearsome in many ways, but ... he told me in no uncertain terms that, you know, that nothing was barred to me. Now I think he'd been – and he admitted it actually – he was influenced by another woman who would I think take an openly feminist stance in the sense of her involvement in organisations that looked after women's, you know, pursued women's rights. So I think she had paved the way and made it easier, and awakened his awareness.' This is an example of how paying attention to gender facilitates women's inclusion. Another example is provided by a community worker who, despite experiences of women being marginalised in senior positions within her sector, nevertheless felt that much of her experience was beneficial for women: 'Certainly my experience in the community sector as a woman was different from that in the church because there's more of an acceptance of gender issues in general. And women's groups are quite frequent in community circles and they are looking at women's issues as well as a whole range of other social issues. So probably the awareness is a bit more, a bit higher.'

A second factor contributing to a sense of inclusion was identified by some of the women in positions of church leadership, namely that of good processes. In these situations where women's participation in formal leadership was a change from established practice, women commented on the importance of careful procedures that involved the whole congregation. One woman spoke of how she became a member of the leadership team of a sizeable congregation. A fairly open process was conducted over time which allowed for individual members to state their views, 'and so it is a large church and only two people, you know, objected on the grounds of me being a woman. And one person left over the issue', but overall, 'I have very, very rarely felt, you know, that people have not received me as a woman.'

The third factor that helped in women's experience of inclusion was an emphasis on gifting and team work. In one sense this is part of good process in providing leadership of a congregation. Unlike the above example, however, those who spoke of an emphasis on gifting or team work did not necessarily highlight the importance of gender. As one woman employed by her church commented, 'The [church leader] is looking for people who will work with him and make things happen, and he seems to have a very healthy regard for, I don't know how to put it really, but people who have particular gifts, he wants to make – to utilise them and make them happen. And I don't think he's honestly terribly concerned in terms of the male-female issues.' A male church leader made a similar point: 'We here in this church have one woman on the staff and she's the first to ever have been in this church. When she came I deliberately made no mention, or no drawing attention to the fact that she was a woman; it was never mentioned that she was the first and all this kind of stuff. She was an individual, she was a minister, she was part of a team, and I never wanted to draw attention to her gender, really. I didn't think it wasn't an issue ... We try to make it not an issue. She is a person, she has a ministry, she has gifts and she just gets on with using them ... I'm pleased that there hasn't been any reaction against her, the fact that she's a woman.'

These stories demonstrate that it is possible for women to experience inclusion when they cross the sexual division of labour. Such inclusion, however, is by no means guaranteed, as is clear from the following experiences of conflict encountered by women *because they are women*.

Experiences of Conflict

One possible way to present the types of conflict that women encounter *because they are women* in their involvement in church, community and politics, would be to consider separately that particular opposition experienced by women in positions of religious authority which is based on biblical interpretation. The reason for isolating this kind of conflict would be because the exclusion of women from such religious leadership has a legitimacy within evangelicalism, since it is bound up with biblical interpretation and church tradition. Treated this way it would be relevant to consider the manner in which those opposing women in religious leadership behave towards women who occupy these positions and also how they generally deal with challenges to their understanding, accepting the fact that there is a theological rationale for their view. Certainly, the biblical debate about women, men and authority is considered in chapter five and is not the focus here. There are, however, a number of difficulties with an approach that separates the conflict concerning women in positions of religious authority from other kinds of conflict women experience in their church, community and political involvement.

The first difficulty is, at what point does one draw the line? For some, it is women's ordination that should be prohibited, but not necessarily their preaching or participation in directing public worship. For others, their understanding excludes women from formal ordination and teaching roles, but not from other forms of lay leadership. Another view is that women may not take part in any kind of ordained or lay leadership of the whole church, but may contribute in the leading of public worship. Some who would prohibit women from any kind of leadership nevertheless allow women a voice in the affairs of a congregation through formal mechanisms of church meetings. Other congregations do not have women participating in any of these ways. In short, it is not possible to identify clear lines within evangelicalism which mark out those areas of religious activity in which women either have or have not the authority to participate.

The second reason for not isolating conflict to do with women in positions of religious authority is because some of the types of conflict that these women experience are also encountered by women in the community and political sectors and by women in the church who are not ordained. In other words, while particular circumstances differ, there are some common elements in women's experiences of conflict. Forms of harassment, for example, have been experienced by women in leadership both in and outside of the church, and by women in the church who do not occupy positions of formal leadership. The phenomenon of not being taken seriously is common to most women at some point in their engagement in church, community and politics. Further, women experience this kind of treatment from Christians (including evangelicals)[5] as well as from those who espouse no such personal faith. Such similarities, elaborated below, suggest that a consideration of conflict concerning women in religious leadership would benefit by first being placed in a wider context.

Finally, following on from these similarities, it is clear that the difficulties that women encounter are not restricted to women in formal religious leadership positions. This indicates that opposition or hostile behaviour towards women in leadership positions in church and society is not operating in isolation from particular attitudes towards women in general. This is not to say that anyone holding the view that it is biblical to exclude women from positions of religious authority are those (both women and men) with particular attitudes towards women, although they may be. Rather, it is to acknowledge that beliefs about women in leadership occur in a context of attitudes and assumptions (conscious or otherwise) about women's nature and place and amid established structures and practices that affect women's experience of their church, community and political participation. In this sense it is possible that conflict regarding women in religious leadership highlights existing issues around women rather than creates them anew. In other words, the question of inclusion is about how women and men relate in all areas of life, not simply how they negotiate spheres of religious authority.

This chapter, then, considers a variety of conflict experienced by women in church, community and politics. Some examples are more overt than others. By overt, this does not mean that a particular situation has high public visibility. Rather, it is more easy to identify by the woman concerned. Some conflict is more hidden in that it is harder to articulate even though women have a sense of having experienced some kind of prejudicial treatment because they are women. This kind of conflict may be hard to confront because frequently those responsible for the prejudicial treatment are unaware of the import of their actions. Unfortunately this also can be true of overt opposition that women experience which the instigators sometimes justify to themselves.

EXCLUSION

The experience of exclusion has a number of forms and can be harder to identify than might be expected.

One form of exclusion is prohibition from participating in certain areas. This is most obvious in church contexts in those congregations which restrict women's activity to communal hymn singing. For example, 'The men were allowed to pick the hymns, but the women, all you were allowed to do was stand and make up extra volume by singing them ... It just is so absurd that you almost had to laugh, otherwise you were going to cry about it, you know.' Not conforming to a congregation's accepted norms of gender participation is a rare event: 'When it came to the Lord's table it was some brother gave thanks for the bread and wine, and a friend of mine who on one occasion when they didn't say, "would some brother", she gave thanks, and there was shocked silence. You know, we could not do that. That was not part of our role, and there were certain things that we just were not allowed to do.'

In these kinds of situations it is very hard for women to find ways to express themselves. Speaking of her mother's experience in such a congregation one woman commented, 'She was very aware that she had learned an awful lot over the years as a Christian, and it was all being taken in but not being used, and although she was too timid to use it in any way, she felt at a certain level that she would like to have the opportunity to.' Those who do wish to contribute in some way have to find other avenues to do so: 'Anything that was in me in terms of a sense of what God wanted me to do, I always found fulfilment outside of the local church as opposed to inside it.' A community worker commented, 'I would have the skills of being a good leader, but within the church setting I have never been given the opportunity to exercise those.'

One aspect of women's experience of exclusion from positions in which their gifts might be used can be living with the knowledge that the man who is appointed is not as able as they are. Speaking of a university Christian union which had to be led by a man, one woman said of the male leader, 'I really felt that I had more ability than the guy, but just because he was a guy, you know. And I mean I just couldn't get my head round that.' This is an experience that contrasts with the view (discussed in chapter two) that equal opportunity measures can lead to women being appointed on the basis of their sex and not necessarily their merit. The experience of this woman and of others is in fact the reverse, that men who are not necessarily the most able are appointed to positions because of their sex.

One effect of the exclusion of women from certain offices, functions or responsibilities within a denomination or congregation is that there appears to be an absence of conflict concerning women's participation. A male church leader commented that at a congregational level his church did not experience conflict over women's participation because there were no women on the ruling body of the congregation. Another man said of a group of churches, 'I don't think they've engaged in this [issue], and as a result haven't had any conflict, but for the churches that will go for it, if they do there will be.'

Certainly, if everyone adheres to and is comfortable with the assigned gender roles then there really may be an absence of conflict. However, an absence of open conflict is not necessarily the same as an acceptance of the status of women's involvement. One woman who felt that the question of women's participation had not been a source of open conflict in her church described 'just feeling frustration, but not conflict. In my own church I would feel very frustrated, now. Women aren't – we don't take part in communion or anything in our church, and we wouldn't have any role at all [like the] men.'

As already noted, women from such churches often find avenues outside of the congregation for more Christian activity. In doing so, conflict is avoided because they find fulfilment for their gifts and abilities elsewhere. This path may be the most realistic option for many of these women, but it avoids or diffuses rather than confronts or resolves conflict over women's church participation. Further, a consequence of the apparent absence of any conflict within congregations means that if women do raise the question of their inclusion they are usually seen as creating the conflict while what they are actually doing is revealing a situation of conflict that already exists.

Another form of exclusion women experience in relation to religious organisations is, in the words of one church worker, 'a barring of an opportunity to be in certain places'. Ordained or lay women may not receive invitations to participate in services in particular congregations or at events, whereas their male counterparts are invited. One interviewee knew of a group of ministers who played golf together but did so at a club that did not have women as members, automatically excluding any women ministers who might wish to join them.

Women also experience exclusion by being treated as irrelevant or by being ignored. A church worker and a community worker both spoke of how they saw their work being undervalued or bypassed in a church context because of their involvement as women. Another community worker in a church-connected project told of how her reporting of her work was only believed if what she said was endorsed by a male colleague. A woman in politics reflected how, despite her activism, she was not considered as a party candidate until the point when 'they were stuck' for someone to stand.

Women are also excluded when they are the ones doing the work but receive no recognition (and hence no support) for it. One woman recalled, 'I can remember sitting in that church and they'd call the men up to pray for them – what they called the pillars of the church, let's pray for all you men. They did nothing and there'd be me sitting there and all these women, who worked there, you know, sitting. You've no idea how that makes you feel as a teenager, you know, and all these men getting prayed for and you're just left sitting.'

An all too common form of exclusion is the experience of being invisible, when women are frozen out, ignored, overlooked or deliberately snubbed when they are present in person at meetings and events. The only woman at a small church group of invited members, one interviewee found there was not even a chair provided for her. Speaking of being the only woman participant at a religious gathering among a very large group of men, all but one of whom ignored her, one interviewee said, 'I thought if I had been part of the ladies who served the tea they would have spoken to me. But because I was there and they weren't sure who I was, what I was, they didn't speak.' Aware of a friend's similar experience of a religious group, a community worker pointed out, 'it's that rudeness that I think she finds very difficult'.

A woman involved in politics described her experience of invisibility in political settings. While men indicate they want to contribute with just 'a flick of their eyes or gesture with their finger ... I put my hand up like at school and I wave and ... they can see anything else around the whole table except me.' She spoke of, as a woman, being ignored when formal introductions were taking place and of not being invited to join in with everyone else socially after meetings, 'where the chit-chats were going on, you have to go [so] I just opened the door and walked in and that was it, silence'.

This kind of exclusion can be very hard to confront or deal with. Recognising what is happening doesn't necessarily make life easier for women who encounter this behaviour. One woman who had a range of experience at work, in the community and in politics put it like this: 'What happens if I get into a room full of men and they just ignore me? And everything you say is surplus to requirement, and that can be very difficult to deal with, because you always feel then that you're just wasting your time. And I've had that experience over and over and over and over again, where you would go into a room and you'd make some contribution to the meeting, and it's almost as if you haven't spoken ... But as I say, you know, there's different ways of dealing with conflict. If it's open in your face you can deal with it, but it's not always like that ... I mean I've been in a room [with] quite learned men, you know ... but you can be frozen out. Almost like, "well she's a woman, like, she's not saying anything of any value," and that can be very hurtful also.'

Finally, in considering forms of exclusion, one woman reflected on the exclusion women experience in terms of the handling of biblical tradition. She articulated a sense of alienation she encountered when being led in a meditation around the story of Jesus calling his disciples. She and the others present were directed 'just to sort of think about that story and try and put ourselves into that, you know, into that place, and just think about it, just sort of picture it, and, you know, all of this. Then we were to say what we had experienced through that. And actually what I had experienced was, I was actually saying in my mind's eye to the Lord, "well, these were all men," you know, and where is – I was aware at that stage of that sense that men knew what their role was but women weren't too sure. [I think also about] how we read the Bible, and the role of women in Scripture, and how often it's played down or not talked about at all, and yet there was a place there, you know. And how whole theologies are built around that.'

Exclusion, then, has many forms. It may be experienced when women are present as much as when they are absent. And it operates both organisationally and conceptually.

CONDESCENSION

Something that many of the women talked about was their experience of not being taken seriously. In the forms of being patronised, belittled, ridiculed, not listened to, unacknowledged, and shown disrespect, this condescension was experienced not only by women in positions of leadership and in male-dominated spheres, but by women who were involved in areas of traditional and generally accepted women's activity. From listening to their stories it is hard not to conclude that a culture exists in both church and society that disvalues the contribution of women, and by implication, women themselves.[6]

Not being taken seriously is something many women are aware of. Referring to her work as a teacher, one woman spoke of staff meetings where 'I really felt that men's opinions were taken more seriously than women's.' Commenting on the dynamics in a church committee another woman observed, 'The people with the power on the committee are men, and they seem to listen with more respect and more attention to what men say.' This was the experience of another interviewee who found her clear directions as chair of a para-church committee meeting being ignored, with the male committee members paying no attention to her.

Women active in church, community and politics spoke of times when they made a contribution that was ignored, only to have the same matter given attention when raised by a man. Speaking of a political context one woman reflected, 'Are your ideas and thoughts as acceptable as a man's? The man can stand and say gobbledegook and he's listened to, but a woman comes on with something sensible, she's not listened to. I have found ... that I would make a proposal, something that needed doing ... you know, something that was an issue. And it was sort of going to the general sort of discussion. Two minutes afterwards a man would pop up and say [virtually the same thing] ... And I'll think, that's exactly what I said a couple of minutes ago, but it wasn't picked up as anything sort of sensible. And yet when the man tries to say exactly the same thing, not in maybe the same way ... but he will be listened to. And I'll say, right, hold on a minute, I said that first of all, but they don't think it's sensible when it comes from a woman.'

A woman active in her church noticed this same phenomenon in house-group situations where 'I might make a comment and it will not be viewed as being as authoritative as ... men who may say something [and] it'll be listened to as being more significant and authoritative because of who is saying it. And many women do the same. It isn't just men who'll listen. I think many women listen to men and say, well he said it, it must be okay.'

In fact, one woman was so used to not being taken seriously that she could identify the precise incident when she felt her opinion was heard. She had moved to a different church and had been asked for her view on something relating to the church building: 'I think that was the first time I ever really thought my opinion was important in the church. I would have had opinions before, but wouldn't have felt they were important.' Not paying due attention to what women say is a common phenomenon.

One part of not being taken seriously is ridicule, and this often happens when the matter being discussed concerns gender. For example: 'It has happened to me at work; if one takes a position where one is advocating equality, then it is met with, I've seen it met with derision, which has been quite hurtful ... and actually an awful lot of just total stupidity in terms of coming off with stuff – either they've gone off down a kind of sexual route or else they've actually just treated the thing without, you know, with a total lack of seriousness.' If women protest against the ridicule they may be accused of being humourless and of taking themselves too seriously, whereas the difficulty actually is in them not being taken seriously enough. The more women protest, the more the very issue they are trying to raise is used to undermine them.

Women also experience being patronised. A woman related how men in the church had suggested that women could not greet people at the door of the church building before a service because it would be too cold for them. Other women mentioned how they were addressed; for example, 'Men tend to sort of call you "dear" when you get into an argument, which I find most condescending. "Now dear" – now I find that insulting.' Speaking of a political context in which women were a minority, another woman remarked: '[At] first it was terribly obvious, you know. "Thank you gentlemen" at the end of a meeting, "oh and ladies". And opening doors, which is fine and very polite, but they kind of over-did it for a while. You know, they were bending over backwards because there were women present, but they've stopped doing that ... At the start sometimes they were patronising and condescending, but that seems to have stopped a bit as well now. They argue with us just as much as each other ... They've got used to us.'

A community worker was very aware of being treated differently when she became a mother: 'After I had [my child] I wasn't taken as seriously. I certainly wasn't taken as seriously when I was pregnant, and sitting, even heavily pregnant, in meetings, definitely not. Definitely a lot patronised and definitely not taken seriously.'

Another aspect of not taking women seriously is taking them for granted. One woman spoke of how she established a particular community project which was given very little attention by the management board and which she did voluntarily. When it became a viable project as a result of her work and creativity it was taken away from her: 'This is what I'm talking about not taking the women seriously. [It was] all going really well, and then they thought maybe that there was an opportunity there for sustainability and wages and that. They brought in a business manager.' A similar experience was related by another community worker: 'I've done all the ... hard work and they're going to pass it over to a man, you know.' Both of these cases were church-connected community projects.

Other women were simply overlooked and their contribution unacknowleged. Several women told of achievements in their particular sphere of activity that were not recognised.

Women also spoke of occasions when assumptions were made about them. A community worker and para-church worker both told of being mistaken for secretaries because there were so few women present in the respective meetings. The community worker who was the lone woman delegate at a meeting told of how the person concerned actually said to her, 'I'm sorry, I just assumed you were someone's secretary.' In her own words, 'It never crossed his mind that a woman could possibly be one of these leaders. And I found that extraordinary, because ... at that time I'd quite a high profile [in regard to that context]. And I found it extraordinary that he just – it didn't click on him, you know. Whose secretary was I? And why would I be there? Nobody else had a secretary.' Another woman was taken for the administrator of the course rather than the person actually providing the training. Despite her appointment by a church for a specific non-domestic role within it, one woman told how she thought at first it was a joke when 'one of the workers said to me, "Ah good, now you can help with making the tea and stuff and making the buns, you know, on the workers' days." And I laughed and then I looked at him and I thought, you're serious.' A further example comes from a woman relating the time she attended university open days in order to help her choose which subject to study. She went to a number of traditionally male departments with a genuine interest in their subjects and said of one of them, 'I think they assumed I was there to follow the boys around, you know, and there was that kind of attitude still.'

A further way in which women experience not being taken seriously is by a questioning of their ability. Despite a general level of acceptance, a political activist pointed out, '... whenever you seem to go that wee bit further, there's a question mark over a woman's ability and they don't think a woman's quite up to it'. Another woman spoke of how a friend of hers had been appointed onto a church committee but had been told by one of the men that as they would be discussing something she would know nothing about, she need not participate. A female minister had difficulty getting workmen to discuss with her the repairs to the church building: 'They weren't really going to discuss with me. I thought, they're just thinking what could this girl possibly know?' Another woman found that people assumed she had achieved her position not by 'getting there by right, [but] I was getting there by who I was sleeping with. And that's a kind of a scary thing, that people actually think that because you're a woman you can't make it any other way.'

A community worker was very aware of the contrast between the way women's abilities were used in spheres outside of the church, but not recognised within it: 'Being in an almost all-female organisation, the chairwoman is a woman, the treasurer is now a woman, and so on. All the roles, managerial, everything – run by women. Property matters run by women, you know. And yet in the church all those jobs are given to men, or taken by men. And I feel it's, you know, there's a massive gap between the two, because you go into your work situation and you're used to, you know, having responsibility or other women having responsibility, with money or whatever it is, and then in the church there's a feeling – I feel there is a sense that you can't trust the women with those big matters, you know, like property and money, and . . . so on. And there's a lot of women sitting in the congregation in very responsible jobs outside church, but in church they're just sitting there, you know, and they're put on the cleaning team or the tea rotas or whatever . . . that's it, you know, and that really frustrates me.'

Only one woman was able to identify a positive side-effect of not being taken seriously. In the context of working only with women, 'We're not taken quite as seriously, so I think we get away with more, and I think it's worked out to our advantage. I think we have dealt with issues that maybe some of the sort of [male organisations] have been scared to deal with, and because we have dealt with them then it's made a way for them to move.'

While most of the above examples describe incidents where individual women were not taken seriously, other women spoke of occasions when condescension was not directed to an individual *per se*, but to women as a group. A woman who worked with a woman's organisation in her church spoke of how men left the room when the women's report was being given. While the men had listened to other women speak on other matters, 'it was the fact that I was talking about women's work, a woman's movement, that's not interesting. We don't – what do we want to know about that for? ... we're not interested. It's that, it's the perception of a woman's group, a woman's organisation ... Where they might respect an individual woman, but it is showing disrespect for ... a gender.'

Another woman observed this kind of dynamic in relation to the Northern Ireland Women's Coalition as opposed to other women politicians: 'There was the whole Women's Coalition thing which seemed to end up being a – for a lot of people – a subject of mockery more than necessarily be taken seriously. And for there to be, you know, women politicians who are taken seriously, that would certainly be something that I would feel strongly about.'

The suggestion here is that disrespect of individual women is intrinsically connected to a disvaluing of women as a group. In the words of one interviewee: 'I think we're a long way from getting that respect. And even in the most educated circles. Even in the circles of the church. I mean you're miles away from getting that respect, because you're just a wee woman, you know, and like what would you really know? And, you know, even women who have done sterling work here in the political scene are still treated like that, you know. They're still treated like, oh, well like, you're women. Let's give them a wee committee and they'll talk a sentence to death. Even in this project here.'

NUMBERS COUNT

One factor hindering women's full inclusion in various ways in church and civic society is the dynamic created by the numerical imbalance between female and male participants in any situation. The idea of the token woman is probably the best-known example of this numerical factor and certainly has been experienced by some of the women interviewed. It is not, however, the only way in which the numbers of women and men involved impact on women's experience of their church, community and political participation.

On a very practical level, women can find being a lone woman in a group of men intimidating. A woman active in the church reflected on how she had become aware of this: 'I think I have noticed being a woman on committees or whatever that there is – people talked about it and I at first, when I was younger, didn't see it, but I see it now – there's a confidence problem that you have. If I'm sitting as the only woman in a group, not so bad if I know them all very well, but if I don't it's hard to break into the general conversation, unless you're very, very sure of your ground. And because I would be by nature fairly shy, I sometimes do find that a problem.' Another woman who did not consider herself shy or lacking in confidence or the ability to assert herself, also commented on the experience of being one of few women in a committee context: 'It was incredibly difficult to have any sort of a say because it was all – it was very male-dominated, and the men that were there knew each other extremely well, so really only listened to each other, and never ever opened the door up to allow me to have a comment.'

One woman spoke of the reaction when she did find a voice in a numerically male-dominated church setting: 'I asked a question, just a legitimate question ... and it was the most amazing reaction, it was "we've got a woman's voice here", you know. People were turning round and staring at me ... I must say the chairperson, to give him his due, although he'd [used exclusive language throughout] ... he knew me and he called me by name and said something, but I think most of them were so stunned that they actually heard a woman's voice that it was lost. And it was a general question, it wasn't anything gender specific, it was to do with whatever they were talking about.'

Women's numerical minority experience often ties in with them not being taken seriously. As a woman involved in politics commented on being the only woman in certain political contexts, 'While [the men] are very courteous, I wouldn't exactly say I would be part of ... I wouldn't be one of the boys, sort of thing, in meetings and that, and there are one or two exceptions to that now, but by and large you wouldn't be treated as an equal, you know... Now there would be ... exceptions to the rule, but the bulk would still carry that prejudice that you're a woman, and like, what would you really know?'

Encounters such as these contribute to a sense that women's presence may often be just tokenism, that is, for the sake of having *a* woman present, but not necessarily taking women seriously or expecting their equal participation. One woman felt that tokenism accounted for the presence of a woman on the leadership team of her church: 'It was a token ... I'm just more comfortable where it [that is, women as leaders] is accepted and encouraged.'

This is a difficult arena to negotiate for women who may only get 'token woman' invitations to participate and yet can use that opportunity to try and make a contribution. For example, 'I suppose in reality I get invited onto things because it's good to have a woman. But then we all represent various constituencies at various times, we're all invited to do things because we've a particular interest or whatever, so you know, it's kind of fair enough. So I suppose in a way ... if I hadn't been a woman I probably wouldn't be involved in as many things, I guess.'

Not all women feel the same way about tokenism and, indeed, not all women feel their participation as lone women to be tokenism. Even when there was an element of tokenism involved, some women spoke of being well received by their male colleagues when they were either the only woman or in a minority in an overwhelmingly male-dominated setting: 'I'm able to be on as many committees as I want, it's more a case of turning them down, partly because there are so few women [in this sector] and they all want the token women presence ... But I'm never made to feel that I'm on as a token woman or that I'm on as a minority and sort of what do the women think. I would say I'm generally accepted as a colleague and that's that, by and large.' Another woman who also had felt included as a lone woman in a church leadership team wondered if it was being the only woman that actually made her acceptable to her male colleagues because as a lone woman she was not a threat to them.[7]

Other women indicated their dislike about being part of tokenism for example, 'And in terms of representation on other committees, in fact at times I get far too many of those because they're always looking for a woman. There are so few women around. So I end up being the token woman rather too often and that can get irritating.'

What some of these comments reveal is that with fewer women in various leadership or brokerage positions (that is, those positions that are deemed to qualify a person for committees, organisations, boards, councils) the fewer women there are to call upon to participate in various ways and, hence, the potential for over-involvement of some individual women.[8] For this reason one male church leader felt that there was an imbalance in the numbers of women involved in church structures. Given the relatively small number of women ministers overall in his denomination, he considered that their involvement in denominational processes amounted to a form of 'reverse discrimination' (described in chapter two as affirmative action). If this is an accurate assessment, it is perhaps inevitable if women's voices are to be included in these structures.[9] While it would not be possible where ministerial representation is concerned, in other contexts where women's participation is sought, one way the evangelical community could address this situation might be to reassess the criteria on which invitations for participation are based. This need not mean reducing the qualities expected of people, but rather widening the understanding of suitable brokerage positions.

Of course, a woman may be given a genuine invitation to participate in something even though she ends up being a minority woman in the group. Here the problem can be the same as in cases where tokenism is operating at some level, namely, that there are assumptions that one woman can represent all women or that a woman can speak only on issues perceived to be women's concern, and in either case, that one or two women are sufficient for the purpose. Hence, while all the individuals involved contribute towards the nature of the experience of a lone woman in a group, it is also evident that the numerical balance between female and male participants in any situation affects the extent of inclusion a woman may experience.

INCLUSIVE LANGUAGE

While there are more issues surrounding gender and language than the question of inclusivity,[10] language is a powerful tool to either include or exclude women as they participate in church, community and politics.

The most familiar way this happens is through the use of generic terms such as 'man', 'mankind', 'he', 'brothers', 'brethren', 'chairman'. These words refer to males but when used generically are said to either include or even at times solely refer to females. In effect, however, such generic terms make women 'linguistically invisible'.[11]

It is women themselves who can best express how important it is to be linguistically included:[12]

> I love to hear people saying 'sisters and brothers' – I don't even like 'brothers and sisters' when they just add 'sisters' on. I like people who've thought further to say everybody needs to hear this so you put 'sisters' first ... I do like it, it just makes me feel this is about me.

I can't bear to hear 'him' ... I just can't bear it now, it's become, you know, grating on my ears now. And I think there's no excuse for it anymore. I mean I exist and I don't exist as part of 'him' and I just can't bear it, but that's a dodgy issue. People think that's being petty, but I don't think it is, I don't think it is being petty at all. I could change it round the other way and start by saying, you know, 'her' and 'womenkind', but the men wouldn't be too long in objecting about being left out.

It's so important that you're not addressed just as 'brothers'. I mean basic things like 'sisters and brothers'. I mean still at times at [the annual gathering of the church], we would be addressed as 'fathers' and 'brethren' or 'you men in the ministry'. Or 'if a man does this' or 'if a man does that' or, you know, 'the right man for the job'. And I find that offensive, you know, because it's just a total lack of thinking, insensitivity, unacknowledgment of the fact that there are other people here who are not men.

I would not be into insisting on politically correct language. I never have been ... But I have never ever felt as uncomfortable in a meeting because everything, the language, the approach, everything was orientated to men. And they had four women sitting there and two of us had bright red jackets on.

I'm very angry with ministers who get up and pray for the men they are training in the college. I was thinking of one who I know is anti-women ministers, so it would be deliberate, you know, but he won't even acknowledge that there are women there training. And I found that, you know, very, very difficult because I feel, just as a Christian, he's really demeaning them, he's really saying, you know, 'you're not there, you don't matter'.

I notice it when it's not used all the time. Every time it's not used and it should be. Oh yes, yes the guy leading the worship at church last night talked – in the prayer or something – talked about you know, 'all men'. And I'm thinking, hang on a second here ... I was very shocked actually that he wasn't using it, you know, inclusive language there.

Just from a purely practical and emotional point of view, I'd rather be included as not. And I think language is one symbolic way of people being included.

There are a number of reasons for advocating the use of gender-inclusive language. There is the difficulty in determining on occasions whether a term is being used for males or is being used generically, and sometimes the same term is used both ways within one sentence. In addition, the meanings of words themselves have changed in usage. As a community worker put it, for those people 'coming from a non-churched sort of background or whatever ... "he" means "he", "she" means "she"!' Another community worker made the same point in thinking about her church: 'No matter what people argue, you do feel left out. You think, okay well we know that what they actually mean here is all of mankind, but I'm sorry that isn't what it says to me today. It may have meant that and it may have quite blatantly meant that in the past or women may not have even realised that potentially they could be included in that. But I think language has changed so much. But then you could say it's all to do with, not just inclusive language, but language which is actually meaningful to us today as opposed to things that we have to translate that folk can actually understand what it says. So I think the two things are tied together. I think it's a change as well in the way society uses language and therefore the inclusive language is probably becoming more important.'

A further reason for gender-inclusive language is that exclusive language is a means of perpetuating the idea of maleness as normative humanity from which femaleness is a subset or divergent. It can do this because language is related to the way we think and behave.[13] Chapter one pointed out how attention to gender raises awareness that humanity is both female and male and that when this awareness is absent it is usually women who get overlooked because there is a tendency to prioritise maleness in our thinking. Using inclusive language counteracts this unsaid equation between humanity and maleness, an equation which can be illustrated in the following sentences: Man is the only primate that commits rape; Man being a mammal breast-feeds his young; Man has difficulties giving birth.[14] The strangeness or otherwise of these sentences depends on how we picture the generic term 'man'. If the latter two sentences seem odd or funny it is because when we use generic terms we think of males rather than of both females and males. Inclusive language helps to overcome this omission in our (often unconscious) thinking about humanity. 'Seeing speech as a kind of action'[15] is a helpful way to understand the role that language plays in either making women invisible or including them, and in defining humanity as either male or female and male.

A number of women recognised the place of language in excluding women: 'I think subconsciously it must, you know, ingrain into people the dominance of the male because all the time this is what we're singing, praying, listening to, whatever ... It certainly sends out messages, I'm pretty sure about that.' One woman had come to this understanding afresh, having encountered the importance of language more generally: 'Recently I have been very much aware of the fact that actually what you say does make a difference ... The kind of language that we use in any area, it makes a difference because it keeps on reinforcing something ... I used to think, you know, they're on their hobby horse and do you really need to make a fuss about that. But increasingly I'm realising what you say matters and especially if you keep saying it often enough. It reinforces certain things. It reinforces certain ideas and principles.'

A number of women, though supporting the idea of inclusive language in many cases, had reservations about making an issue of it. In some cases this was because they felt inclusive language was awkward, or because insisting on such language caused its (usually male) opponents to become entrenched in their view. Some felt there were more important issues to be addressed and others reacted against gender-inclusive language because of its association with feminism.[16] For a number of these women it was the overall context in which the language was used that was important. So a woman involved in church leadership was prepared to 'give people the benefit of the doubt where I really know that they are pro-women and it's maybe, it is a slip of the tongue or just a slight lack of thought or something like that.' Similarly another woman active in her church commented, 'Sometimes people will ... talk about chairman but they actually, instinctively you know they're meaning female as well and you know that, you know, by the way they're saying it and the context. But there can be other contexts when it's not meant and that really irritates me.' As a community worker put it, 'The words don't bother me so much, as long as everyone is included in the group ... even down to the basics ... that whoever's speaking, or at the front, or facilitating the meeting or the session or the discussion, includes everyone, has eye contact with everyone and doesn't direct their conversation to their friend, who's usually the man, which I see a lot of.' In the words of another community worker, 'I think some people can use the wrong language, but still make you feel equal.'

For other women, however, benign intent did not necessarily reduce the impact of encountering exclusive language: 'Well, it really matters to me that the language is inclusive ... I mean sometimes people use it quite unknowingly, especially in worship, and I mean the tradition of the church is to have this very male language, and therefore they're using exclusive language without meaning to exclude you, and yet you are excluded.' As another woman put it, 'It's all very well dismissing it as being, you know, sort of people getting het up about things they don't need to get het up about, but the problem is that once you have thought about it you can't go back. It's instinctive. It becomes – it has become an instinctive thing and, you know, when I read something that isn't [inclusive] … in an order of service it hits. And you can't stop it hitting. And that's just the way it is.'

These comments indicate that exclusive language, that is, generic terms in masculine forms used for females, cannot be relied upon to include women. As Margaret Gibbon points outs, 'If generic terms in their use or understanding actually exclude women, then they are not generic.'[17] She also comments that arguing over whether language reform is a priority among the many issues women face is 'to miss the point. Language is the vehicle for the other forms of discrimination.'[18] This was understood by a political activist who herself was not concerned about a number of contexts in which exclusive language was standard usage. Nevertheless, 'I think there are certain cases, for example when people say things like "the right man for the job", that's – that's not on. Because that defines in people's minds a man. And automatically we lose out fifty per cent of the people who could be the best person for the job … Certainly in documentation and things like that it's important, when you get down to the kind of written recorded stuff that's important, where you're talking about things like the best man for the job it's important, because you're defining certain characteristics in what you say.'

When women do raise the matter of inclusive language they can often find themselves not being taken seriously. Hence, language is another site of condescension towards women. In this sense women experience a double victimisation – first they are excluded by the language used, and then they are ridiculed for drawing attention to their marginalisation. A young community worker felt it was just another way in which she was labelled as odd: 'It's like [them] going, "oh you and your things," you know, your vegetarianism, your women, your language, you're just strange, you know, that's just you.' A woman involved in politics made a similar observation about the treatment women may receive in the church: 'I'm thinking about a friend who's very well educated and she would be in for political correctness.[19] And in many ways people treat her as a joke. You know, people say, "here she goes again." And in fact I've known men say, "well, if she's going to continue to talk in these meetings I don't think I'll bother coming back," and it's almost as if what you're saying is irrelevant.'

A community worker with experience in discussing inclusive language within the church pointed out, 'If that language question isn't taken very seriously, if it's felt okay just to laugh at that, then women's status is being laughed at as part of that, I think. And there is a need to engage with the issues and somehow raise some awareness around the fact that maybe these are real issues and that there's a need for them to be taken seriously and for the people who are raising them to be listened to ... I've heard all kinds of arguments against it from trying to have these conversations, but I do feel that if the church is about everyone and the ministry of Jesus was about everyone, then there's a need to look at how that's lived out through church life. Whether that's talking about Sunday morning service or whether it's talking about the life of the church and the membership in terms of what they do. And I suppose the invisibility I think is a big thing. I mean I suppose one of the things I've been trying to do in having those conversations is just make the point, you know, you can't just assume that this is okay. Say a reading or a hymn where everybody sings or everybody just listens to it and that's fine, you know, and it's like people don't hear the maleness of it. And so part of it is just about raising the issue. Well, I have difficulty with this. I am a woman and I have difficulty with this. There may be others who don't, which is often what's held up as a response to that. While lots of people have no problem with that, it's also about saying well, I'm a woman and I have difficulty with this and I don't feel included by that language. So it is, I think it's a crucial debate ... because it does reflect what the thinking is and how things work and it does also then shape what happens after that.'

While concerns over inclusive language may often be trivialised, at the same time language continues to be used negatively towards women. One woman involved in politics spoke of how her party Assembly members[20] (who are not all male) were referring to themselves as assembly*men* and that this was a means of opposing the NIWC who insist on the term 'member' being used. She described this as 'silly politics', but it is a deliberate use of language to exclude women.

By way of contrast, a few women spoke of occasions when inclusive language was actually used to mask sexist attitudes and behaviour. A community worker remarked, 'It's easy to use language to kind of cover up what you really think, to be PC[21] on the surface, to be kind of correct and all the rest of it, but deep down to actually still think that women should be at home by the stove or – do you know? And I think that I'm much more interested in how people actually behave rather than what they say ... It was very important to be seen to be saying the right thing, but very often I felt that people didn't do the right thing, and I think that you need to do both really.'

The question of language is not isolated from other issues that need to be addressed in order to facilitate women's inclusion. In the words of one interviewee, 'If people are actively trying to include women, then there should be an activeness in trying to change language.' As another woman put it, inclusive language 'is one of those things that eats away at a problem, doesn't it, and helps to bring some kind of positive light on it'.

While the importance of gender-inclusive language is often down-played, particularly by those (mainly men) who use masculine terms to refer to women, the importance attached to language in other contexts speaks otherwise. Talking of her church's discussions around a new service book and in particular the 'whole furore' over the term 'Mother God' that appears in one passage: 'Now if language doesn't mean anything, why did that cause such extreme reactions? Now if language is not emotive, why get carried away by this one word, what's so disgusting about the word Mother?' What is relevant here is not whether it is appropriate, good, wrong or heretical to refer to God in this way. Rather, regardless of how controversial within evangelicalism this particular example is, the point is well made that language does matter. It matters when speaking of God, and it matters when speaking of women.

QUESTIONING

In their dealings in religious contexts women sometimes have to handle being questioned in some way about their participation. This may be done subtly or more often very directly. While some do so courteously, more often women speak of the rudeness involved. Further, while it is more usually women in some kind of leadership position who experience this questioning, women in less prominent roles also encounter it.

Ordained women spoke of people coming up to them to tell them how they did not agree with women in ministry. While those holding this view may do so on biblical grounds and at times present their opinion as 'nothing personal', the experience for the women concerned may be far from abstract. For example, 'I mean two weeks ago I visited somebody who took his Bible out and as soon I walked in the door started to quote verses at me. And was quite aggressive about, you know, "you say you're a Christian, but you obviously can't be because you haven't read this". And as time went on, I mean I really wanted to walk out, but I stayed and we chatted. He was sick and I prayed for him. And he said, you know, "I don't want there to be any hard feelings and you're very welcome in this house." It's a very strange mix of, you know, I like you and I appreciate your ministry, but I don't think you should be doing it. And that was, much as you try and wipe off, it is difficult to come across somebody like that.'

Sometimes the comments reflect curiosity and an implied question mark over a woman's ministry rather than overt opposition. Another ordained woman spoke of an encounter she had after the first time she had led a church Bible study. A man questioned her about how the meeting had gone. Eventually he got to the point and said, 'Well, I suppose it's the first time they've had a girl in charge of them.'

This questioning is not only for women in ordained ministry. A non-ordained church worker commented, in the context of being well received overall, 'I've had two people who have come and said, sat down and, you know, addressed it [that is, gender] and said that they never wanted me appointed.' In addition, non-ordained women also find themselves confronted with men questioning the legitimacy of women in ordained ministry to the extent that it reflects upon their own legitimacy, even though they operate outside of the areas that these men say they think should be exclusively male: 'I've had a number of debates with some of the guys who would say, excuse me I don't believe women should be ministers. I don't believe they should be in positions of authority as in being ordained, either as an elder or a minister ... I suppose what I do think is that because a lot of them struggle with or would hold this view ... then they do struggle with knowing how to relate to the role that I have.'

Women in positions of lay leadership within congregations also experience questioning. One lay leader spoke of being approached at events that included lay leaders on a number of occasions and being questioned about her participation. One of these incidents led to a prolonged conversation about her role: 'And the person literally, literally couldn't understand how I as a female, with plenty of males there, was [part of the leadership]. And that would be fairly common.'

Other women face questioning simply for their usual participation. A male minister used to confront one woman active in the church: 'I had accusations that my spiritual life wasn't good and things like that.' She and her friends attributed this to the minister finding her threatening in her activity in the church. Another woman who worked with young people found herself questioned 'because I was a married woman, at that age [with young children], that I was out doing evening work, as opposed to that I should have been in the house with the children or whatever, I'm not sure'. She reflected on the underlying currents and the unhelpful comments that 'every now and again' would be made: 'Whenever you're, as I say, a married woman within the church, some churches, I'll not say all of the churches, but some churches have an idea of what the role of a married woman is within Northern Ireland, especially in the rural areas, very especially in the rural areas. A wife should be at home and should be cooking her husband's dinner and, you know, should not be, for example, going away on a weekend with young people, you know, that's really not on.'

Sometimes the questioning may be done in a public manner. One woman spoke of incidents in church in which 'I wasn't even advocating feminist ideas or practices, but I was labelled as one – and in a very aggressive public manner actually, which just absolutely stunned me, amazingly so.' Chapter one noted how the feminist label can be used as a weapon against women, to discourage or even discredit them. As another woman pointed out, 'I've only ever been called a feminist by people who are trying to deny my faith.'

For one young woman her brief visible participation in a church event at which she publicly thanked a number of people involved in a particular project produced a pointed response from a male minister present. He 'basically said, I hope you enjoyed that moment because it'll not happen again. And I know that's what he meant, it was said in a relatively light-hearted way, but I felt expressed very strong opinions under the surface. And it was something that really stuck in my mind because I just felt … like, you know, he was genuinely expressing a lot. It was unnecessary…'

She knew this person and was aware of his views and so 'I suppose to me there wasn't a great concern about what that said about his value of me as a person, but I just felt it was a very unnecessary comment. I didn't take it particularly personally, but I just felt that if that was the kind of natural reaction how hurtful it could be to a lot of people.' A further implication for her was his words 'enforcing the fact that that is very likely the case because there aren't those openings for women so naturally. Not a big issue for me, I mean I'm far removed from the feminists, you know, but I suppose it's a matter of respect.'

That this kind of questioning can hint at an overall approach to women's participation and place was experienced by a number of women. A clear example is provided by a young woman speaking of her student experience in which the 'guy who was the student leader, just … can't deal with people and especially women'. She spoke of that student experience as 'being negative towards women; our student leader and sermons were basically saying, "oh yes, women should submit to all men", and blokes and the student group going "oh yeah, that's so cool".' While the question of authority in gender relations is considered in chapter five, it is relevant to make the connection here that the questions faced by women in some kind of visible leadership within churches are not unrelated to attitudes to all women.[22]

ACTS OF PROTEST

The description of incidents that most obviously involved what might be called acts of protest related to women within church leadership, and particularly those in ordained ministry. The validity of women particularly within ordained leadership remains, to varying degrees, a vexed notion within the three main Protestant denominations, each of which ordains women.

A Church of Ireland leader stated that, 'Knowing the wider church, there's been huge conflict, and remains huge conflict, and some of it I think still causes a great deal of pain both to the women who are perceived as the cause of the conflict and to the men and women who somehow feel hurt because there are women doing things that they feel women shouldn't be doing. So there's huge conflict at that level in the wider church in certain areas.' In the words of another Church of Ireland leader, 'Northern Irish nominators are still reluctant to appoint a woman.'

Similarly in regard to the Presbyterian Church in Ireland, a male commented, 'I think also ... within the denomination, our denomination, [there's a] quite a widespread antagonism towards women in ministry, and even in many places in the eldership.' Speaking of the same denomination another male interviewee pointed out, 'I think that women who are [involved in denominational structures] have found significant difficulties. I think it's hard particularly for the ministers who are female, and whilst I think that situation will change, I think it'll change only very slowly.'

A male leader in the Methodist Church in Ireland saw outstanding issues in his denomination: 'I think in a sense, to be open and honest about it, now I'm talking about ordained women in the ministry, there isn't even yet a total readiness for congregations to receive women ministers.'

Highlighting this situation in regard to ordained women should not be taken as suggesting that it represents the total experience of women in leadership, nor even always the predominant one.[23] The point is not to characterise female leadership experience only by the difficulties encountered, but rather to acknowledge that, in practice, this can still be an area of conflict despite the formal access to ordination and amid good experiences for women.

The interviewees described a number of acts protesting or opposing women's ordained or lay church leadership participation. There was one man who would not listen to a woman preaching, but left the church auditorium. A non-ordained woman visiting churches to take services found the minister deliberately absent. At other times women were allowed to speak from the lectern rather than the main pulpit. An ordained woman helping to serve communion was not only kept from handling the bread and wine, but was not offered the elements herself by the visiting ordained man in charge of the service. A church member stopped attending communion when a woman was officiating; another man refused to take communion if served by a woman. A number of women spoke of church members who left when they became leaders.[24] Most of these could be incidents experienced by individual men because of various areas of personal difference or disagreement. However, in each case described the act of protest was because the person involved *was a woman*.

From the point of view of those who oppose women in leadership, to consider these examples perhaps begs the question (which is considered in chapter five). From the point of view of the women themselves who experience or witness this behaviour, however, a different assessment would be made.[25] The following observation from a male church leader indicates that a difference exists not only in attitudes towards women in leadership, but in regard to how this difference is handled: 'I think the presence of more and more women and the higher profile that women have now has made some men maybe more vigorous in their opposition to the role of women in the church. And I think for some, unfortunately, it has made them maybe less courteous. Because they are so determined I suppose to obstruct where they can in this whole, in this whole process, that maybe that makes them less than gracious, and I think that's the accusation that has been levelled, and I'm sure it has probably been levelled at me. I have not been knowingly or deliberately should I say ungracious or discourteous, but I think sometimes if you're opposed to something it can be perceived to be ungracious even though you're desperately trying not to be.'

The question of women in leadership remains an ongoing issue for the church, not least within evangelicalism. Another male church leader commented that a number of ministers say they are not against women in leadership, but that they would have problems in their congregation if a woman was appointed: 'So again it depends, if you like, how high up the tree you're going to place the woman, as to how great the difficulties will be with that situation.'

IT WOULDN'T HAPPEN TO A MAN

In addition to the variety of conflict that occurs around women's participation in church and civic society described above, women can experience difficulties that are not on the surface about them being women or to do with gender. When recounting these incidents the women often reflect that the way they are treated is not something a man in a similar situation would experience.

Speaking of a challenge to her political involvement by a male colleague which would also have existed if a man had been in her position one woman asked, 'Would the same person go after a ... man? Now the threat that he would probably feel would be undoubtedly greater from [another] man ... but I don't think he would go after a man just so hard. You know, he'd push me further, because he would think that I'm an easier touch ...

so I'm an easier target.' An ordained woman spoke of a similar dynamic in a church where there was disagreement with her over her attitudes to community issues: 'But people have felt freer to hassle me about that, some people because I'm a woman, who mightn't say it to the [ordained man]. Other women find it easier to put you down about something they disagree with you on not because you're a woman, but because they can say to you as a woman why they disagree about the way you think. They're the sort of women who are into respecting the authority of the male minister more.'

The idea of a woman being viewed as more able to be criticised was articulated by a woman lay church leader: 'It only happens now and again, but people feel that somehow they have a right to, you know, with my up-front job, sometimes I feel people feel they have a right to make comments and they have a right almost, there's almost an ownership of me and I can get some criticisms. I don't mind constructive criticisms, but it can be around almost petty things, you know, if I make a mistake in the announcements, somebody would be very quick [to comment] and there'd be strange comments ... And it sounds even petty saying it, but it's there and I think part of it's being a woman to be honest. I think people say things to me they wouldn't say to a man. And I think part of that, maybe that's the price you pay for ... being visible. And I think when women are visible, people feel they have a right to make comments on your style of speaking or your dress even. But that irritates me. The comments I got were so, I don't know, they were so petty and quite critical in a destructive way ... it was a getting at me, I think ... I think some people still feel it difficult that women can be at ease and be comfortable in that sort of setting.'

Another example comes from an incident that occurred at a gathering of ordained ministers (male and female). Referring to the contribution of one particular woman at that meeting her female colleague told of how the men who were present reacted. The interviewee felt the woman concerned was 'pompous and domineering and all that, you know, what they fear most had come upon them. And there was this kind of nervous, derogatory laugh and I really bristled at it. And I thought right, okay she is like that, but had it been a man sort of reacting like that, nobody would have passed a comment.'

Another woman spoke of a time when she was chairing a particular religious meeting at which some controversy, not related to gender, arose.

A senior man in the particular organisation took over the position of the chair to deal with the discussion. He asked the woman's permission but she wondered, 'would he have done that if I was a man? ... But it's just probably an example of whether it, you know, it may be a nice thing to do to have a woman in leadership, but when something really critical happens, let's play safe and pull the thing back.'

A consequence of these kinds of incidents is that it can be hard to identify them as gender related because the presenting issue is not overtly to do with the woman *as a woman* or with gender issues in general. However, such incidents are intrinsically related to gender relations because a difference is being made on the basis of the person's sex. The dynamics involved in this are expressed by a woman referring to her professional life: 'In work I think it's interesting because I think actually although the structures are in place for equal opportunities and so on, and although, you know, there's all sorts of sexual harassment regulations and things like that ... underneath, legislation doesn't actually change people's attitudes. And I would say for a lot of people, some people are quite overtly sexist in their approach and in the way they relate, and other people actually are very fair and equitable, but at a certain level there are kind of inherent ways of dealing with people that come out, which are different, you know, on their part for when they're relating to a man or a woman, and I've come across that.' She clarified that the differences she refers to are neither necessary for the issues in question nor appropriate for the situation: 'No, they're not, and again those are very difficult to actually deal with because people very often don't realise they're doing it. Yeah, so that's caused me a lot of grief on various occasions.'

That the phrase 'it wouldn't happen to a man' is applicable in a context where there are formal measures in place designed to protect women from discrimination illustrates the pervasiveness of such hidden sexist treatment.

SEXUAL HARASSMENT

A final difficulty described by interviewees which may be encountered by women who participate in church, community and politics is sexual harassment. The Equal Opportunities Commission for Northern Ireland, which describes sexual harassment as 'a serious workplace problem in Northern Ireland',[26] defines sexual harassment as 'unwanted conduct of a sexual nature or other conduct based on sex affecting the dignity of women and men at work'.[27] It elaborates this definition indicating that many forms of behaviour can constitute sexual harassment including physical conduct of a sexual nature,[28] verbal conduct of a sexual nature,[29] non-verbal conduct of a sexual nature,[30] and sex-based conduct.[31]

This kind of abuse can occur directly with those instigating it being identified, or anonymously through letters and telephone calls. Several women interviewed spoke of these kinds of experiences that had happened to themselves and to other women they knew, talking in terms of being bullied, intimidated, threatened, disturbed, sickened, discriminated against, abused, and sexually and physically harassed.

This harassment of women occurs not only outside the Christian community, but also within it. While in theory such behaviour seems incompatible with a faith profession, in reality it co-exists, even at times is endorsed by a religious ideology. One woman employed by her church in a leadership capacity described the treatment she received from her male boss: 'If I voice an opinion, he is down my throat and he talks to me in such a rude and ignorant way that he would never dream of talking to [male colleagues] ... I can't cope with abusiveness and my boss would be abusive, you know, he would shout publicly in meetings, he would shout across the room at you and tell you "you're subordinate to me" and things like this ... He would shout publicly, he would demean me publicly and I find that really hard to deal with.'

When experiencing sexual harassment women can be subject to a double victimisation. There is the harassment itself and this can be compounded if the body, institution or employer they turn to for help does not intervene.[32] Speaking of her experience of such a situation in which the appropriate parties 'didn't take it seriously at all' and did nothing about the matter, one woman commented, 'I find church dynamics and government probably the most threatening thing that I've come into.'

In trying to understand something of the dynamic involved in sexual harassment, including the fact that men may not be aware that their behaviour is harassment, Carol Becker points to the prevailing sex-role stereotypes that 'present women as sexual beings but continue to reinforce the view of men as organisational beings, no matter what they do'.[33] In this scenario women are considered responsible for bringing sexuality into a workplace which, until their participation, was presumed to be asexual.

This is illustrated by two women interviewed. One talked of being the first woman in a group of male church leaders and how 'sometimes – and they'd probably have been shocked if you'd pointed out to them – [they used] almost overtly sexual jokes in an effort to cope with this female who was there in what had been an all-male domain. And yet they probably didn't even realise they were doing it.' The second woman spoke of being in the presence of two male church leaders who made lewd comments about another woman who was unable to hear what they were saying. 'The crudeness even within the Christian church is despicable,' was her verdict. When she drew their attention to their behaviour, 'they just laughed. And went "oh that's the female perspective on it".'

Viewing women primarily as sexual objects can be perpetuated even with an increased awareness of forms of harassment. Carol Becker records how men complain they cannot even compliment a female colleague on how she looks because it could be misconstrued: 'It may be true, but it's not the fault of women. This is exactly the bind. Even if women are spared the experience of harassment, they are still held responsible for the fact that "we all have to be so careful".'[34]

A context that views church and various workplaces as asexual until women participate does not foster in men responsibility for their own sexuality. It is just such a responsibility that is alluded to in Jesus' comment that 'everyone who looks at a woman with lust has already committed adultery with her in his heart'.[35] Mary Evans comments that in these words Jesus is not disputing the idea of lust being sin, but rather he is challenging the assumption 'that the primary function of women was to be man's sexual partner and that the automatic result of contact between the sexes would be lust'.[36] In other words, Jesus considers men accountable for their own sexual natures, rather than projecting this responsibility onto women. Mary Evans also remarks that the words of Jesus indicate that 'Women are to be recognised as subjects in their own right, as fellow human beings, fellow disciples, and not just the objects of men's desire. Their life and rights are to be recognised as important and not to be endangered by the natural desires of the men.'[37] While she applies this to the situation depicted in the gospels where there were female and male disciples who followed Jesus with no suggestion of sexual misconduct, the stories of some evangelical women in Northern Ireland are witness to the continuing pertinence of these words of Jesus.

Towards Inclusion

The various difficulties women may encounter *because they are women* illustrate how women's participation in church, community and politics does not necessarily guarantee their full inclusion in these endeavours. Clearly, more is involved in women's inclusion than can be 'legislated' for even by forms of affirmative action. A woman in politics remarked that because of 'my involvement in a number of spheres, not least my job, and the politics sphere as well, and seeing the under-representation of women within politics, [I know] that it's not direct discrimination, that it's indirect discrimination that is doing an awful lot of the things, and attitude barriers and things like that.' In the words of another female interviewee, 'You know, we can have all the rules, and we here would say we have no discrimination, we [have] equal opportunities and so on and so on. But the tongue – what is said – and much of the experience is we are not all equals, it is still male orientated, you know. The males feel that they have to be controlling, and that women should really be in subjection, and therefore ... "you might be right, but we're the men, we decide", still dominates.' These kinds of mindsets inevitably permeate women's experience of involvement in church, community and politics, and can produce the various forms of conflict discussed above. Many of the interviewees mentioned the need for a change in attitudes and mindsets in order to have women more involved in church and civic society.

This is not to suggest that attention to equal opportunities or affirmative action is therefore futile. Such measures can be the means not just to facilitate women's participation, but also to foster their full inclusion. It is not a question of making a choice between concentrating on either mechanisms to aid women's involvement or a change in attitudes. Rather, both are involved in bringing about a situation in which women not only participate but are also fully included. A male church leader expressed this in regard to his denomination: 'Well, there are two ways you can change [women's low involvement in the government and leadership of the church]. You can change the way you run elections and have places reserved for specialist groups – women, young people, whatever – or you can change attitudes. The first sometimes is necessary as a short-term step, but without the second it's going to get nowhere. I would be reluctant to push the first too hard because I would be much more concerned to change attitudes and see lasting change. But I think sometimes ... if we did [have reserved places for women in the denominational structures of the church] we would begin to change attitudes at that kind of level. I think sometimes therefore the step is necessary. But at a more local level I think you can work much more by changing attitudes. And the way to change attitudes is ... if you have the opportunity to do so ... get women in there doing the business – there's no way attitudes are going to change quicker than if people see women in action.'

A community worker also saw the need for attention to practical measures as well as mindsets: 'Sometimes I wonder about recruitment, you know, about active discrimination in terms of quotas and things to get women into positions because they must be there, it's just that they're not coming through for promotions and things. I mean I wonder about the Equality Commission whether it will address some of those but I think attitude-wise there is still such a long way to go. I suppose it's attitudes and culture and the ways of doing things and all the support systems that are needed for childcare and just more flexibility in general.'

It is good that some women have successfully participated in the area of their choice and can speak of experiencing inclusion in many ways. However, the prevalence, extent and nature of the conflict experienced by women involved in church, community and politics witnesses to the fact that simply moving women across the existing sexual division of labour is insufficient to ensure that the experience is one of wholehearted acceptance. This is because inclusion is about more than adding women into areas previously dominated by men. Rather, as the following chapter explores, it concerns the way women and men relate together and what happens in and to the spaces that men are now finding themselves actually or potentially sharing with women.

4

The Difference Question

When women do participate in various roles across the sexual division of labour, the question remains as to the nature of their contribution. Are women included in order to participate on the same basis as men or because they have something different to offer? And even if they are there to do the same task as men in a particular job, do they actually do the task differently to their male counterparts?

At the heart of the debate over women's increased participation and inclusion in areas previously dominated by men are concerns about sameness and difference between women and men. If women are to be included on the same basis as men, do they lose their sexual distinctiveness (whatever that is thought to be)? In other words, do they have to become like men (however that is understood)? And if women are included because their contribution is different, is it possible to safeguard against their unequal treatment, something that frequently occurs when women's difference to men is emphasised?

These concerns touch on matters of personal identity and are intrinsically bound up with how women and men relate to each other and function in church and wider society. They account, in part, for why some women wish to disassociate from matters around sex and gender, wanting to be treated 'just as a person', and also why other women assert their identity *as women*, whether to endorse their femininity or to highlight the sexual discrimination they experience. Concerns regarding women and men's similarities and differences also contribute to men's sense of who they and the way men respond to sharing their once exclusive male domains with women.

The purpose of this chapter is to explore the significance that the notion of difference has in women's church, community and political participation and in the way women and men work together. It is not concerned with directly addressing the matter of whether the difference that women may bring is innate or part of women's socialisation, or indeed a complex interaction between these two, assuming that this is even the best way to conceptualise such a debate.[1] Of course, aspects involved in the 'nature verses nurture' debate will inevitably appear in a discussion on difference. The debate impinges, for example, on the type of activity in which women are expected or considered able to engage. Hence, there is the idea that innate differences in women raise the question as to 'whether it's true to say that women can do any job that a man can do on a public level',[2] or that women with excellent teaching and preaching gifts 'would be few and far between',[3] and that 'women in ordained ministry might be the exception rather than the rule [because] the kind of gifts and orientations that women naturally have ... will not lead them to that kind of position of leadership ... because they're not suited to it'.[4] Such beliefs are countered by others who consider that 'women are pretty much like men ... it's like saying when you go to another country the culture's different but people are basically the same',[5] or that 'individuals are different, but men and women are not more different from one another than there's differences in one man and another man, or one woman and another woman'.[6] But whichever view is taken of any differences between women and men, whether these are believed to be innate or otherwise, there remains the significance attached to the notion of difference, and the extent to which the question of difference is both helpful and impeding to women's church and civic participation, and this is the focus of this chapter.

Of course, sex difference is not the only difference between women and men, nor should a focus on this difference imply that women do not differ among themselves. A number of women considered that factors to do with age, political viewpoint, national identity, and economic status were of equal and in some cases of more importance to them personally and to those with whom they worked and served than the matter of sex or gender. One of the difficulties in focusing on differences between women and men is that it can eclipse other divisions and concerns that women have (chapter seven returns to this matter of priorities in people's lives). However, the matter of sex and/or gender difference remains a key component to a consideration of women's church and civic activism and it is this focus that is addressed here.

The Value of Difference

The difference that women bring to church and civic life is one reason given for supporting the greater inclusion of women in church, community and political spheres. In the world of politics, for example, without an increase in women's participation both numerically and in key positions in electoral politics, issues that are important to women (and children) remain largely unaddressed.[7] One woman involved in politics commented on the attitude of male party colleagues that when policy discussion arose around 'sex education, teenage pregnancies, abortion, they didn't want to know'. Certainly, in the Northern Ireland talks process that resulted in the Belfast Agreement, it was the NIWC who ensured that women's rights were stipulated in that Agreement.[8]

The community sector which is populated by women frequently focuses on concerns of women and their families, because women know what these are and are motivated to address them. As a community worker put it, 'a lot of community issues are to do with social need [and] a lot of them are women's issues probably because women are in the community on a daily basis struggling with the different issues of community'.

Awareness of women's contribution in regard to domestic concerns was expressed by those active in church life. One male church leader reflected, 'I think we all have blind spots, and I think that some blind spots are not gender-specific, and some blind spots tend to be more gender-specific – speaking of generalisation. I think if you get a bunch of men together you can end up being very strong in some respects, but also having significant blind spots ... Some of them are perhaps to do with children, you know. I think that men tend to fail to – fail to take into account the needs or the place of kids in a church environment. I think that women are much more aware of (a) the needs of the children, and (b) what will work and what won't work for them. And I think that men can get a bit idealistic about children ... and that can be unhelpful.' Similarly, another male church leader said of women's involvement in a church committee: 'When it comes to seeing practical things that need doing about the buildings and the difficulties for the elderly or for women with babies and so on in using the facilities and resources we have, those things don't have to be pointed out to them; they see them, you know.'

Connected to the idea that women are concerned with certain types of issues relating to women's interests is the idea that women bring a different contribution to their involvement, arising out of their domestic familial concerns.[9] This different contribution concerns women's ability to relate to the needs of others and be concerned for their personal well-being. The idea of women being more compassionate, caring, nurturing, empathetic, understanding, able to listen, tolerant, calm, sensitive and soothing, was repeated by almost half of all interviewees, and stated as reasons for including women more in church and civic life. For example, one community worker considered women's participation in church and society as 'essential. I think women have a different perspective on life than men have, you know. And I think even with the whole kind of family – there's such a compassion and an understanding I think some-times in women... Women do have much more of an ability, I think, sometimes to be able to come alongside people and listen, and understand.' Another interviewee echoed similar ideas in her reflection that women were more caring and aware of the everyday stresses that people faced: 'Having gone round lots of churches in Northern Ireland, women are kept in their place I feel very much. And I feel it's wrong, because I feel that they have, very much have a special ministry within that ... I feel that women can be more caring and I feel that they can be more supportive of other women and more understanding of the stresses. Especially I mean to reach out into the community, so much hurt out there, you know.'

A male church leader concurs with these assessments: 'My experience has been that ladies – particularly in the context of [lay leadership] – are much more conscientious when it comes to the pastoral concerns. More conscientious in visiting. Perhaps, dare I say it, more caring, more sympathetic, more – more on the ball in terms of being intuitive and linking in with how people feel. Whereas men, generally, and it's a terrible sweeping generalisation, but a lot of the men I've dealt with have not necessarily had very good person-to-person skills. I think I have regretted that more women are not involved in leadership.' Another male church leader identified women's relational orientation as being fundamental to their different contribution: '[Women] are better at relating ... they relate more easily, and they see relationships as the core of things rather than propositions and statements and theologies – now that's a vast generalisation. But I think that at the core of it for them is how do I relate to someone else? Whereas for men that may not be at the core.' Certainly 52 of the 70 women interviewed specifically identified working with people, making a difference in their lives, and being involved with their development and concerns, as among the elements they most enjoyed about their particular participation in church, community or politics.

An attitude of care for the person is also reflected in the comments of two political activists who followed the debate in the Northern Ireland Assembly on abortion.[10] They were interviewed soon after the debate had occurred and both women were struck with the lack of sensitivity they discerned in most of the speakers. Both commented at length on the absence of compassion for women who experience a crisis pregnancy in the general tone of the debate:

> I was very disappointed with the attitude from both sides of the house. Like I felt there was no human compassion or love with them. I felt that if our Lord was standing in the middle, our Lord wouldn't have it. And I felt, I don't agree with abortion personally, unless it was incest, rape or some of the really drastic things. I think a woman, and I feel strongly that a woman has to have a choice, that as a woman, you know, it's her conscience and everything else. I don't like men making decisions for women. I feel that that '67 Act was men making decisions. Now we've come a further thirty years and there's been all the developments. I think that it has to be women deciding. And I felt that [in the debate] those men weren't listening, you know. And I listened to people shouting about murder and killing and I found it was hurtful and sickening. You know it really did upset me ...

There's no love and there's no caring and I mean that's what I feel, there's no understanding.

One of my disappointments in that whole debate was just the lack of understanding and compassion that was there from people who to a large extent I agreed with. Because I wouldn't be, well, not pro-abortion, I don't believe anybody is, but I wouldn't necessarily believe that abortion under the '67 Act is a good idea. And I found a lot of people who were arguing the kind of case that was argued against that Abortion Act had a very, I don't know, it – it seemed to lack any compassion for the people who made those choices when it was difficult, and I mean as a Christian I find that frustrating. I find it frustrating for people to stand up and talk about murder and, you know, these people, and … no morals, and … they're murdering babies, and all this kind of thing, because murder is wrong, but then so is making someone else feel that bad all the time, and that kind of lack of compassion and understanding, to me as a Christian, is every bit as wrong. So I find it very frustrating when I read that kind of high-handed moral argument without any thought for the people involved. It just jars with me … because I just felt that the tone of the debate more so than the content was just – there was something not quite right. In many ways the people who seemed the most arrogant and bitter and twisted seemed to be the people who were speaking against abortion, and the cruelty of abortion, and yet I thought that in themselves they were being very cruel about people put in that situation … It was a case of a very negative, very negative debate. There were no solutions, there were no alternatives. To me those people who spoke against, spoke only against and had nothing positive to say, had no understanding of probably the reasons why people feel the need to make those sorts of choices. Or even for that matter for the kind of effects that making those choices has on people.

These two women actually contrast the absence of compassion for women who experience a crisis pregnancy in the general tone of the debate to Christian values, which they felt were largely absent, and not to the sex of those involved in the debate. However, in the main it was the women MLAs present who either opposed the outright ban of a consideration of the extension of the 1967 Act to Northern Ireland or who offered some alternative way of considering the situation of unwanted pregnancies. As Jane Morrice MLA herself commented in the debate, 'It is my perception that all the interventions this afternoon from women Assembly Members have either been in favour of our amendment or against the motion.'[11]

When the original motion to oppose the extension of the Abortion Act 1967 to Northern Ireland was put to the floor, all seven of the women present when votes were recorded voted against endorsing this proposal.[12] This is not to infer that they were all in favour of extending the Act as it currently stands (although some may have been), but certainly it indicates that the women considered simply endorsing the motion in itself an inadequate response to dealing with crisis pregnancies.

Alongside this emphasis on women's relational focus was a sense of women's practicality, ability to multi-task, reliability, and conscientious-ness, often consciously linked to their lives as mothers: 'I think that sometimes women do have an intuitive response to things. And that they are more sensitive, now not always, and therefore able to empathise with people. And yet women tend to be also extraordinarily practical because we have to be really. And the other thing I think and this is purely my own surmising really, women can think of a lot of different things at once. Men can only think of one thing at once. That's a very generalised state-ment, but do you know what I mean? I think that's a wonderful thing about women. That they can, you know, that they can, I know it's diffi-cult, but they can hold down a very good job and yet at the same time they are probably the ones who have to be thinking, are there clean clothes for the children to wear in the morning? have we got food? et cetera, et cetera, somebody's coming or that room needs to be cleaned, you know. Whereas a man doesn't think like that, finds it difficult to do two things at once.' The ability of women 'generally' to see detail and organise thoroughly was also linked to motherhood by another woman active in her church: 'We can focus in on things and we are better organisers because if you're a mother, you're constantly organising. And those organisation skills are there in every mother because they've got to be. And men don't see, they have a more general mind. Now our pastor's a very focused mind, but they've a more general mind in knowing what they want to get done, but maybe don't pay the attention to detail as to how you get there.'

Clearly many people value this sense of different contribution that they see women bring to the various activities in church and society. Women bring a focus to certain issues that would otherwise be neglected, and an ability to their endeavours related to their domestic concerns (whether innate or learned) that can have a positive impact on areas of church, community and political life. For many, the difference in itself is valued, in the words of one lay church leader: 'I would like to see more women [involved in all areas of life], but I'd also like them to recognise that as women, they've not to lose that because they want to be equal with men. Because I think women can bring an awful lot about the age-old accepted qualities, you know, the nurturing and the caring and the dealing with the emotional side of things, intuition, being able to [attend to] all of the things at one time. I mean I think women are very good at juggling and prioritising.' As another interviewee articulates, this assertion of difference is made in the context of feeling that an identity involving sex/gender difference is under threat: 'We live in a society which wants to make us all the same and we are not the same. There is a difference between males and females and that is how God made us and that's how he plans to keep us. And we don't do either sex any favour by trying to say we're all the same. I think we have been made with unique differences and [we shouldn't try] levelling it out and trying to make it all the same.' However, while for many people the notion of difference is valued, the concept is not without difficulty in the lives of women.

The Discrimination in Difference

While, in some ways, an emphasis on the difference women bring to their church and civic involvement may be viewed as beneficial, concentrating on difference can also have negative consequences.

Highlighting the difference of women can lead to marginalising them into women-focused concerns (around children and care) and away from other church, community and political issues. A woman who had held down a responsible management position in her employment situation spoke of her initial difficulty in 'using the gifts and talents that I was given outside the church in it ... In the church I'm a woman and therefore I'll do this [work with children], whereas I could easily have been managing something ... It's different for a man because if he's an accountant outside then immediately we put him as treasurer.' Another woman observed a similar demarcation occurring in a secular context in which a female had been appointed to a management team with two men: 'The female is the people person, the caring person and I've thought to myself, she's been appointed because of that caring image. She's the caring third of senior management.'

It is worth reflecting whether there is possibly a connection between the gradual involvement of more women in church leadership and the emerging emphasis on the pastoral role that such leaders need to be addressing. Certainly one male church leader made this connection when he commented that ministers and lay men who had difficulties with women being ordained nevertheless 'could more easily have lived with it in the eldership than ... lived with it in the ministry ... I think a lot of people recognise that often at congregational level the people who are, who actually have the gifts to do pastoral work, are female and not male. And therefore, if the eldership really is about pastoring then it seems amazing that they're not there.' While an emphasis on pastoral concerns is good in and of itself, the potential could be that women are included only to fill these functions, and excluded from other aspects of leadership.

In the world of politics, while women may be accepted when dealing with certain women-oriented matters, this can change if they engage with other political issues. Citing an example when the contribution of an Ulster Unionist Party female member was well received at the Northern Ireland Forum for Political Dialogue, Kate Fearon comments that the male members were capable of showing respect to women speaking on women's issues, but 'it also seemed to confirm that they were only prepared to show respect to women who fitted neatly within their mould'.[13] This is acceptability at a price and demonstrates how 'inclusion as well as exclusion can work against women'[14] for their inclusion is conditional and restricted.

Not only can difference lead to women being marginalised, but women's participation itself may be understood differently to that of male counterparts. A community youth worker reflected on this in regard to how she was viewed: 'I suppose there's a sense of what I do, because I'm female, I'm about doing nice things and being nice to people, a bit of a do-gooder and that kind of attitude, which I don't think would be there if I was male. It was very much like, "oh, she's a nice wee girl" and "she's trying to help those poor wee children", you know. Whereas I think if I was a male in there doing the job it would be a much clearer sense of, I suppose, purpose or whatever, you know, they would see much more clearly. They wouldn't see me just as some nice wee girl.' A stereotypical view of women's political activism is vividly illustrated by the experience of the NIWC who discussed the content of the Coalition's TV 1998 Assembly election broadcast with two male communications consultants, both of whom suggested the NIWC 'depict its candidates as "mummies" keeping the bad boys from fighting and making everything all right'.[15]

In these scenarios, activity in the margins is not viewed as the place where the real work is done. Speaking of a community project one woman commented, 'Even in this project here – I mean women have been to the fore of leading this, it was a woman actually founded this project and did the most amazing stuff, and we've had women directors since that, but still with all it would be seen [as] ... "oh, it's just something the women do", you know, childcare, crèches and all the things that women are interested in ... They're wee soft issues, you know. The men talk about all the good, the big, hard issues, you know. [This work here] it's seen as just something women do.' Other women also spoke of men's unwillingness to become involved in aspects of community concern that were considered women's domain, one community worker attributing this to the strong gender stereotyping that still existed: 'Some of the issues that men do get involved in are the big physical infrastructure things, you know, about an environmental improvement scheme or something like that. Or, you know, negotiating with housing bodies on redevelopment issues. I mean they get involved in those kinds of things that are almost physical and tangible or whatever. But things like health issues or community care or even educational ends of things, you know, it's been more difficult. And part of that has got to be just society, you know, conditioning to think, well women are responsible for looking after people and, you know, taking the kids to school and arranging childcare. I mean that is so strong.' While women are expected to immerse themselves in the so-called soft issues, they are not always welcome outside of those imposed margins. Another community worker spoke of the sense detected in her project of 'why can't the men look after the real jobs in this place?'

Along with the marginalisation of women that confines their sphere of activity and often interprets that activity as being qualitatively different from that of men, there is a value system that perceives women's concerns as less important than so-called mainstream issues. Hence, so-called women's issues (dealing with reproduction, care and welfare) tend to be 'relegated to the second division of politics'.[16] They are not considered of importance because they are perceived to be concerns (or even 'problems') for women. This, of course, poses a difficulty for women: women who address such issues increase their own marginal status within the political world, yet to avoid them simply confirms the secondary status of these concerns.[17] Even the potential routes to political involvement with which women engage are consigned a lesser significance with 'extensive official unwillingness to treat as serious expressions of citizenship what women do in their communities'.[18] In this sense women's groups are the 'second sex' of the voluntary sector, itself lacking equal recognition with trade unions, business and farming interests.[19]

This devaluing is accompanied by men either actively distancing themselves from or simply ignoring issues focused around women or perceived to be women's concerns. A male church leader commented on the fact that the church is made up largely of women: 'Now the pitfall is that men, some men, can then say, "oh, that's a women's business", you know, and can be alienated even further from it, and the same can be true of community [participation] ... men can say "oh, that's a women's thing, I won't ..." and they are repelled even further.' His choice of the phrase 'repelled' is telling because it speaks of the sense of disassociation from issues considered women's domain that is part of a value system that diminishes the worth of women's contribution or the importance of their concerns. Hence, when the Scottish Parliament debated domestic violence, 'an issue which affects one in five women in their lifetimes and as many as 100,000 children in Scotland alone – the press gallery was virtually empty'.[20] While the press ignoring this issue in part may be attributed to the disinterest of the (predominantly male) media correspondents with the style of debate which did not involve 'division, acrimonious splits and barnstorming speeches',[21] an observation has also been made of the Welsh Assembly that 'lobby journalists tended to listen to the male Assembly Members and leave the Chamber when women were speaking'.[22] A similar dynamic was commented on by a woman attending her church's annual gathering at which, when the report of the women's organisation is presented, 'most of the men leave the room to get coffee'. It is a small step from this disinterest for so-called women's concerns to disdain for women themselves. One church woman spoke of how in her denomination 'the trouble is men will not listen to women in leadership in [our church] circles. No, no, it's immediately devalued depending on who says it. It's not what you say, it's who's saying it and that's very sad, but that's the way it is.'

A community worker commented on how difficult it was usually to get volunteers for a sub-committee to address aspects of the work in which she was involved. However, in attempting to organise a new sub-committee, 'when I said [it was about] "planning" and "direction" and "strategy" the three men immediately volunteered to be on that sub-committee. I thought that was fascinating. I haven't really worked out in my head what that's about, but I think it's possibly about power. I really don't know... But I mean I do recognise in working with that committee that in fact there is a lot of control invested in a small group. You know, they – they do have a lot of power, so maybe I should think about that!' Her sense that it was the relative importance in terms of power that had drawn the men into taking part is indicative of the value scale that operates around things associated with women and men.

Regardless of the particular details, common to each of the above examples is a value system that attaches lesser worth and importance to those things that are associated with women. As Mary Stewart Van Leeuwen points out, despite cultural diversity in the way tasks are allocated on the basis of sex,

> What is universal is the higher status of whatever is considered 'men's work'. If in one culture it is men who build houses and women who make baskets, then that culture will see house-building as more important than basket-weaving. In another culture, perhaps next door, where women construct houses and men make baskets, basket-weaving will have higher social status than house-building.[23]

She argues that even biological differences in regard to men generally having greater physical strength and women's childbearing capacity, 'acquire differing values only within the framework of human culture'.[24] In other words, the fact of these differences cannot account for the tendency in human culture to give higher esteem to those with greater physical strength than to those who bear children.

In addition to the marginalisation and devaluing of women that occurs, a further difficulty with the category of difference is that the difference usually under consideration is that of women's difference to men rather than differences between women and men. Indeed, this chapter has talked in terms of women's difference because it is dealing with the matter of including women in areas traditionally occupied in the main by men. In other words, the discussion is about women's entry into an existing framework that has been formed, developed and inhabited largely by men. Herein lies the difficulty. The norm has been established largely without consideration of the experiences or concerns of women.[25] Hence, talk of difference in these contexts is talk about women's differences from men, which can often be viewed as their deficiency from a male norm, making them unsuitable for the tasks that men carry out. They are therefore marginalised and their contribution is seen as less important.

It is in this context that an emphasis on women's equality with men and the downplay of differences occurs. An emphasis on women's difference rather than on their sameness to men has been used against women to undermine them. In order to avoid the pitfalls of an emphasis on difference, many want women to be included in greater church and society participation on the basis of representation, that is, simply because this more accurately represents the population. It is a matter of justice. Several women active in politics made this point, one commenting: 'Being an MP or being an elected representative isn't just a job, it's about representing the people, you know, who sent you there.' Another expressed something similar: 'I feel that in public life there should be a gender balance.' 'After all,' a third political activist said, 'I don't think any world should be a man's world, you know. Women make up half the population. We have something to say.'

Some women involved in their church also considered the matter of representation as reason for having women within church leadership: 'There are many more women than men who are members of our church. So I think that it would be good that women were represented.' A male church leader endorsed this idea: 'The facts of life are that most worshipping congregations on a Sunday morning in church are 60 per cent women and 40 per cent men, I think. I don't know. Even, you know, even more in some places, and certainly even in some up-and-coming new churches, it's still I reckon the women [who] are the larger grouping at worship. Therefore I think there has to be a reflection of that in the whole government and ministry of the church. So as far as I'm concerned that needs to be constantly addressed.' Some interviewees gave this idea theological backing, as in the words of another male church leader: 'If the leadership of a church or political assembly or any grouping is predominantly one sex it's unhealthy and unnatural, because God put us on the planet to live together.' As a woman active in the church expressed it: 'I just think that men and women, when you put male and female together, together we reflect the image of God. It's very hard to put it into words how that is so, but it just is so.'

The idea of representation does not deny difference. Indeed, it affirms its importance: it is because humanity is made up of female and male that women need to be included. However, difference ceases to be a confining criteria in regard to the nature of women's participation.

Of course, given that women have a different social as well as physical embodiment, it is possible that they have different experiences that inform their lives and which are part of the human enterprise. Hence, it is relevant to ask whether these different experiences have a bearing on the way women participate, even if they are not made the criteria for women's participation in the first place.

Participating Differently

A politically active woman talked about how she had changed her view on the way women participate in politics. When she first came across 'all this stuff about how women think differently and act differently than men', she thought, 'I don't think I do act differently.' However, 'over the years I think that the way I participate in debates is different, and that is something that has come to me against what I thought initially. I mean I would have been loathe to say that I thought differently to my [male] colleagues, you know. I thought, oh, we're all the same. But I think we participate in different ways. I don't think my policies would be different from a lot of my male colleagues, but I think I participate in a different way to them.' In talking in terms of *participating differently* this woman is trying to encapsulate a substantive reality that she and many of the other female interviewees expressed about their church and civic involvement. Regardless of whether women are included because of the difference they are said to bring, and whether any such difference works in their favour or is used against them, many interviewees, both female and male, spoke of sex and/or gender-related issues surrounding *how* women participated.

It is more accurate to talk of gender-related rather than gender-specific traits. The former indicates a tendency rather than an inevitability of finding certain behaviours in women and men. In reflecting on the differences between women and men the interviewees frequently qualified their observations, speaking in terms of generalisations, and noting that the same traits are in fact found in the other sex (a number of the quotations cited in the first section of this chapter demonstrate this clearly, as do the ones that follow below). Another example is found in the words of a male church leader as he considers the involvement of women in the pastoral care in his church: 'There are, if you like, feminine traits within women that I know some people say you find, you know, you can't say it's a feminine trait because you find it in some men, but I think there's maybe, in a general sense, there are maybe more gentle, caring aspects to the nature of women that maybe aren't so predominant in men ... And I think they maybe have a more compassionate heart at times.' When it comes to women's different participation, similar generalisations need to be borne in mind.

Indeed, not all interviewees believed that women did participate differently. One male church leader stated: 'I don't honestly see women and men as that different when it comes to leading the house group, when it comes to deciding something about ... the buildings ... setting strategy and mission statements ... I don't think it brings revolution having women involved. I think they should be involved, but I don't think it brings revolution. We need a revolution to get them involved!' Other interviewees, however, were aware of gender-related issues concerning women and men's participation. The two main areas raised were, on the one hand, women's concern not to participate in the same way as men, and on the other hand, the potential for an emphasis on women's different participation to be confining. Hence, as with the notion of difference, there is both value and disadvantage for women in focusing on the different way they participate.

NOT LIKE A MAN?

One of the concerns that women expressed was their determination not to participate as church leaders, community workers and political activists in the same way as their male counterparts. A church leader said of her preaching and worship leading, 'I think I've been very determined ... not to do it in a male style, you know, to try and do it from my perspective.' Another woman had thought much about becoming part of the leadership of her local church. She felt that if she were to do this, 'I would be doing it in my way and my style. And wouldn't want to become a man doing it, you know ... a woman doing it in a man's style ... I think that's what we need to be careful of, you know, of women taking up leadership roles and then automatically taking on the male way of doing it. So I tend to try and be true to myself and not sort of absorb another way of doing things.' A lay church leader contrasted her own style with that of another woman: 'I'm thinking of one lady who ... preached her sermon, and she just came across as very male in how she worded things, and her structures, and I thought she'd lost her femininity in that, and I feel if I lead the morning worship I don't try and do it the way a man does. I do it as I am, and I think that works, whereas if I tried to be male in how I do things it's false... And I think in committee meetings and things like that ... I just thought this is really hard to maintain the feminine side of me, rather than getting into this aggressive sort of male way of speaking and doing.' These women clearly consider they participate differently to men and do not want to adopt what they view as 'male ways'. The kind of style or female way envisaged among the interviewees was one that emphasised the importance of considering others involved, be this in decision-making, preaching and teaching, or in organisational matters; and being true to their own self-expression in the way that they speak and in what they speak about.

In the area of leadership a number of women favoured a more consensual rather than hierarchical mode of operation. A community worker saw this as part of a community ethos: 'I think you can be in leadership without having a big L leader title. So I mean a lot of the courses and stuff we would do would be about community leadership and it's really about, you know, being a good group member. It's to do with taking responsibility for new people coming in and for decisions that are made. And I think the groups that work best are groups where people are all leaders and are trained as such and skilled up as such and see themselves as leaders together rather than a big L leader who's up at the front ... I remember someone recently saying, you know, that [this geographical area] has a lot of people who see themselves and act as chairpersons, that kind of chair role, compared with a facilitator role. I think that's something to do with how power is viewed. And again the chairperson role is usually seen as a kind of a male thing where you tell people what to do ... Whereas some of the workers, many of whom happen to be women, maybe consciously it's women who do it, would be more facilitative in terms of enabling a whole group of people to get consensus of some sort and move together. Because part of the problem being, you know, individualism and fragmentation rather than a collective kind of ethos. So I think good leaders have inherent authority because of who they are and their experience. And I think it's a lot more about responsibility than about power in the popular sense.'

A church leader also recognised this collaborative approach from her own experience: 'Women will talk round and round and then reach a consensus ... It doesn't mean that all men are like that or all women. [But] generally men will discuss and they will give what they see as their viewpoint as logically and concisely as they can and you'll disagree with it or agree with it, but not talk round and round it the way women do. And men do tend to feel, "What are women getting at?" and yet women do reach a consensus that way. And men, especially men chairmen, can get a bit impatient and not listen to it all. And the process of talking through something I think is more important to women.'

This emphasis on consensus and inclusion was attributed by one community worker to women's experience of subordination: 'We maybe bring a softer approach to things. We maybe are slightly more considerate of other people's feelings and other people's abilities. I'm not saying that men aren't. I wouldn't say that, but maybe we see it more clearly. Maybe because women have been the underdog for quite a while and they know what it is like to be disadvantaged socially or snubbed in a committee or seen only as the tea-maker. So maybe women realise that it's all too easy to walk over people. And to focus only in on the task to be done. Whereas we should see other people, we should see the wider contribution that everyone else can make.'

A male church leader compared all-male leadership team experiences with those that involved women and men: 'The mixed meetings do tend, I think, to run better by and large, to be more relational, to be more polite as well. More civilised maybe is the right word to use.' While sometimes, he thought, women's 'concern for how people are feeling and doing' could slow things down when 'what you want is a straightforward business meeting that it's bang, bang, bang. Let's make some decisions and get going, [at] other times when you're too businesslike you actually miss some important issues, and it lacks the sort of human dimension.'

Another male church leader commented on how women's inclusion in equal numbers in a newly formed group was a different experience to the usual all-male groups he worked with. He found it 'very difficult to define ... [but] it was a totally different dynamic'. He did observe that 'the fact that a woman is present often changes the way in which men deal with each other in that at times they're ... they don't tend to be so kind of judgmental or hard and harsh, always kind of using forms of discussion that close options off, you know, rather than opening them up.' This enabled the whole group to function more productively. An important qualification is needed here. This leader himself recognised that it was the equal numbers of women that enabled the healthy dynamic to exist. He therefore noted that while it would be good to have more women involved in the usual leadership channels of the church, simply having a few women would not be as effective. Rather, 'it's much more significant when you go into a sub-group of some sort working on a particular issue, and the numbers are more even. When you put them down in the large group it, you know, it changes things, but perhaps not as significantly as you might expect.' Here again is evidence of the importance of the numbers of women involved – there needs to be sufficient numbers of women for them to make an impact on proceedings.

The difficulty in a so-called women's way of participating is that such 'women's ways' are perceived as weak and soft. A political activist made the point that if people saw a woman politician or party spokeswoman appearing on 'the television or whatever and taking a sort of a soft line on something and whatever, it's difficult for them to say, "oh well, she would be a good politician", because what we see as being a good politician is somebody that is very aggressive and puts forward a point of view and goes for the other person'. She understood how a woman could sometimes find herself falling into the trap of thinking, 'I'd better say something, you know, because they're going to think I'm weak.'

In particular, expression of emotion is often viewed as weak, and out of place. One woman in church leadership spoke of shedding tears in the very difficult context of personal attack: 'I'm a crier. But I say to myself . . . that's what women are, you know. I'm not saying that we're all criers, but sometimes women do cry. I cry easily, you know, and I've cried in meetings. You know, I've cried in annoyance. And then afterwards I've gone out and felt, what are you crying for? Well, then I've thought to myself, well no, this is what I am. The church, I mean we're not, we just don't fall into let's all be stiff upper-lipped, pseudo-men, you know. Let's be what I am, this is what I am, a crier. If things annoy me I'll cry and get angry, you know ... People just get embarrassed. Women feel sympathetic, men feel, oh dry your eyes girl, you know... But it's my personality coming in and I'm not going to become one of these cold, repressed people just to suit men and tradition ... They can't cope with that either, that I'm this emotional human being sitting in front of them. They can't deal with that either, they go, silly woman!' For this woman, tears were not only an expression of hurt (as commonly would be interpreted), but also of anger at unjust treatment. They are an expression of deep feeling about herself as a person.

However, this kind of different participation is not always valued, and the idea of not only its weakness but its inappropriateness for church leadership or public concerns still pertains. There is still a belief that 'rational discussion necessarily precludes emotion, or that an objective perspective, detached from personal involvement with an issue can be attained – these are founded in a male world of independent individuals who "forget" their connections to nature and the body.'[26] In the words of a female church leader, 'We are so ruled by our heads and somehow, someway, sometime, the hearts are going to have to be addressed and the hearts and the heads need to join up. Because I'm not negating the head, it's terribly important, but there needs to be a two-way traffic and people, and maybe men especially are so scared of their hearts and maybe that's one area where women can introduce them. But then you see they have a stereotype of women in which they regard heart as being emotionalism and heart has nothing to do with emotionalism ... A heart knowledge is something very different.'

It is worth noting that despite male defence of rational deliberation, the reality can be a little different. Speaking of a church leadership team without women, one man commented, 'there was a greater tendency to enter into ideological controversy'. He contrasted this to working with groups that involved women: 'My experience was that women tended to be less confrontational and less prone to – to argue, and to take ideological positions in argument or theological positions.' He then added that men 'tend, we like to think we're theological, but I think we probably weren't just quite as purely theological'. This suggests that despite an absence of overt emotion, male deliberation does not necessarily consist of 'pure rationality'.

A community worker strongly disputed the idea of women's softness as weakness: 'I just think women are softer but their softness is not the same as weakness because I think they're softer and I think that's an important contribution ... It has been perceived as weakness by women and men, yes, very much so. Therefore some women nearly feel, "I have to be as good as a man in order to be taken seriously." And in some instances maybe that's still the case. But I feel we just need to be ourselves and be good at what we're doing.'

A male church leader also spoke of the importance of women being themselves: 'I've said to the female members of staff that they must feel free to be themselves in a way that actually encourages the men to be themselves. By that I mean that if there are emotions floating around or if people get upset, they are to feel free to physically be upset. The tears, the laughter, whatever emotions there are. You know, in my experience women are better at expressing them, and I'm trying to, I'm encouraging the – the female members of the team to just do that, and that it will actually have a positive impact on the male members of the team. And that that is an important part of their role, to just encourage all of us to be more open and more honest … I do think it has had an impact on us. I think it's making us all more human essentially. And it's making us more complete, and it's again all to do with this balance of things, and that we're gradually, this is a growth process, you know, and it doesn't happen quickly, and there has to be trust built up and developed, which I think there now is. But I think yes it is happening, that we're becoming more like the Lord wants us to be, I think.'

The numbers of women involved in part influence the extent to which women can be themselves. One woman commented on her experience of being one of the few women in church leadership: 'What I am facing is [people] needing to understand that not every woman is the same as the last woman they [met] … which is about accepting diversity amongst women like we accept diversity amongst men, and there are so few of us that it's a bit hard to really get a grip of that, but it's the truth.' This speaks of how women may be viewed in a particular way that actually constrains their participation according to the expectation of others. In such instances, the benefit of emphasising how women participate differently can turn into a burden.

ONLY LIKE A WOMAN?

Given that so-called women's ways of participating are viewed as 'soft', ineffectual, and inappropriate, 'women are expected to be like men if they want to succeed. But, the more they do act like men, the more they are criticized.'[27] Many men who themselves operate hierarchical, task-oriented, sometimes competitive and even aggressive styles in their participation and leadership, will adversely judge women who act in this way. A woman involved in politics faced this impossible dilemma: 'You're never going to win, you know. You're, you know, I don't mean to swear on this, but you have to be hard. If you're hard then you're a bitch. You know, in the broadest possible terms – I don't mean that as a swear word, but that's how you're classed in many respects. In a man if you're ruthless that's great, you're going to get on, if you're a woman you're just [a bitch].'

A double standard is operating here. What is acceptable in a man, is not acceptable in a woman. So, as one interviewee elaborated, 'for example, going to a meeting, you know, if a man comes in with a pile of papers he's very busy. If a woman comes in [like that] she's disorganised. You know, things like that, where women should never go into a meeting without lipstick, they should never go in [without being smart] – whereas a man can come in, you know, tie open, all those kinds of things, and he's just busy. But a woman will not appear sharp and will be undermined unless she is, I'm not saying power dressing, but you know what I'm getting at? – she may not be coping.' Clearly a different evaluation is being made on the same behaviour depending on whether it is observed in a woman or a man. If these kinds of situations pertain, it suggests, in fact, that women can never receive a fair assessment of their contribution because *as a woman* contributing, they are already judged more harshly and by stricter parameters.

In particular, two attitudes about the way women participate were identified by the interviewees. First, the notion that women were followers rather than leaders was apparent to a number of interviewees who noted how men expected women to defer to their opinions. A woman involved in politics had experienced this: 'Men have this sense that we're – we're the leaders. We're the authority, and we tell you what to do. And even though a woman could be equal in every respect she still doesn't have that – in a man's mind she's still a woman. I mean as I said earlier … we're still in a very macho situation. I mean, I know people … who would be involved perhaps in talks about different situations [relating to community issues], but when it comes to the actual decision-making women are left outside, because like, women couldn't really make decisions, you know.' A community worker observed the chairman in community groups 'just assuming that the women agree with what he is saying … or, you know, if there's other men, that they're maybe all together on it, and then they assume, you know, [that women will defer to their opinions].'

Another community worker spoke of her early experiences working with male colleagues: 'I found that they patronised you quite a bit, you know. They expected me to just automatically agree with [them]. They were the leaders, and I was there, and I was all right as long as I was typing letters and agreeing with all of their kind of decisions, you know. But once I kind of started to have opinions of my own – I've kind of talked to one of the people [involved] and I said, you know, "You were fine with me, as long as I agreed with you, but once I started to say 'I'm not sure if that's right' … once I started to kind of have opinions of my own our relationship changed," and they didn't handle that very well at all, you know.' Another interviewee spoke of how a male church leader accused a woman of cross-examining him when she had asked him questions in a particular meeting to which they both had been invited.

This expectation that women will not take a prominent part in discussions or, if they do, will support male opinion and decision-making, reflects the way that, on the whole, men take a more visible role in discussions. A number of interviewees remarked on how men more easily contributed to debate, conveying knowledge or expertise in an area, which on reflection they did not necessarily possess.

A woman involved in the leadership of her church had observed this dynamic: 'If you say to a man, "will you speak on this?", you know, I've watched this in the past and [they] sort of went, "yeah, I'll do it." And you know fine rightly they haven't a baldy notion, they're going to go home and panic, but they don't say, "well, I don't really think that's my [expertise]." Whereas a woman will say, "well, I don't really know if I can do that. Well, if you really want to me to try it, yeah", you know. It's just a different attitude.' Similarly, a woman in politics recalled a female Westminster MP speaking 'to some women about politics, and I remember her giving the definition, the difference between a man and a woman is that if a woman is asked to stand for a political party she'll say, "let me go home and think about it." If a man is asked he says, "yes", and then goes home and thinks about it. And that's the difference.' A male church leader concurred: 'When it then comes to leadership and active roles, women often put themselves down. Partly because of expectation, partly because … now this is all terribly conjectural, I think men are greater chancers, you know, they will, I mean, when I see people operating leadership I will see men bluffing more than women, and, you know, my perception is that women are much more honest in terms of assessing their abilities and gifts, whereas men say "oh, sure I can do that," and then sort of think "oh, I wonder how I'll do it."'

A politically active woman observed the dynamics operating in her political party: 'You often find that [a] debate has more men involved in it than females, and I don't think it's because the females don't want to say anything, but I think they're afraid of saying something in case (a) it's not going to be agreed with, (b) they're going to be shouted down for making a stupid remark, but I mean I often think, do men think before they get on their feet [and say to themselves] I'm not going to say this because it's going to sound really silly? Because I have heard numerous men get up and make points and I think to myself, what – did he really think about that before he said it? And I think women think more about what they're going to say before they actually say it. That might be a generalised thing, but ... I don't think females are very good at bluffing, and I have seen many bluffers in my time! But I just don't think females are as good at that sort of [thing] ... If they have something to say they say it and that's it. There's no sort of big grand entrances and exits to their speeches.'

Another woman involved in politics wondered whether the tendency for women to participate in discussion in a certain way was actually self-perpetuating. Expressing her observation of women's participation that 'there are an awful lot of silly women running about who have, you know, a great deal of opinion for their own thoughts, and they perceive themselves as having much more ability than they do actually', she commented that 'women's contributions aren't necessarily judged on their merits. And I wonder – I've thought about this a lot actually, and I wonder how much of it is because – I don't know if you've ever noticed this, but whenever men speak they just make statements. And it's taken for granted that – you know, reasonable enough. Whenever women speak their conversation is peppered with repetition, and I think, you know, opinion-based things where they can be contradicted, and they're always seeking reassurance by saying "Isn't that right?", "Do you know what I mean?", you know. And so they almost set themselves up for – not disbelief but you know what I mean – for query if you like, [of] the merit of what they're saying, the wee question, because they need constant reassurance, whereas men just say. I just wonder how much that has an impact.'

Opinions differ as to whether the scenario this woman describes simply reflects the different interactive cultures of women and men, or whether it is attributable to the power relationships between women and men in which men are dominant and women subordinate, and in which it is the less powerful who need to be polite or gain permission to be heard.[28] Whichever analysis is thought to account for women's tendency to speak in this qualified way,[29] the above interviewee is suggesting that women's hesitancy perpetuates the idea that women are not as able or qualified to contribute to discussion and hence to direct deliberations. So, the idea of men having an authority that arises out of greater knowledge and expertise is sustained. Speaking of a situation in church where there was some confusion over the specifics of an event, one woman had experienced being disbelieved when pointing out that the information a man had provided was inaccurate. As it turned out, she was correct, but 'one of the other men said that [the man] had expressed his view with such conviction that he believed him'.

The second attitude towards women's participation identified by the interviewees, in which women's way of participating is judged differently, is the assumption that their contribution is not based on skill but on some other more elusive quality. A community youth worker spoke of her mediating skills in the context of a dispute among male adolescents in the youth club. In addition to having to overcome the view of the male volunteers who 'didn't want females to be involved in conflict', her own skills were put down to her being female rather than her abilities: 'I think their way of dealing with conflict situations is so heavy-handed and if I'm dealing in a conflict situation that diffuses or moves on quicker, quite often they will attribute that to the fact that I'm a woman rather than to just different methods that are used. Which is, which can be a source of frustration because I know ... that the fact that I am a woman would influence the way – most of the young people we work with are males and it would influence to some degree their reaction to me. And yet there have been other times when I don't think it has made much difference at all. You know, they're perfectly capable of being very aggressive to me as well. But I think sometimes it's almost a scapegoat in terms of, well, you're a woman, of course they're going to react better to you, rather than looking at, well, what's the difference in how we're dealing with the situation?'

Another youth worker described the same phenomenon with the unemployed males she had worked with. In contrast to their experiences 'with bosses, who, you know, were very, very strict and you stepped out of line and that was it, I saw [my role] as a very different thing, that it was,

I was there in a more supportive role and maybe they did feel that I let them off with too much and that kind of thing. I would have got that kind of feedback and think they'd have thought that that was because I was a woman, rather than because that was my style of leadership or because I felt that was something that needed to happen in that kind of environment.'

This experience of having their skills undermined was also spoken of by a woman of her experiences in a church context. While the first reaction of male colleagues was to dismiss her point and think, 'Oh, she's just opinionated and what does she know anyway ... when what you actually say becomes evident and has a measure of truth to it, or that your insight actually is spot on, then there's almost like an admiration and then it's, you're valued because you've got this intuition.' This intuition, however, is not 'an acknowledgement of skill and experience ... And I did struggle with that, you know ... you almost do diminish its place in the broader team approach if you just say it's because I'm a woman I can see these things because the assumption then is all women are insightful or intuitive or have some capacity then to reflect or to see but it's not a skill that's learned.'[30]

A woman with a preaching role in her church commented on the surprise men had expressed about her ability to preach when she first began giving sermons: 'People would have said, the men especially, you know, and they don't even realise what they're saying half the time, "well, I was really surprised, but I really enjoyed that this morning." And they didn't even think, you know. Because they thought they were being encouraging and saying how well you had done, they didn't hide their sense of surprise that it could be good because you're a woman. So those kinds of things were amusing and they never upset me or anything, but it was obvious that it did kind of make them think, oh well you can get something out of a woman teaching or preaching, you know. And that it was a revelation for them. And quite often, I mean even now someone would say, you know, "that was very good" and would add on something like, "for a woman", or something like that.' Even amongst intended endorsement, the phrase 'for a woman' casts some doubt over her ability. The fact that she is female is part of the assessment of her gifting. The comments are not just about what she does, but about who she is. The question of difference does indeed touch upon identity as much as activity.

Difference and Identity, Status and Power

Part of what contributes to women and men's sense of personal identity is an understanding of how each sex relates to the other. This understanding is embodied not only in interpersonal and family relationships, but in social structures, religious organisations, and public institutions. The way women and men view each other does not necessarily have to be constructed primarily around sex or gender difference. Nor does an acceptance of such difference inevitably preclude endorsing commonality.[31] However, when gender differences in power and status are part of what forms and maintains personal identity, changes in personal, social, religious or public structures and behaviour that challenge this gender hierarchy can be profoundly threatening to people's sense of who they are. This applies to both women and men, although in different ways.

THE THREAT TO MASCULINITY

It was clear from the interviewees that part of the issue in women's participation in church and society was the way men may find women's participation threatening to their identity and status. One male church leader, drawing on his own experiences over a number of years, reflected at some length on this: 'If men lose out in a debate, in a decision, do they find it more difficult to lose out if women sway the argument against them than if a man does? I don't know the answer to that. I think ... I think it might be more difficult to lose an argument to a woman than to a man ... Within the church context, why is it hard to lose an argument to a woman? I wonder if maybe one feels that one's masculinity is threatened by it. I think it depends a little bit on who you lose the argument to. I think if it's a woman whom you respect and are comfortable working with, it's not that big an issue ... I think if it's a woman whom you don't see eye to eye with generally speaking, then it is more difficult to lose it. And if it's an issue that you feel strongly on then I think it's more difficult to lose the argument to a woman, because again I think you feel "I'm a man and I am failing, you know, by losing an argument to a woman," and I suppose it comes back to that, you know, having been taught that the man is the leader. I mean I'm speculating, but if that's the case, these issues were much more difficult for me ... years ago. I mean I'm not really encountering difficulties now ... I don't find it as threatening, but I did find it, I did find it, to be perfectly honest, quite difficult in my younger years to lose an argument to a woman.'

This man went on to articulate the role theology had played in endorsing this idea that it undermined his masculinity if a man lost an argument to a woman: 'If you take the male leadership, female follower-ship role it is very difficult to teach that without implying that the woman is a second class, is – is in some way inferior to the man. And although, although you may preface it by saying, "of course, in God's eyes men and women are equal", I think it is nearly impossible to teach it without – without the reality being that the woman is viewed as a second-class citizen. And I suppose if that's where you've come from, to feel that you're losing the argument to a second-class citizen, you know, to someone who is in God's order inferior to you, then it undermines your perception of yourself, you know, and so I think that, I think that has been part of my difficulty in the past probably.'

The sense of superiority over women that he describes as part of masculinity does not have to be endorsed theologically. Any male identity formed on the basis of being better than women, and/or on a distancing from behaviours and attitudes associated with women, will be threatened if those boundaries are broached by women's inclusion across the sexual division of labour. This may well be exacerbated if women do not participate on the basis of bringing a different contribution, but rather concern themselves with the same issues as men. In either case, men find themselves exposed to women's abilities, which inevitably at times will equal or exceed their own. Whether or not men themselves are able to recognise and then reflect on this sense of challenge to their identity, it is often women who are more aware of the underlying dynamics at work. One woman active in the church commented: 'Some of the conflict that was there was because I was female, and ... one person in particular felt I was a threat. Now I think if you tackled the person on it they would be aghast at it, but their behaviour was such that they felt threatened ...' Another woman very involved with the church said of her male colleagues: 'I think half of them are frightened of me at some level because, I mean, even if you take [particular occasions] where sometimes I'd be making a speech or a presentation and I'd be looking at them, and their whole body language is crossed and away from me, and some of the senior guys wouldn't even look at me.'

For other women, the hostility they encountered appeared far more conscious on the part of the men concerned. A community worker knew that her male colleague was 'very uncomfortable with a woman being on a par to him'. Another community worker found a male employee did not like taking direction from her as his senior in the organisation. One of these women also spoke of how she had offered an alternative view of certain events at a meeting to that expressed by a male community worker and knew that 'this guy would be annoyed because I as a woman challenged him in public, as well as the content of what I was saying'. A politically active woman, speaking positively of her earlier experiences in a community endeavour, also was aware of the initial difficulty her participation created for some of her male colleagues: 'Men were gracious to me, but I, a woman, and a woman who spoke, and who challenged, was a little uncomfortable for one or two for a little while, until they realised that I wasn't doing it for any ulterior motives!'

Even when there is a willingness to include women, men may still find the actual practice more difficult than they anticipated. Speaking of her church in which there was 'a willingness to, you know, allow women to take quite key roles in the church,' one woman reflected, 'but I think they kind of do struggle with the reality of that, you know, there's very much a sort of spoken willingness to, but in reality I think it sometimes feels, I think some of the men can feel a wee bit threatened by it in reality'. So in practice, therefore, despite their willingness to involve women in the leadership, 'in reality again it's very much the men that take the lead, and kind of fall, I think, kind of fall back on their maleness to have the final say, you know, and kind of intimidate or dominate in order to be eventually the ones that – that take the lead.'

With these dynamics at work, female challenge to male opinion may be averted by men in ways that are detrimental to the women concerned. One woman spoke of how, 'men find it very threatening that I would [express my views, so] they would say I was calculating or I was being, they would just find ways of deflecting the actual issue onto, you know ... they see it as this is about me being a feminist or something and I'm just being, you know, it becomes very easy for them to deflect. I almost feel scapegoated then ... OK send me out, I'm the representation of all that you fear, but the issue still stands and somebody's got to call it ... [but on a couple of occasions] the immediate reaction was, "no, you're wrong", and I just did feel that if I'd been a man I wouldn't have had that. There was just something threatening about a woman challenging.'

Another woman commented how churchmen had dismissed a woman's viewpoints by describing her as 'a single angry woman, and it's like, just because they challenged something that's not, had nothing to do with being a woman, or single, or anything'. She commented further, 'unless the ideal [of including women] gets broken down into, well, how are we going to do this? what problems does this address? what makes it difficult? or whatever, then the same patterns just fall back into it, even though, like, it might look like there's equality. In reality, you know, unless you start really challenging and talking about how to, you know, redress inequalities, it's very hard.'

Redressing the realities of women's inclusion will also involve addressing the matter of power. Despite much talk of leadership as service, two women identified power as integral to the question of women's participation in the church. A woman had talked to a female friend in the church about the possibility of appointing women to the leadership in their congregation, which currently is exclusively male: 'We've got to take things slowly, which is one of the things that gets me here; everything has got to be slow and I tend to like to move up speed. And the comment made by one of the men to [my friend] was, "It's the only area we have left in terms of our authority." And that's where it's at and I think they feel, well it is the only area they've got left. You know, "I'm being bombarded in the workplace by women who are breaking the glass ceiling and it's not fair, it's not right, I can't handle this, so give me a safe little place in church, where I can exercise power without fear of somebody, you know, biting at my ankles." And women have not mobilised sufficiently to do that. I think probably we're too gracious to do it.' Another woman put it bluntly: 'It's a power thing, you see, if you can't get power outside, you'll get it in the church, and I think that's where a lot of abuse comes in the church, that people can't get their power elsewhere but then they bring it into the church – abuse in the widest possible sense.'

The notion of power these women are observing in some men is a negative one, a matter of power over others rather than power that is enabling of people. Carol Becker observes that part of the problem in this regard is in 'viewing power as a limited commodity'.[32] While power is restricted in hierarchical structures, it does not necessarily have to be so in collaborative ventures such as church leadership teams (nor indeed in community or political organisations), where the emphasis ultimately should be on the empowerment of all. What is needed is a 'vision of leadership that is no longer based on "I win; You lose," because "my power depends on your weakness."'[33]

Even in churches where women are encouraged in their leadership and preaching participation, there can be male concern about the numbers of women being included. While a desire for balance in leadership appears reasonable, one woman was very aware that in her context, where it was the few women who were participating in preaching and church leadership, this concern was motivated by male anxiety: 'At times the men would talk about, you know, we have to, where we have to be careful and we have to make sure, keep a balance et cetera, et cetera. And you sort of feel, well I mean we have been so totally off balance for so many years, that if we go unbalanced in the other direction for a while, I don't really think it's such a big deal. You know, because women have had to listen to men for such a long, long time ... They talk about balance in terms of, I mean, women now have a reasonable amount of input, but certainly not anywhere near fifty per cent ... I also think it's amusing in terms of how they talk about even women in leadership and all those kinds of things and are very quick to talk about how we must hold the whole thing in balance. And, you know, I find myself continually pointing out, but there has been no balance for all of these years, centuries, et cetera, and it's a bit ridiculous, you know, because we sort of sat without saying anything for a long, long, long time. And also I think we're not really in danger of going out of balance, to be truthful!'

Commenting on the kinds of difficulties experienced by men who form their identities in oppositional terms to women, one male church leader said: 'I honestly think that some men have a problem when they find a very gifted woman and they find it hard to know how to handle this. To see somebody who's not going to sit down quietly and go into a corner and sort of demurely agree with everything. I mean I think a lot of the problems of the church are actually men's problems.' It is certainly true that what has so often been viewed as 'women as the problem' is in fact a problem that men have with women's participation. However, as one woman involved in politics noted, 'Sometimes it's oversimplified that it's the men that are stopping you getting ahead.' For it is also true that women themselves find their own identities at risk by some kinds of participation by other women.

WOMEN: 'THEIR OWN WORST ENEMIES'

The idea of women being their own worst enemies was either stated explicitly or implied by about one third of those interviewed. It speaks of some women's resistance towards other women's (or indeed their own) participation in certain areas, particularly those that cross the sexual division of labour.

In part, this resistance was attributed to women's own lack of self-esteem wherein they lacked a belief in themselves as able or worthy to participate. As one woman put it, 'We should place equal value on what women do, and, you know, we should bring our little girls up, and our children in general, we should bring our men and ... women up to value whatever role anyone has in life. And then it's, wow, it's like, it's a sweeping statement, but ... if we could put that value on the role a woman has then she would become a valuable member of wherever she was – church, or her home, or, you know, whatever ... But it's, it's doing that. And women are as guilty of it as men are, I mean, you know, I'm not going to point the finger and blame men for that. Women do it too, we can be our own worst enemies at times. It's getting women to value who they are, you know, where they are. It's a self-esteem thing really, isn't it?' The consequences of not doing this were expressed by a woman in politics: 'We also in a way have ourselves tuned up that women shouldn't really do well, and when they do then we have to ask why.' Certainly an ethos that has confined women to particular roles and at the same time assigned these roles a lesser value, can foster in women a belief in their own inadequacy or relative unimportance. Being undermined in this way, they are unlikely to challenge the male dominance of the status quo.

Not unrelated to this lack of confidence some women display in their own abilities or sense of worthiness to participate more fully in church and society, is the idea of women's place, and of what activity or behaviour is proper for a woman. This notion of place, and the sense of threat to female identity that comes when it is challenged, also contributes to some women's resistance to crossing the sexual division of labour and often does so in a more overt manner.

Intrinsic to the idea of women's place is the idea of what a woman should be and what she should be doing. This is often uncovered by the perceived absence of these qualities or behaviours. One woman spoke of the difficulty she had in relating to the women's organisation in her church: '[They] can't deal with me because I never wear a skirt, I always wear trousers. I don't conform to their image of what a woman should be.' A community worker related how 'I was never what I would call a "woman's woman", a female woman. And I think sometimes that women put women in boxes.' Her experience outside of 'the box', outside of women's place, had created difficulties for her from other women who felt she should fit into the stereotype of an at-home mum. A woman working in her church also found attitudinal difficulties from other women: 'I think [they] probably feel at some level I should probably go home and look after my children, and [that] I probably don't look after them very well.'

A woman involved in politics saw the same tension at work in her party, relating this to a generational difference: 'There's an elderly ladies thing I think that it's not the proper job for a woman to be involved in elective politics. They certainly have been involved in the party throughout the years and very much so, doing things that made it possible for the men to be elected politicians. But they don't see their role as elected politicians, and because of that they don't see [the] role [of] ... the young people coming up through, as elected politicians. So I think that's a problem for females within the party when they go to selection meetings. It's sometimes their own sex that's not electing them.' Referring to women in her own church declining to be involved even in welcoming people to church services when they entered the building, another interviewee said, 'What would anger me most is some of the women didn't want to take it on because "it's not our place".'

Those who do not conform to this women's place are labelled as outside of the norm for a woman. A community worker had experienced this through difficulty with how she was perceived by another woman who considered her threatening: 'I think ... there's an underlying kind of assumption that any women who are involved in jobs that are seen as being leadership aren't the norm.' Another community worker felt this was true not only for women in certain community roles, but also for women in ordained church ministry: 'I think that sometimes where women fall down, when they're not in normal jobs, when they have to take the risk, that sometimes other women are hard on them and they're hard on themselves ... It must be very difficult if you're stepping out ... if you're not conforming, you're not the normal.' If women express antagonism towards women who are not conforming to a female norm, it indicates the need some women feel for gender conformity for their sense of personal identity.

This norm can involve assuming a subservient role. Despite the fact that in church circles women 'very often are the power behind the throne', one woman noted that they 'keep themselves in a second class or even a third class, if you can talk that within church communities'. Another woman observed of some women in her denomination that, despite many of them being quite able professionally, in the church 'they like the male authority figure and they like their minister to be an authority figure; they like to be dominated'. In this sense she described them as 'the stronghold of patriarchy', that is, they are the ones who, in some ways, act as guardians of male dominance. In the words of another woman, 'there are some women, who make sure [discrimination against women] is perpetuated'. Speaking of a past experience she stated, 'That really made me more angry than anything else, that women were perceived as being subjugated to men, that they were perceived as having a certain role, that is, the housewife ... And I mean it was women ... who, you know, it was blatantly clear to me that that was their attitude and I was stepping out of line, you know, give me my beret![34] And that's not helping, really not helping. I suppose that made me more angry than the men. I just thought what, you know, what are you saying about yourselves, what are you letting happen to you. And I think it's a lack even of understanding in them or realisation of what they're letting happen to themselves or what they're doing to themselves by letting that happen.'

The irony in many of these situations is that women can perpetuate the idea of women's place by the way they view and behave towards women they consider are stepping out of that place. So one woman said of the treatment she had received from some other women, 'I feel that it's almost like, if anything at all to demean, to cut the feet from under you, to bring you down to size, you know, to let you know that your place is with us, it's not up there with [the men].' The emphasis is very much on, 'for goodness sake, don't rock the boat'. Another interviewee spoke of 'problems with women who work around me, who would very easily do anything to help a man, but who never think of doing anything to help a woman, you know. In my position, my equivalent as a man they wouldn't hesitate to do anything that would help them out voluntarily, but there isn't the same willingness, neither voluntarily or necessarily in the job, you know ... but that actually ... perpetuates the system.'

The threat to women's identity that comes when other women step out of place was articulated by a woman about political participation: 'There's a certain truth in the idea that sometimes we're our own worst enemies, because I don't think we necessarily do support women candidates. I think if some women decided to stand you don't necessarily want to support them because we don't want to see women progressing more than we have ourselves or something. I think that there can be a bit of a catty nature within women at times, and a certain assumption that – why should they be able to take on that role?' Another woman observed how there had been problems in her church over the years: 'If there was a woman sort of way stepped out, you know, in a leadership role, they're pushed back again. That's the women as well that have done that, you know, it's not just the men, it's an overall thing. And maybe it was the women who complained more about the women being up there. But that, sometimes I saw that as a jealousy that they, they didn't want to accept that a woman could get up there and do that because they weren't doing it. So women are their own worst enemy.' As a politically involved woman commented, 'even in our own minds as women, if a woman gets on there's all that jealous aspect, "oh, I wonder where she got that?", you know, "what did she do more than anybody else?"'

The idea of women as their own worst enemies was spoken of by a male church leader in regard to raising the question of women and men in his own denomination: 'The people who have objected to us looking at personal identity in relation to male and female, and particularly the role of the female, have been the females. Because they had felt there was a role carved out for them, they were happy in it and they were matriarchal in it, and so to actually say to them, "you actually can join this leadership group, you actually can participate along with the males," they have been more reluctant sometimes than the males had been to have them, because they have been conditioned and they have presumed upon themselves a role, a model, an ethos that they lifted up and was convenient, and didn't want out of their comfort zone. So it wasn't just the males saying no ... It's not just a male mindset. It's a female mindset that has been either conditioned – certainly been conditioned by whatever...'

For whatever reasons they maintain it, women's resistance to members of their own sex participating outside of traditional gender roles in effect supports those men who work to retain an identity of different status and power. Critics of these positions argue that the gender roles have in fact been determined by men, regardless of the extent to which women now make them their own.[35] These are not easy matters to resolve precisely because they are part and parcel of how women and men form their sense of self.

The notion of difference is viewed both positively and negatively. For some people, women's difference is a reason for their greater inclusion in church and society, in the particular contribution they bring and/or the way that they participate. For others, an emphasis on difference in these situations has been a means of marginalising and devaluing women. It raises the issue of whether it is even possible to maintain the notion of women's difference while at the same time valuing the contribution that women bring. This in turn is connected to our sense of personal identity and the extent to which it is formed and maintained by holding differences of occupation, power and status at its core. Whatever stance is taken, however, for many Christians, and not least for evangelicals, the nature of women's involvement in church and society is ultimately determined by the giving or withholding of a divinely sanctioned legitimacy to participate. While no consensus amongst evangelicals exists on this matter, the following chapter demonstrates that the question of authority is enmeshed in the participation of evangelical women not only in their faith communities, but also in the society in which they live.

5

The Question of Authority

This chapter addresses the question of whether men have a divinely decreed authority over women; in other words, is it God's design that human gender relationships, while being open to a multiplicity of expression in different cultures, times and individuals, should nevertheless always adhere to a model of male authority and female submission?

In the question of authority, as in the question of difference, essential views of women and men are involved. Innate differences between women and men are said to make it appropriate for women to be subject to male authority (however that is understood) and to be and behave in certain ways. There exists a 'far-reaching presumption, barely obscured by the modern ideology of feminism and equal-rights legislation, that the natural place of the man is the public world of influence and power, while the natural place of the woman is the private, domestic world of the home'.[1] That said, however, for many evangelical Christians, the determining factor in establishing male authority over women is the understanding that this is a divinely ordained ordering of human relationships. It is

> the principle of 'masculine headship'. Variously interpreted as having operative jurisdiction throughout the whole of creation, or only in marriage, family and church relationships, this is the difference which underlies all other differences between men and women, and because this principle is laid down by God, it cancels out any other considerations which might modify or contradict it.[2]

Hence, while allusions to physiological and psychological differences between the sexes occur frequently when speaking of whether and how women should participate in church, community and public life, the ultimate question is one of authority.

There are two main evangelical viewpoints on this matter.[3] While it used to be generally thought that to hold a view other than male authority over women was to disregard the authority of Scripture, that is no longer the case. A biblically argued case against male authority over women is now made by evangelicals who hold to a traditional evangelical understanding of Scripture, namely, the Bible as the word of God, authoritative in matters of faith and practice. The actual outworking of these two views can vary quite considerably. In particular, a view of male 'headship' which in some contexts means a woman may not pray aloud in mixed gatherings, in other contexts allows women to participate in nearly all aspects of church life, including preaching and communion, providing she is under the authority of a male church leader. However, the main distinction remains: either women *as a sex* are subject to male authority or they are not. As Andrew Perriman comments, 'there is no clear middle ground in this debate: the authority of the man may be mitigated in various ways, the contribution of the woman to family and church may be enthusiastically promoted, but in the end the one either has authority over the other or he does not'.[4] This chapter considers the biblical case for each of these two positions and then explores their application in women's church and civic participation.

The Bible and Male Authority

PRELIMINARY CONSIDERATIONS

Before outlining the biblical case made for and against the idea of male authority, it is important to make some general comments pertinent to the debate.

The language of the debate

The language employed to speak of the notion of 'headship' has changed. Two decades ago the terms hierarchical and liberation were applied to the views of male authority over women and the counteraction of that idea.[5] More recently, however, the terms used are more likely to be complementarian and egalitarian respectively, and the terms dominance and subordination or subjection have been replaced by leadership and submission. For both viewpoints this probably reflects a change in language that is more in keeping with social sensibilities in an age that adopts the public rhetoric of female equality. The view of male authority now stresses male responsibility rather than male rule, and complementarity perhaps evokes a sense of partnership and working with the strengths of each for the best of everyone rather than a sense of men 'lording' it over women. However, a divinely ordained male authority over women remains the distinguishing feature of this view and is not diminished by the change in the language used to describe it.

A two-way debate

While those advocating the second view that does not understand 'headship' as authority have always of necessity countered the arguments of those who advocate 'headship' as authority, the latter are now more likely also to address the counter arguments to their position. Hence, for example, there is more of an awareness by those holding a view of male headship of the need to acknowledge the abuse of women by men that at times has been justified by a dominance/subordination model of male/female relationships and indeed to distance themselves and their position from such behaviour.

Another example would be the discussion around the designation 'helper' applied to women in relationship to men. Those advocating that 'head' does not mean male authority have always pointed out that the idea of helper is not one of lesser value or worth and indeed supports the idea of equal status socially as well as theologically. Now those advocating male authority also are giving more consideration to the value of the notion of helper, albeit without changing their viewpoint on a divinely ordained order of gender relationships. This suggests that the biblical debate has impacted on evangelicalism to a degree that can no longer be ignored by those who have in the past been more able to assume the unquestioned acceptance of their position. It is probably too much to claim that a real dialogue has developed, but certainly there is a greater awareness of the issues of the debate by all involved.

The use of Scripture

A distinguishing characteristic between the two positions is their use of Scripture. The traditional evangelical viewpoint stresses particular passages and words and has a tendency to isolate these in support of its stance. Those advocating that male 'headship' is not about authority over women do consider the same passages in detail but place these in the overall context of biblical material in order to interpret their meaning. Commenting on the Church of England's discussion regarding women's ordination, John Martin notes that in addition to examining the usual texts employed in the debate, a significant component that contributed to a biblical acceptance of women as priests was a hermeneutical shift to considering the 'whole sweep of biblical theology and what it might say to the issue in question'.[6]

'Headship' – a misnomer?

The question of male authority is usually addressed under the name of 'headship'. It is worth pausing to reflect on the term itself. R.T. France comments on 'headship':

> The word is heard so often in discussions of the respective roles of men and women today that some people may be surprised to learn, firstly, that there is no Greek noun in the New Testament which corresponds to the English abstract noun 'headship', secondly, that the metaphor of the man as 'head' occurs only twice in the New Testament ... and, thirdly, that in at least one of those uses there is no reason in context to think that the metaphor has

any relevance to the issue of women's ministry in the church: it is ... simply a way of expressing the marriage relationship.[7]

Without pre-empting the following discussion regarding male authority, the point is simply that a notion of 'headship' is accepted within evangelicalism without many of those who adopt it necessarily having an understanding of its construction from the biblical text. It has taken on a standing of its own, in a similar way to another evangelical metaphor – that of being 'born again'. Again, the phrase 'born again' appears only twice in the New Testament,[8] in a context that many consider suggests the phrase 'born from above' to be the more accurate meaning.[9] This is not to negate the relevance of the idea of the metaphor of being born again *per se*. It does, however, illustrate that it is possible for ideas (supposedly) rooted in biblical concepts or words to take on a life of their own, with less focus on the original connection to the biblical text.[10] Attention to the scriptural grounding of a concept, how it comes to take on meaning from the biblical text to our lives today, is the task of hermeneutics. Hermeneutics is necessary if 'the authority of the evangelical tradition' is not, 'in practice if not in theory', to take 'precedence over the authority of Scripture'.[11]

Outlines of the two principal viewpoints are given below. Not all the arguments presented are necessarily made by the proponents of each view. Further, the arguments for each case made by its advocates are far more detailed and complex than these outlines allow.[12] However, they do indicate the main arguments usually presented in support of and counter to the view of male authority.

THE CASE FOR MALE AUTHORITY

The case for male authority comes from the New Testament statements that 'the husband is the head of the wife' (Ephesians 5:23) and 'the man is the head of the woman' (1 Corinthians 11:3).[13]

The passage in Ephesians[14] draws a parallel between the relationship of husbands and wives and that of Christ and the church. A wife is to be subject to her husband, who is her head, in the same way that the church is subject to Christ, who is the head of the church. Husbands are expected to behave towards their wives as Christ acted in respect of the church, namely, in self-giving love.

The passage in Corinthians[15] is concerned with the context of public worship. It makes no specific mention of female subjection but rather focuses on the propriety of a woman having 'authority on her head'.[16] Variously understood as some kind of physical head covering or a particular way of arranging her hair, in either case referring to appropriate attire for a respectable woman, the emphasis is very much on the proper relationship of women to men, which may or may not be expressed through wearing some kind of actual head covering today. For 'while wearing head coverings no longer speaks to our culture, there is an abiding principle in this text that is applicable'.[17] This principle is that 'God has ordained that men have the responsibility to lead, while women have a complementary and supportive role'.[18] In this passage, the idea of God being the head of Christ is paralleled with that of Christ being the head of every man, and men or husbands being the head of women or their wives.

The term 'head' in these instances is taken to denote authority. This meaning is derived from its use in these passages and other places in the New Testament,[19] and also from verses in 1 Peter[20] which, while they do not use the term 'head', nevertheless speak of wives' submission and obedience to their husbands. Usage outside of the New Testament in the Septuagint, that is, the Greek translation of the Hebrew Old Testament, and in non-biblical writers are also cited in support of interpreting 'head' as authority.

In summary, Christ's evident authority over the church is the pattern for the authority of males over females. The Corinthian reference to God as Christ's head indicates that the model of submission does not involve an inferior essence or nature, but a difference in role or function. Hence, Christ is of the same nature as God, but submits himself to the Father for the purposes of redemption.

Male 'headship' is further supported by an order of gender relationships established in the creation narratives in Genesis 1–3. While Genesis 1[21] establishes the creation of humanity as both female and male, in the divine image, and the dominion of both sexes over the created world, it does not speak to the ordering of their relationships. This is established in Genesis 2. The description of the man being created first, the woman being created from the man, her being described as his helper, and the man naming the woman, all indicate, not a superiority of the male, but a leadership function. This stands alongside their equal status before God established in Genesis 1 and speaks to its outworking. Hence, the joint dominion over the earth given to female and male in practice means that 'the initiative, the ground-breaking aspect of that rule, lays with the male ... because the man was made first ... Man is to be the pioneer'.[22] Raymond Ortlund goes further and suggests that while Genesis 1 does not address gender relationships directly, 'God's naming of the race "man" whispers male headship'.[23]

In this view, Genesis establishes the sexual distinctiveness of humanity, with a difference in function though not of being. While open to a variety of cultural applications, this sexual distinction is intrinsic to humanity's creation, and is not, therefore, the result simply of socialisation and, hence, open to alteration. Rather, the difference in role is part of being female and male: 'A man, just by virtue of his manhood, is called to lead for God. A woman, just by virtue of her womanhood, is called to help for God.'[24] Humanity's fall into sin depicted in Genesis 3 does not alter this basic created order although it certainly results in 'a painful distortion of the existing hierarchical relationship noted in Genesis 2'.[25] Redemption in Christ, therefore, offers the possibility of restoring the ordained gender order from its misuse and abuse, not obliterating it altogether.

The creation narratives are alluded to in both the Corinthians passage and in 1 Timothy.[26] The text in Timothy states, 'I permit no woman to teach or to have authority over a man; she is to keep silent.'[27] It then refers to the creation narrative stating that as well as Adam being formed first, it was Eve who was deceived and became a transgressor.[28] Supported by a further instruction in 1 Corinthians[29] that women should be silent in the churches, not permitted to speak, but be subordinate, these passages have been variously applied. For some they prohibit women from participating at all in public worship involving men. Others, because of additional instructions in the Corinthians correspondence and evidence of women's ministry in the New Testament, permit women's participation in public prayer and prophesy providing they do so with an attitude that respects male leadership. And some consider that women may teach even mixed groups, including preaching in public services, if in doing so 'they are not usurping any improper authority over [men]'.[30]

Clearly there are significant differences in these positions. Indeed it may be thought that a view of male authority is greatly reduced in its restriction on women if it permits their participation to the extent of public preaching. However, this view, as its proponents and opponents would both emphasise albeit to different ends,[31] still maintains a proper gender order which sees leadership intrinsic to maleness and complementary support intrinsic to femaleness. Hence, while J.I. Packer argues that 'the burden of proof regarding the exclusion of women from the office of teaching and ruling within the congregation now lies on those who maintain the exclusion rather than on those who challenge it',[32] in the same context he writes:

> ... a situation in which a female boss has a male secretary, or a marriage in which the woman (as we say) wears the trousers, will put more strain on the humanity of both parties than if it were the other way around. This is part of the reality of creation, a given fact that nothing will change. Certainly, redemption will not change it, for grace restores nature, not abolishes it.[33]

There are of course implications of this in the outworking of women's community and public involvement in addition to their involvement in their families and churches.

Part of the support for women's greater participation is their obvious gifting. While this is not usually denied by any of those advocating a view of male authority, the debate is over the context in which women's gifting may be exercised. Hence, for some:

> A woman is not permitted a pastoral or governmental position over men in a New Testament church. No ministry that places her in such a position is open to her. There is no question but that a woman may be every bit as spiritual and spiritually gifted as any man. That is not the point. The place of public ministry and pastoral government is not open to her, 'not turned over to' her by the Lord, as the literal force of 1 Corinthians 14:34 has it. The Lord will give her fitting opportunities to exercise her gifts.[34]

One final point to note is that while today a view of male authority is usually presented in terms that affirm women's equal spiritual standing with men, this has not always been the case. Existing within the history of the church is a line of tradition that taught women's inferior spiritual nature, a line that continues into living memory. The idea of women as bearing a secondary image of God still has an influence in a number of more conservative Christian groupings, at least on some middle-aged and older women who learned this directly when young. Hence, while most commentators would not speak in such terms today, holding rather to a view of women as 'spiritually equal but functionally different', a belief in women's spiritual inferiority continues to exist. There are still women in Northern Ireland today for whom the idea of their spiritual equality before God is either relatively new or even yet unheard of.[35]

As expounded today, a view of male authority affirms the equality of women with men in their status before God. The biblical statement: 'There is no longer Jew or Greek, there is no longer slave or free, there is no longer male and female: for all of you are one in Christ Jesus'[36] is seen as endorsing the equal spiritual standing of women, slaves and gentiles and not to speak to the ordering of social relationships. This view of male 'headship' maintains a spiritual equity in women and men's standing before God but posits a distinction in terms of social relations whereby men not only take priority but hold a divinely given authority over women. This is not to be understood as dominance or authoritarianism, and not to be exercised abusively. It is seen, rather, as men's role to give spiritual leadership and to exercise overall responsibility as leader in marriage and church relationships and even in other social contexts.

THE CASE AGAINST MALE AUTHORITY

The case against male authority involves a different understanding of the metaphor 'head'. It argues that while 'head' is used today to denote some kind of authority or authoritative position, such as headmaster, this is not the only possible usage of the metaphor. Indeed, nor is this usage one with which Paul's Greek readers would have been familiar. While the Hebrew word for 'head' can be used metaphorically in the sense of 'chief over' (although arguably with a sense of priority rather than rule), a common Greek usage of Paul's time was source or origin, as in head of a river. This is consistent with the Greek understanding of the heart 'as the source of thought and reason, the head ... seen rather as the source of life'.[37] 'For a wife to think of her husband as source would not mean that he has power over her, but that in symbolically coming from him (as woman came from Adam) she is of him and one with him.'[38] This meaning can also apply to the usage of 'head' in other New Testament passages when it is said of Christ, who is portrayed as the source of the church's life.

Another metaphorical understanding of 'head' is 'that which is most prominent, foremost, uppermost, pre-eminent' and therefore is 'spatial or temporal, not hierarchical or organic'.[39] Both Septuagint and non-biblical writers support this understanding. While those who are described as 'head' because of their pre-eminence often will be in positions of authority and leadership, these latter are not what is being referred to in the metaphor.[40] In regard to men, therefore, the metaphor 'head' speaks to the 'dimension of visibility, prominence, eminence, social superiority' occupied by men in society and family and not to the 'dimension of authority and subservience, for which other terminology was available'.[41]

Whichever view is taken, that of source or pre-eminence, the point is that authority is not the intended meaning of the metaphor 'head'. Others have pointed out that the use of 'head' to describe the relationship between women and men applies to the marriage relationship, not to general relationships between women and men. The same words are used for 'woman' and 'man' as for 'wife' and 'husband' and, hence, while the passages in both 1 Corinthians and 1 Timothy concern corporate worship, they nevertheless refer to the relationship of a wife and husband in that context and not to the ministry of women within the church community.[42] This does not mean that 'head' needs to be understood as authority in marriage. Rather, a mutuality of relationship is being portrayed. For self-sacrificing love by a husband is reciprocated by a wife's submission. Hence, in Ephesians 5, 'the subjection of the wife and the love of the husband are in fact to be expressions in different ways of the mutual subjection called for'[43] in the preceding verse that exhorts the Christians to 'be subject to one another out of reverence for Christ'.[44] Wifely obedience is never instructed by Paul, although obedience is mentioned in other social relationships, namely that of children to their parents and slaves to their owners. Indeed, the only time Paul specifically mentions male authority towards women is in the context of conjugal rights in marriage in which a husband's authority over his wife's body is reciprocated by that of a wife's authority over her husband's body.[45]

In this view, the two other passages that mention authority in relation to women do not support male authority over women. The Corinthian reference is to authority on the woman's own (literal) head, that is, her own authority to participate in worship.[46] Indeed, the fact that these verses refer to the way in which a woman prays or prophesies, means that the later verses in the Corinthian letter about women's silence cannot be a total prohibition on their public participation. The passage in Timothy that speaks of authority actually uses a different word than appears in the other texts.[47] Not only is it not the usual way authority is spoken of, but this is the only occasion in the New Testament in which it appears, making its translation more difficult. So if Paul's intention was to say 'that no woman may ever be in a position where she has authority over a man, he has chosen an unnecessarily obscure way to say it!'[48] The church in Ephesus, where Timothy was, faced particular difficulties with false teaching and a general undermining of marriage. What is being prohibited (given a closer examination of the word that is translated as authority) is domineering, inappropriate behaviour by the women in the church (or again, by wives in regard to their husbands), as those lacking the skills necessary to teach, attempting to assume that role. Women are therefore to learn – not in silence (the usual word for silence found in the Corinthians passage is not used here) – but in quietness of temperament, the necessary attitude to foster the learning that was needed.

Further, in Timothy, the reference to Adam and Eve[49] does not relate to a creation order of gender relations but is more likely a reference to the Genesis narrative in order to refute false teaching that venerated Eve. The statement that Eve was deceived[50] does not have to imply that by nature women are more easily deceived and hence never able to teach. Apart from Paul's statement in Romans that it was Adam who was deceived,[51] the reference to Eve's deception serves as an illustration of what was happening at Ephesus; in the same way it is also used in 2 Corinthians[52] of both male and female members of the church being led astray.

In this view, the Genesis narratives do not describe a divinely ordained order of gender relationships that give men authority over women. Genesis 1 portrays humanity as male and female made in the divine image and sharing dominion over the earth. Indeed, 'neither is given dominion over one another'.[53] This is not contradicted in Genesis 2. The fact that the man is depicted as being created first gives him no more priority than the rest of creation has over humanity in its prior creation. Indeed, man plays no active part in woman's creation.[54] She owes her creation to God and not to the man's rib. In the same way the man owes his creation to God and not to the dust from which he was made. The description of woman as a 'helper' for the man indicates her parity with him, her sameness, her suitability because she is like him. She is a 'companion corresponding to' the man.[55] The notion of helper does not signify secondary or subsidiary activity; frequently it is spoken of as God's action towards humanity. Rather, in Genesis 2 it speaks of someone equal to the task, 'expected to engage fully in the same activities'.[56]

Finally, the man's naming of the woman does not signify his authority over her. Some argue that the proper naming formula is not used in Genesis 2, others that whenever naming occurs, it is the context that determines whether authority is involved in this act, not the act of naming itself. Hence, when the man names the woman as when, for example, Hagar, the slave girl, names God,[57] no authoritative relationship is implied.

In this view, hierarchical gender relations arose after the fall depicted in Genesis 3. Hence, redemption in Christ offers the possibility of restoring the original non-hierarchical way of relating between the sexes. Such interdependence is depicted in the Corinthians reference that 'in the Lord woman is not independent of man or man independent of woman. For just as woman came from man, so man comes through woman; but all things come from God.'[58]

This counter argument against male authority pays particular attention to the context to which the more difficult passages were addressed. It also views these few texts against the weight of the New Testament evidence of women's participation in the life of the early Christian church. With the Spirit poured out on women and men alike,[59] women shared in prayer,[60] prophesy,[61] decision-making,[62] and teaching[63] in the church. They had churches in their homes[64] and they were among Paul's co-labourers in the gospel, such as Euodia and Syntyche.[65] In particular, Phoebe was a deacon of the church at Cencrecheae, and Junia is described as 'prominent among the apostles'.[66] Some argue that 1 Timothy refers to women deacons and not to the wives of male deacons.[67] After reviewing the ministry of women in the early church, Andrew Perriman states that 'we may discern in these fleeting allusions a very appealing model for the unselfconscious, collaborative ministry of women. There is no apology for their work, no apparent segregation, no fussy attempt to demarcate their sphere of activity, no overt subordination of their work to male authority.'[68]

In the view against male authority, this understanding of the practice and life of the early church is consistent with a reading of Jesus' own attitude and behaviour towards women in the gospels. Sometimes viewed as being notably better than the prevailing situation for women within Judaism,[69] Jesus makes no role distinction for his disciples on the basis of their sex. They were among his followers as disciples and included with men in spreading the good news.[70] The choice of twelve males as his closest companions cannot be taken to signify exclusively male leadership in the church any more than it can be used to indicate that only Jews should hold such positions. More likely, choice of the twelve disciples relates to the twelve tribes of Israel, indicating continuity with Israel.

In this counter view to the idea of male authority over women, social equality goes alongside that of spiritual standing before God. The facilitation of women to fill roles of leadership and teaching within the Christian community and society is intrinsic to the good news of restored relationships with God and each other. This is not simply to serve the self-fulfilment of women, but for the sake of the church and the world, which otherwise would be deprived of women's wider contributions. Such an idea does not obliterate differences between women and men or obscure sexual distinction. Rather it conceptualises the relationship between women and men differently, in which women and men function together for the good of families, society and church, according to their gifting and abilities, with a mutuality, partnership and reciprocity between the sexes.

Headship Applied

While it is possible to clearly outline a position advocating a view of male authority, there is much diversity in its practical outworking and application, not least in the fact that while some apply headship to marriage, others apply it only to the church, while for others it covers both contexts.

IN MARRIAGE AND FAMILY

In talking about the outworking of headship for wives and husbands, the interviewees drew on their own experiences as well as their observations of the marriages of their parents, siblings, and friends. In terms of the understanding of what headship meant in practice, two main ideas were presented. The first was headship as an exercise of power and control, viewed by those who spoke of this as detrimental to women. The second revolved around the leadership role of the husband, which on the whole was defined as his prerogative as decision-maker in the home.

Headship as power and control

The interviewees who spoke of headship as a means of men exercising power over women were not endorsing this view. While some did not adhere to any notion of male headship in marriage, others did, but understood it in terms of a husband's leadership, rather than control. Certainly the kind of dominance and authoritarianism that they describe as one outworking of headship is generally rejected by contemporary advocates of headship. However, women's encounters with this type of behaviour by men in regard to their wives witness to a form of headship that has impacted negatively on the lives of women.

In this application the emphasis is on male authority and dominance. Rejecting this view one woman recalled, 'I mean I grew up with it very, very much so and I mean it was preached on often, the whole thing about Christ head of the church and man head of the household and all that kind of thing. And, you know, a lot of authority, I mean that was very much linked with authority.' In the words of an unmarried woman, 'I would tend to resent having to bow to what might be regarded as the headship of a man ... I tend not to be in that kind of situation, so how in reality I would react I don't know, but then maybe that's why I'm single. The thought of ever being dominated by a man. I suppose that's the way I view it – domination.' Another woman spoke of two occasions when she came close to marrying. However, 'both men tried to rule what I was doing and I said, "forget it".'

Women related this type of headship with the denigration of their sex: 'If a woman turns out to be an equal then that's when the hostility kicks in ... [Men] have to be taking you down, you just can't be good in your own right. And I think, you know, I don't believe that's something perhaps we'll ever crack. Because that's the way the world is, and that's the way we were reared through the churches, that men are the head of the house and women are subservient, and all that.' A woman involved in community endeavours spoke of the minister's wife in her church who believes in being 'a step behind ... I don't know any women in our church who would have the same views as me, you know, that we're – we're equal. Yeah, I don't know anybody that would. Or maybe they have and would be frightened to say.' Another community worker contrasted her vision of equality with 'the evangelical sense of headship', of 'thinking in terms of somehow women's role is to sort of speak when spoken to almost, you know, that kind of thing'.

Aware of changes in her congregation over the years one woman commented that in the past 'I would have called [the men] MCPS[71] on some occasions, in no two ways about it, because there was a level of abuse of authority which they had assumed. I don't mean collectively and I don't mean in the church, but there were a lot of them and their personal attitude toward women would have left something to be desired. And I don't think that's the case now, but I mean that was, that was a reflection of society as a whole. Society as a whole, fifty, a hundred years ago treated women extraordinarily badly.' For other women, this exercise of male dominance was not simply a thing of the past. A woman in politics commented, 'I think, in Northern Ireland they still expect the man to be the head of the house and make the decisions. It may work in some places, in some partnerships, but I think male dominance like that, I don't think that's really Christian.'

For one woman, there is nothing benign about headship: 'It's done more damage to women, the Christian women in this land, than anything! It permeates everything ... even women who don't really say they believe it, it permeates them, you know. It's a curse. I believe, and this might sound extreme, I believe that the church in Northern Ireland has done more damage to women than anything else, than any other organisation, I really do. I think because they've taught inferiority. They've taught [the women] that you'll be needing these men. And I think it's responsible for a lot of the problems with men in our land, because Northern Ireland men, especially working-class men, they've a wire about themselves. You know, they strut about and they are something because they've somebody beneath them, it doesn't matter how lowly they are in society, they've got somebody beneath them and it's the woman. And whether we go to church or not, there's an ethos that just permeates ... I'm talking about ... Northern Ireland Protestants, the ethos is, as a man I am something because you're beneath me, you know. So that's why you've all these arrogant young men running about. Where does the idea come from? It comes from centuries of the church, nobody else said it to them. It's the church that's done it. The church has come along and said, you men are heads. It doesn't matter whether you're an eejit, it doesn't matter whether your wife is cleverer than you, you're still over her. And it's permeated our whole society. I've been to wedding services in [different denominations], which made what that woman was entering into as a contract like a prison contract. Where the minister has preached a half-hour sermon on her role and what she is expected to do and her position in the hierarchy and how he was the head and he had to make decisions.

And I sat there and [thought] this sounds like somebody signing up for slavery, you know!'

The precise nature of the relationship between the church and the rest of society in perpetuating such a derogatory attitude towards women is no doubt complex. However, the prevalence in Northern Ireland of disparaging attitudes that accompanies this type of headship offers some explanation for the negative and hostile treatment related by women in previous chapters. Other interviewees, however, perceived headship differently.

Headship as decision–making

The women and men who advocated male headship operating in marriage painted a different picture of what that meant in practice. A few spoke of the role of a husband to provide spiritual leadership in the home. For one woman, this was consistent with the way she was brought up: 'Well, being brought up with my background, men have the headship in the home and I would hold to that ... Now when I say male leadership, I don't say male dominance. And there's been a lot of growing there. I see marriage as an equal partnership and as a shared role. But I see the man as being responsible for, in the home, for the spiritual well-being of his family. I would see that as a responsibility, a God-given responsibility, not left to the woman as it usually is. I would see that as being the male responsibility.'

In most cases, male headship was interpreted as giving the husband the prerogative of making decisions. An unmarried woman spoke of her expectations of a husband: 'While I absolutely believe that marriage is a partnership, my personal feeling is I would like a husband who was the head of the household. Not to lord it over me, but in, I suppose in the biblical terms, where, as Christ loved the church, you know, that kind of stewardship, and looking out for somebody, and taking decisions for the good of the family, albeit together, but, you know, that's the kind of marriage that I would like, if someone, you know, where we both make sacrifices for each other, and that there's no kind of – no competing. You know, a partnership although where the man is the head of the house and will take decisions if necessary.' One woman said, 'It's just such a relief that [my husband] can make the final decision on something.'

This is not to be understood as excluding women from the decision-making process: 'I would certainly think we share things and we make decisions together ... but at the end of the day I would probably go with [my husband's view]. There's part of me looking to do that. No, I would probably say yeah; if [he] thinks it's right then that's okay.'

Frequently the kind of decision-making alluded to in male headship takes place in the event of disagreement between the couple. In the words of one woman, 'I'm not an ardent feminist and I do feel in marriage that both should, that by and large it should be a consultative process, not autocratic. But that I suppose given, if both can't come to an agreement, I do feel it would be the man's prerogative to exercise headship.' A male church leader expressed something similar: 'In a marriage ... there's a dual leadership, and – and things are discussed. If at the end of the day for the sake of the family a decision needs to be made then my understanding of Scripture is that the man has responsibility to make that decision.'

Such beliefs are not merely theoretical. Some women spoke of having faced these kind of situations; for example, 'I see ... our home situation as a team situation and at the end of the day where a decision has to be made, no matter how difficult, and that has happened, [my husband's] decision goes.' Knowing that such a circumstance could arise was influential in one woman's approach to marriage: 'I had made a very definite decision that I was not prepared to marry someone unless I was prepared to promise to obey him. Because I knew in myself that I am strong-minded enough, and pig-headed enough, that I would see it could be a disaster, and unless I felt I had enough respect for him, because I recognise that at the end of the day somebody's going to have to make the decisions, or potentially make final decisions, and ... unless I was prepared to submit to him, [that] would be [a] non-starter in terms of relationship, and I'd actually recognised that in a couple of other relationships.'

While all of these people advocate a headship in which the husband provides leadership that involves him in making family decisions, it is also quite clear that this occurs in the context of a relationship envisaged very much as an equal partnership in which there is sharing, discussion, mutual respect, often joint decision-making, and a sense of working together. Any sense of dominance or autocratic leadership, the kind of behaviour referred to by the interviewees as power and control, is rejected. To some observers this appears an incongruous pairing: equal partnership with male prerogative for direction and decision-making.

However, it is not for those who practise this application of headship. This is articulated by a male church leader: 'In terms of headship I would see the biblical picture as one in which there is equality in Christ, and the Bible tells us to submit to one another so there is a mutual submission in Christ as brothers and sisters. But I would see headship as giving to man the role of ultimate leadership, if you like … It's not a case of the husband gives the orders and the wife carries them out, it's not a doormat, it's not the colonel and the private, you know, one gives the orders and the other one does what he's told. It's a case of mutual respect and reverence and submission. But at the same time I would see the husband as the one who is called to be leader in terms of seeking to determine the pattern if you like of life, spiritual leadership, if you like, to set the tone for the home. But that is a corporate thing, in which the husband and wife need to be together, but yet I think it's the husband has to take the leadership in that. And I suppose also if it comes to the position where there is not agreement between husband and wife on some major issue, I suppose there are two options. One is you either say well we won't make a decision because we're not together on that, or you say well if a decision has to be made and then it's a case of the wife being called to defer to the husband.'

The language of equality that now sits with the theological notion of headship has not been inherent to its explication in past generations, nor necessarily in every contemporary instance. But it perhaps shows how many evangelicals are integrating this aspect of their theology into modern living. Christel Manning explored a similar process among evangelical Protestants in North America. She observed that the feminist norm of equality was integrated into these women's lives as far as their secular work was concerned, but not in regard to the church, which, as is often the case in Northern Ireland, was considered a separate domain operating under different principles, stressing different roles for women and men. However, in the realm of home life, it was harder to make such distinctions because of the 'disjunction between traditional gender roles and contemporary economic realities'.[72] Out of necessity and/or choice women's participation in paid employment outside of the home made them less financially dependent on men and wanting to share domestic responsibilities and thus challenged the traditionally submissive and domestic role of wives. This interface of conservative theology and culture with modern realities led to these women reconstructing traditional gender roles and the notion of headship to include feminist values. While the specific nuances of this reconstruction are different, a similar dynamic exists among evangelical women in Northern Ireland. For some, the rhetoric and aspiring practice of equality that is generally accepted by women in respect of the workplace, although not always in regard to the church, has impacted on the expectations and practice of marital relationships. They advocate equality and sharing, but also concede the ultimate authority to husbands.

This adherence to male headship is not unconditional, however. Some were happy to practise this headship because their husbands had not exploited their position: 'I have no problem with ... if it comes down to it, my husband having the ultimate authority here. But the reason I don't have a problem is because there's no problem in my relationship. In our thirty years of marriage, it's never, ever been an issue. I think there's been one thing that we had a differing opinion about and I, at that point in time, because of how I felt and I still feel, I accepted [his] view.' A similar idea was expressed by another woman: 'You know it's agreement, things I submit to him on, things he submits to me on. But at the end of the day, I'd be more inclined just to say yeah, okay we'll go with what you think is right ... It's a hard one. You know, my theology would say yes, you know, within the home situation the man is the head of the household, but that's easy to say when you're in a good marriage. But it hasn't stopped me saying to people in bad marriages, you need to get out of there – it's too dangerous, don't let him do that, don't, you know. It's, yeah it's not, it's not that simple.' In the face of some evangelical writing that advocates women staying in marriages regardless of the way their husbands treat them, another woman made the point: 'I've been listening to some tapes ... [which] go totally for the whole submissive thing, and wouldn't recommend women leaving their husbands no matter what they're being, have to put up with, and, you know, I was listening to this and having had a friend who was abused verbally and emotionally, I mean her children would have been destroyed if she'd stayed. I think you can take all of this too far, but it's really finding the balance, you know.'

The headship for these women has limits. It must not be exploited and become abusive. Another woman spoke of how it had to be earned by the man in question, rather than automatically derived because he was male:

'I always knew that if I was going to get married it would have to be to somebody that I felt I could submit to, in some way that I could obey and that I would be looking for somebody then with an authority that would be, I was going to say worthy of me, and I, that sounds horrific, but, you know where you are, and you know who you are, and you know what God has given you, and so I wasn't prepared to enter into that sort of relationship with somebody who would necessarily be a distraction to that.'

While this woman would only accept a relationship that honoured her own discipleship and sense of calling, another woman spoke of potentially laying her vocation aside if her husband's decisions required it: 'If I was married ... I would very much submit to my husband. As I've always said, I'll submit to a man when I find a man worth submitting to. I would submit to a husband, I would go along with a husband in terms of the major things. I mean obviously batter it out, have my say or whatever, but if my husband wanted to go to the ends of the earth, I'd go with him, you know. And if that meant dropping a career, if that meant, I suppose the hardest thing would be if it really meant me dropping something I believed God wanted me to do. But even then I would I think because that would be what marriage would be for me. So in that sense, I do see the man as the head in a marriage.'

It was because they clearly believed that any decision their husband made would be for the good of the family that some women deferred to their husband's decisions. As one community worker put it, 'I know the bottom line, if there was a situation we differed on, I would bow to his decision on it. But that's built out of a relationship with him that I know he would only make decisions that are, you know, right for the family, that he would feel right about.' However, a few other women indicated that they submitted to decisions which they saw ultimately working out for everyone concerned, but which observers could say seem to have been made more for the convenience and self-interest of the husband than the benefit of the wife or family. One woman reflected on her marriage and how at one time her involvement in Christian activity occupied more time than her husband liked and 'he started to lay the law down a bit, you know, about what he expected me to be doing here in the house, et cetera, et cetera'. While they discussed this, she felt 'he wasn't being fair. But after a while, I prayed about it, I prayed about it a lot and my attitude towards God is, I know what you're calling me to, therefore if you want me to do this, I'm not going to fight anybody about this. If this is what your purposes are for me, then you will make a way, you will actually influence other people's attitudes as far as I'm concerned.' She understood that her husband was jealous of the time she was spending with others and she waited a few years and 'noticed that there was a softening in the way [God] was dealing with him'. This matter was no longer an issue for them in their marriage and now she felt fully supported by her husband in her Christian activity.

Such trust in God to resolve things without confrontation was echoed by another woman who spoke of how over a number of years her husband learned to share childcare responsibilities in the evenings so that she could participate in church activities outside of the house. Initially he was always the one to go out, something she never resented: 'I felt that that was right, that was okay. And somehow I think I knew that you – that it was okay and it would all work out … The way to deal with that was for me just to let him and trust that God would teach him.' In this and other situations in her home she believed that 'God will sort it out … to everybody's satisfaction, and to the best, and if it is the best that [my husband] has the headship role, if you like, then God knows what he's doing. And I am perfectly happy with that. That doesn't bother me in the slightest.'

For some women this submission infuses their identity and they become uncomfortable acting in ways not considered consistent with wifely behaviour. While she was involved in discussion over issues with her husband, did not see headship as dominance, took responsibility in the home for those things she was better at than her husband, one woman was careful that her demeanour was appropriate to a feminine identity of submission: 'I do think authority is given to men, that would be my view. Whether it's a pastor or a Christian leader or a husband … I try not to be, I wouldn't like to think I'm overruling or being dominant, I think that's very un-feminine even.' In the words of a community worker, 'I suppose within my own sort of marriage and family, I mean, I sometimes think oops, you know, am I sort of butting in here when I shouldn't or how does headship actually work. Not that we've had any real big conflicts over it, but, you know, sometimes I've thought, well maybe I should have kept quiet or, you know, whatever.' Whether this kind of demeanour is viewed as a form of godly femininity or as a form of human diminishment depends on the view taken of the meaning of headship.

HEADSHIP IN THE CHURCH

A number of women interviewed associated headship with both church and family. As one community worker put it, 'Well obviously I was brought up to believe that women were sort of to be submissive to men who were the head of the church and the head of the house and the head of everything. And that would still be the ethos under which like my mother would operate and that's definitely the way we were brought up.' While this woman no longer subscribed to headship herself, another woman expressed her acceptance: 'In our ... denomination you have the minister, you have the elders, who tend to be male, who tend to make the decisions. And because it's always been that way I suppose I accept it. I don't challenge it.' However, it was only a few women who themselves still held in an unqualified sense to the notion of male headship within the church. This did not mean they were all concerned about women's inclusion in church leadership (although some were). While not necessarily against women as ordained ministers, preachers or lay church leaders, because they held no personal sense of calling or desire to act in such capacities, some were generally happy with the male status quo of their churches. So, while there were few women who were enthusiastic advocates of male headship in church, in talking with the women it was clear that male headship of some kind is very much evident in practice in many of their churches.

As with headship in marriage, women spoke both of the exploitative practice of headship in church and the idea of ultimate authority resting with men. In addition, headship in the church involved concerns about women's teaching role.

Headship as power and control

A woman active in the lay leadership of her church spoke of her discussions with male leaders in other congregations: 'Although I've talked [with them] about authority and everything and I do think it's important, I mean I think some of them are obsessed by authority, and just, you know, "oh but, you know, who at the end of the day [will make the final decision]", you know. And you sort of think, but it doesn't, it just doesn't work like this, you know. And again I just think it's a control issue and a power issue. And it seems to me, as you look even at Jesus and His whole idea of servant leadership, there was no sense of him trying to control people in that sense or, you know, dominate people in any sense. I mean everybody sort of softens the edges of it when they talk about it to make it more palatable. But at the end of the day when you dilute it all down, it's still somebody wanting to be in control. And I can't see that that's what it's all about.'

The practice of headship as a means of male power and control was echoed by another woman reflecting on her experience of the practice of male leadership in church contexts which were, on the whole, exclusively male led: 'I've watched men who have had significant roles in the secular world, assume that it was almost their right to have significant roles in church and that's wrong, that's biblically way off beam ... And I've watched other men strive for office and misuse it, who have not been successful in their secular lives, who have got themselves into office because "here's a little place where I can be an achiever". I'm thinking of just ... [those in] perfectly respectable jobs, but not great achievers, not high earners, not significant in the world's terms, but they become little dictators in church. And there's an abuse of power in both areas.' The effect of this kind of behaviour was expressed by a woman who considered that the idea of obedience to male authority led her to put up with mistreatment in a church context: 'I felt so isolated in my situation I had nobody to say "he is out of order here." And I probably put up with a lot – wrongly working under the principle that, you know, you're master and all of that.'

A community worker saw in male leadership a disvaluing of women: 'Women make up more than 50 per cent of the population of the church. If you look at who's actually doing the work, you know, the majority of the people who are Sunday School teachers, who run the crèche, who do all of those kinds of practical tasks, and who do the cleaning, who organise the flowers, who play the organ, all of those things, without whom the church would grind to a halt in many respects, are women. And yet they're given no kind of say in what goes on, not really, except through their husbands, you know. And they're not valued, I think that was my kind of real feeling about it, I felt the distinct lack of value, that it was all right, you could be in charge if you were a man, but if you were a woman you couldn't be because you weren't as important, and I felt that that wasn't – I don't think that's what the Bible's talking about.' Following on from observations made in earlier chapters, it is not surprising that the association of leadership with power, status and importance in an exclusively male domain leads to a disvaluing of women.

Headship as ultimate leadership and authority

Other interviewees perceived headship as something more constructive. For some their view included the involvement of women in church leadership, but again, providing that the highest authority was male. One male church leader, while not wishing to be dogmatic on the issue, stated: 'It has to do with a headship of caring and an ultimate sense of responsibility, and therefore, while I have no problem with lay readers or even ordained ministers, I would have real reservations about a woman being in ultimate charge of a parish or a congregation, and I think that would probably be contrary to Scripture.' Another man expressed something similar: 'By headship, my understanding of that is that you can have a corporate [leadership of women and men], but the buck has to stop somewhere ... My understanding of the Scriptures is that it ultimately ends with the male, and that while that male has a degree of mutual submission to the corporate leadership, if at the end of the day somebody has to make a decision, my understanding of Scripture is that that falls to the man ... I would understand the ultimate authority would rest with a man.'

For others, male headship in the church excludes women from the kind of activities these two men consider valid for women within a headship model. Therefore, another male church leader felt that women could not be lay leaders in the church because 'for me it would come back to the fact that – that we would be placing women in a position where they would effectively be ruling over men.' He saw how this could create difficulties, should they be appointed, for women who would be 'submissive in the right sense of that word in their home' and yet find themselves effectively being placed in authority over their husbands spiritually within the church.

Just because a woman accepts male headship in the church does not mean its operation is unproblematic for them. One woman spoke of the difficulty in submitting to the headship of a male church leader where there was not mutual respect: 'I feel that [for headship] to work, each person has to be fulfilling their role properly ... I find it sometimes very hard to be submissive to – to men that I don't respect ... I think [headship] has been totally abused in an awful lot of instances. Totally abused. But seeing women who are, totally refuse it, and are arrogant against it, there's – there's something not nice about that as well, you know... But I do think for it to work each person has to be fulfilling their role properly, and also has to acknowledge, with respect, the equality of each other within their role ... You know, it's so hard to be submissive to someone and yet they don't really see you the way God sees you. So it, it's hard. It's hard.'

For a number of women who accepted male headship their support was not unconditional. A woman active in her church spoke of leaving a former congregation in which she considered she could no longer accept the stance being taken from the male leader, whom she considered misused his position. However, she was happy to accept the authority of male elders in another congregation: 'because they don't exploit it, I can accept it ... And I think elders are a people with authority, or whoever has the headship has got a far greater responsibility than I have in accepting it. They have in turn got a far greater responsibility in not exploiting, in being worthy.' A community worker only attributed headship to those who earned it: 'Now then, within the church, I have had experience of ministers, male ministers, whose position would deem it, yeah, whose position would denote headship. But the person holding that role has not earned my respect, they have flaunted my respect, they have not, they have abused my respect, therefore they're not head. I don't pay a lot of attention to headship unless the individual has earned respect, I think that's the bottom line on it and it probably would be better leaving it there in case I've said too much.' As with headship in marriage, for these women headship in the church has to be earned by appropriate behaviour and carrying out of the responsibilities without exploitation or disrespect.

Headship and teaching

For some, male headship in the church does not preclude women teaching. As one woman who saw headship as male responsibility for the spiritual well-being of both home and church commented, 'I would see [headship] as being the male role, but the responsibility for teaching and so on, I don't have a problem with sharing that with females if they have the ability.' For others, however, headship precludes women engaging in a teaching role where men are involved. For a male church leader 'the crucial text for me is where Paul says that women are not to teach or to have authority over men. And I know there are those who would see that as cultural, but my understanding is that in the very next phrase he goes on to say that the reason is because of basically the creation and the fall. So that indicates to me that Paul ... was rooting that, not in culture, but in the very substance of what we are as created people and as fallen but redeemed people. So I would, I would understand then that what the Scripture is saying is that because there's a, there's a God-given priority if you like, or leadership/headship in creation, and also that – that in the fall the Bible talks about the woman being deceived, and it was not that we can shift the blame because Adam was equally responsible, but that the conversation that's recorded as between Eve and Satan, and she then gives to her husband, and so I take that to mean that because of what we are, created in the image of God as male and female, and what we are as sinners fallen and redeemed, that God has placed this ... this order.' For this man, such order did not infer that women lacked spirituality or that men were by definition more spiritual. Nor did it mean that women could not be gifted teachers, but this could only be of other women, for it was a matter of God's order, 'it has been revealed'.[73]

While this man's allusion to the biblical record of Eve's deception for him does not imply women are less spiritual or more deceitful than men, such a sense of mistrust of women still is apparent in Northern Ireland. One woman praised women's heart of compassion and yet considered women 'can equally be vicious. They can be jealous, they can be back-biting. This to me is why you need that area of male authority.' Another woman, in thinking about the lack of involvement of Protestant women in more prominent ways in Northern Irish society, noted, 'It is looked on as the male being the important one with the ideas ... and I think that comes from, well I suppose some of the teaching that I had maybe, partly going back to headship, would be that – I'm not sure where it is, where the woman was the one who was snared by Satan. You know, I think it's Timothy. You know, so you don't trust a woman's opinion. That sort of slant. That would be linked up with it, you know, she was the one who caused the man to sin, therefore you can't trust what a woman's opinion is because she's more likely to be having a sinful point of view than the male.' She also commented on a friend's situation whose minister 'didn't like women reading the Bible for themselves because if they did they would get strange points of view'.

This mistrust of women also expresses itself more generally. A para-church worker spoke of being with a group visiting a church which happened to have predominantly women officiating at the service, including in the main leadership role. Many in the group were clearly uncomfortable with this situation and in talking about it afterwards the two males who were leading the group said their difficulty was not on a biblical basis, but rather 'it was just "I'm uncomfortable [with] that number of women leading the church because they're conniving." And I said, but it's because you've just entered into another culture and instead of actually understanding or even looking at that culture you've demonised it, you've demonised the whole crowd of us [women].' As a community worker commented, some men are 'not really sure how to approach women who can articulate their own opinions, and so therefore it's easier not to have to deal with them, by sort of saying "oh well, you know there's this really good verse that says women shouldn't ...", you know, and that's how they get away with it.'

Mistrust of women also manifests itself in attitudes towards sexuality, with women being viewed as a source of sexual danger for men. One woman spoke of the practice of a couple of men in religious contexts who would never be alone with a woman, but would always ensure they were either chaperoned or that the door of their office was open when dealing with female staff or visitors. While this may be considered by some as good practice, the interviewee observed it as measures to protect the men and not the moral standing of the women as well: 'What it's really saying is that women are not to be trusted, women are a danger, a possible source of temptation or whatever. Now how do you foster good working relationships, whether it's at committee level or whatever? It just cannot happen if that's the view that men have of women.' In the opinion of another woman, this kind of distorted relating accounted for some of the opposition to women's greater inclusion in the church: 'I think that a lot of the objections to women taking up positions or for want of a better word, authority, in the church are not theological, they are psychological. And very many of them, again if we took them to their very base would be rooted in some sort of sexual woundedness that hasn't been addressed in its broadest sense.' While many advocates of male headship would disassociate the practice from a maligning of women's character, this

nevertheless has been fed, however wrongly, by a particular interpretation of biblical references.

Headship Questioned

Those who did not subscribe to the idea of headship in terms of male
leadership or prerogative in decision-making did so mainly because of
their conception of either the marriage relationship or the nature of
authority and leadership in the church.

In regard to marriage, the notion of partnership precluded any sense of
ultimate male decision-making. The two ideas were considered
incongruous. As one male church leader put it in rejecting male
authority in marriage, 'I wouldn't want to be in that relationship with
my wife basically.' A community worker spoke of marriage as 'about
equality and mutual submission and respect and working together for a
vision of life and following Christ, and where it was about developing
each other's full potential. And I think within that, then you don't have to
worry about headship as in a "boss" sort of way.' For another woman, the
practice of male headship indicated an immature way of relating: 'The
way it's interpreted so often ... it is just handing some men who haven't
matured enough or been healed enough licence to be dictator or bully
even in their own married relationship. And I've seen it so often, you
know. Whereas if somebody has very bravely and painfully gone on their
own inner journey of reconciliation then it would not be a question of
headship, it would be a question of togetherness under the headship of
Christ, if that makes sense ... In terms of a man and a woman in an
intimate relationship or anything like that, for people who are mature
adults, this would sit very uneasily with [headship] ... Because if you
were a mature adult, you wouldn't be thinking like that, I think.'

Where questioning headship in the church was concerned, a number of
people spoke in terms of a corporate authority that rested with the
leadership of a congregation. One woman spoke of how her church
leadership tried to practise a consensus model of leadership and thereby
avoid the idea of ultimate decision-making: 'Within the church nobody
holds authority in their own right, because it's given by God and because
we're meant to be in an eldership role working together and that's where
the safety-valve is.' The practice of corporate leadership in this view is
seen as a way of discerning God's will, who is the ultimate head. In the

words of a male church leader: 'I don't think the final authority rests with me. I think it actually rests with the Lord mediated to us through his word ... by the Holy Spirit.'

A community worker who saw value in corporate leadership developed this idea: 'I see headship really as a corporate thing anyway. You know, I don't see that it should be a man or a woman ... For any organisation in the church – whether it's the church or any secular organisation – to be run and run efficiently it should be a corporate responsibility ... if everybody's not involved in the process then somebody's going to be left out, somebody's going to be disgruntled, somebody's going to make it not work.'

For others, church leadership is primarily about service. One woman felt many male church leaders had 'forgotten what the biblical criteria for leadership is. A servant heart is at the very core of it. And I think men have missed the fact that women serve, I don't know whether it's by nature, or by custom or convention, but they do. And men don't see that as a validation of their suitability for leadership at all. They misunderstand the servant nature of Christ.' This focus on service was the reason another woman felt that any leadership should be both gender- and age-inclusive: 'I think the whole process of having a ministry team that lead a church, it needs to be across the genders, it needs to be across the age groups. And then it will be a healthy body because it will understand how to serve properly.'

A focus on the gifting rather than the sex of a person was another emphasis that challenged male headship: 'So you see I suppose at the end of the day, the strongest thing for me is why does God give you opportunities, why does he give you gifts, if he doesn't want you to use them? That to me is unanswerable, just, you know, it's always just been like that.'

A community worker was in the process of re-evaluating her views: 'Our minister always taught that women and men are equal in status but different in function ... And I always accepted that, I thought that's quite a good way to put it, yes I believe that. But I don't think I do anymore, I think I have come round to thinking that why should [women and men] be necessarily different in function except ... they are not gifted for it. So that the kind of person you are and what you're gifted to do should be the determining factor in how you're different and function. So I'm really doing a lot of thinking.' As a woman employed by her church commented: 'Who ultimately ends up being the decision-maker at the end of the day? I think if I'm pushed I would have to say, I'm not convinced it should always be the man, because some men, that's not just where their skill and ability lies in terms of being a leader or having the insight or the wisdom.'

To restrict women's involvement by a headship model, in the words of one man, 'to disable literally half the population of the world in Christian service', was viewed as nonsensical and even as irresponsibility towards God. A community worker reflected: 'If God is using people we need to give them the authority to do what God wants to do with them and regardless of who the person is ... I suppose if we're not accepting responsibility and giving responsibility then that, you know, it interferes with His kind of plan.'

It is not that these people were against the notion of authority or accountability and responsibility, but rather, in the words of a community worker, 'I don't think men have any right to have any authority over women just because they are men.' A para-church worker spoke of how her 'conviction and the confidence and the personal authority would lead me wanting to respect all people so I would work hard at that and respecting leadership but I wouldn't, I wouldn't surrender principle just because somebody was a man ... I know that that then challenges the whole headship thing.' This woman is guided by her own sense of moral authority that in turn leads her to treat others with respect, including those in leadership. It was a fear of the loss of women's moral selves that concerned some of the interviewees in the notion of headship. They considered that deferring to male leadership could be used by women to, as expressed by a community worker, 'abdicate responsibility and use it as a cop-out'. Several spoke of how excluding women from formal leadership meant they were not accountable for their often substantial influence through their husbands who were leaders. But there was also the fear for the diminishment of women themselves as moral beings. Speaking of her parents where 'my father was very in charge' and 'my mother did what she was told, and still does', one woman struggled to express the effect of this on her mother's personal development: 'I feel it has left her kind of more ... what's the word, let me think ... affected her ability to make decisions for herself and have, you know, be her own person and all that.' Headship was rejected by those women who saw in it only a sense of personal impoverishment for women.

While the above outlines the main reasons for adopting an alternative stance to headship, the interviewees spoke of a number of routes taken to arrive at their current position. Some women continued to struggle with issues and the practical outworking of their questioning of headship in their particular circumstances. However, it is possible to identify certain factors that made up their journey of enquiry. Often these factors did not operate in isolation, but in various combinations contributed to women (and men) looking at the question of headship for themselves.

INNER KNOWING

Some women spoke of always having had a sense that there was something wrong with the notion of headship. Despite environments, teaching and practices to the contrary, this inner knowledge persisted. As a community worker explained: 'I was brought up as a complete Brethren girl, like, sit there and shut up because who are you to have anything to say? And I just could never, I could not take that on board. I knew that I had very similar views to my male peers, and I knew I was confident and ... had a strong faith ... and had lots to say and all, and I just could never quantify how I, just because I was born a girl, have no way to share that with anybody. That to me was just, I couldn't grasp how that could be part of the way God expected a community of people to work ... I thought there has to be another way for me to express who I am. You know, I can't just go on for the rest of my life suppressing that in terms of leadership and communication, all those things that I was good at ... and I just couldn't see that that could be of God. So I suppose then I just kind of, I suppose I kind of lived with this, well that's what it says, and that's what you're telling me it says, but in myself I just think I can't be like that. That just can't be right.'

Finding out that there was an alternative Christian stance to the one they had been taught gave external support for this inner knowing: 'I was taught it, I struggled with it because it's ... not what I felt inside. You know, there was something that I couldn't quite accept ... And I'd nothing to argue against it at that stage, but just there was no agreement in my spirit with what I was hearing, even though I had to almost accept it with my mind. But there's something not, you know, tallying here. So I think when I heard a different theological explanation, it was like, ah yes, because how I felt and what I was hearing then came together. You know, that was a tremendous relief, not that I feel I now know this is the right thing, but just that it's a different way to think about this.'

For one woman, her inner knowing accompanied thoughtful reflection. She spoke of how at one time she had given much time and attention to the issue of headship: 'I went through a great phase of one time thinking about [headship] and thinking strongly and I'm afraid I couldn't accept it ... But I found that was very difficult in evangelical circles, to always take the man as the dominant one and maybe that's what we've got in Northern Ireland, too much of that.' She went on to say that the idea of 'giving way to your husband all the time on different subjects and different issues ... was making me into something that wasn't me, it was making me as a lesser person'. A man also expressed lack of ease over headship: 'I think temperamentally I was never happy with it, but I recognised that it was there propositionally or theologically or something. But it wasn't there relationally for me, and I was always uncomfortable. I have always been uncomfortable with a strong male headship notion.'

For some women a certain belief in their calling or abilities led them to reject the restrictions of headship as they encountered it. A para-church worker commented: '[Headship] would have been taught and I would have gone along with it but not been that sure that it was right ... [and now] I just believe in my own ability to speak and to challenge.' A woman active in a community project echoed a similar conviction: 'I know a lot of people ... would say that as a woman I shouldn't be involved in leadership in this way. And I know that God has brought me here, you know, and he's made it very clear that this is where he wants me.' Speaking of how at one time others had suggested she consider joining the ordained ministry, another woman stated, 'If I'd felt for one minute that that's the role that God was calling me to take I would have done it without any problem at all, you know.' For these women, a sense of God's direction overrode any objections others may have posed from a headship argument.

For other women it was the experience of progressively getting more involved in various endeavours and increased opportunities to discover and use their gifts that fostered their questioning of headship. What all have in common is a trust in their own sense of who they are and what they perceive of God's intent towards them that contradicts the dominant ethos of male headship around them.

EXPOSURE TO OTHER VIEWS

For some women, part of their journey into thinking differently from the environment of male headship in which they had grown up was their moving into new situations that exposed them to other ways of thinking and behaving.

A woman now involved in church leadership reflected: 'I would say that my view has changed. I would have certainly been of the mind that the woman takes the background role and that would have been largely, culturally conditioned, I think because of the background I grew up in ... I suppose being exposed to a broader range of opinions, my thinking has changed on that, you know ... It would have been moving into [another denomination], through friends and whatnot at school and then going to university, where you'd be exposed to a lot more range of opinions ... And reading a bit wider and whatnot, and then in practice seeing as well, you know, for I see a lot of women, a lot more capable as leaders and so on than some men. So all of that, when you put it all together I suppose, it has caused me to think differently.'

One woman spoke of her exposure to theological education 'where they absolutely questioned everything. And that freed me up then to question [headship].' Another woman elaborated on the impact of a general questioning that she encountered through formal biblical studies. For her it meant 'having the freedom to think something that I'd thought all along but was told I was very naughty for thinking that. And I have found that about a lot of things in my life as I've moved on and encountered people from so many different backgrounds that things that I was nearly scared to think of suddenly I feel are actually right. And I'm allowed to think that.' As a community worker put it, 'It wasn't that one issue, you know, it was like generally expanding my world-view and my lifestyle because of the people I met and the things I was thinking and reading about.'

The impact of friends was also important. For one man it was 'friendships wider than our [denomination]. I'm very thankful to God for that. Over the past ten or fifteen years [it] has been a real help to me to meet people, which I may have thought twenty-five years ago was going to threaten me, and that left me insecure, okay, and I think probably the root of my dogmatism was insecurity ... I've had to acknowledge that some of my presuppositions were just a conditioning of the particular group I was in at that particular time ... So friendships have influenced me, my wife has influenced me, and also the irrelevancy of the church in a secular society to say "hey what's going on here, why are we the way we are?" So I think all those things, and I'm sure a whole lot more have chipped away at me.'

CONTRADICTION IN EXPERIENCE

For others, it was realities that contradicted a headship model that made them question its truth. In some instances this was realising that in practice women were functioning in ways that were accepted by a congregation and yet that in essence challenged the notion of headship. Speaking of how women came to be involved in the leadership of her church, one woman made the point that part of the process in making this change 'was simply because women were doing so much, I mean there really wasn't anything that women weren't doing, apart from being on the [congregation's ruling body]'. Hence, 'we [women] started to ask the questions and started to wonder about things ... [motivated by] something burning inside you that you didn't know what to do with'.

Frequently headship is sustained in theory by the choices of language used to describe women's participation. The phenomenon of 'having a different label for the same activity when it is performed by women than when it is performed by men'[74] is not lost on some women who find themselves subject to this: 'As regards teaching, you know, when people say an elder can teach I say a woman can share and a man can preach. And that's, you know, if I want to share something in church I can, but I couldn't preach a sermon. Whereas what I share may be a sermon, but as long as I say I want to share I can get away with it! ... If I lead the morning worship, which I do, and maybe take a psalm and work my way through the psalm and explain little bits as I go along, well, I think I'm actually teaching maybe a little bit out of that, but they don't see that. You know, that's acceptable, but to actually preach a sermon ... '

Speaking of her own experience involved in church leadership another woman reflected on what that meant for her congregation who opposed women in such positions: 'It would be very fundamentalist, they would have that view of the Bible, black and white and it's all true. And yet they seem to have suspended this passage because of me ... Now they would still read that passage and think, women shouldn't teach and preach, but because I'm standing there and because ... I'm good at [it] and do it well, they've suspended it. They've put it to the back of their mind, right. It's almost like, you know, let's not look at it while she's here.'

It was observing this kind of contradiction where there was, in the words of one woman, 'one thing in theory and another thing in practice', that led some to ask questions of the accepted understanding of gender norms in church. One woman related what it was like to find herself living this contradiction as she became aware of it. Having become increasingly involved in working with women she was asked to participate in a church service focused around women: 'I remember the first time I was invited to speak on a ... Sunday morning service ... And I said well that's fine, never thought anything about it, and I remember sitting at the front of the church, and suddenly realising, "I'm preaching on a Sunday morning service! What am I doing here? Do I agree with this?" You know, it was very, very strange and it was quite funny... Sometimes I feel guilty. Not because the Bible makes me feel guilty, but because I was brought up feeling that it was wrong, you know. So I think listening and experiencing, and studying and learning, I have changed. I have developed a different view of women than the one I was brought up with.'

For other women it was often the stark contrast between their participation in church and their involvement in other spheres that produced internal contradictions for them. For one community worker it had been her school environment: 'In school I would have been in positions of leadership. Now that was an all-girls school and all that kind of thing, but I think I would always have questioned why am I able to do these things and why, you know, have I these gifts and yet in church I'm not even allowed to speak? So I would have been thinking along those lines and thinking about my mother too as a very strong person and she's not allowed to speak and she is probably more able than a lot of these other guys who are.'

For some women it was their work experience that made them question the treatment of women in the church: 'In a way I find it quite difficult to square [my church experience] with my views in the secular world and in the world of work, where I feel very strongly that women should be given a fair crack of the whip, and you know, everybody should be treated equally, and so it's almost like I have these two lives that at work, you know, I would die in a ditch before I let anybody, you know, I mean seriously I feel quite strongly about it, before I let anybody take advantage of me because of my sex, and yet at church I do it all the time.' A lay church leader found that her involvement in a male-dominated profession had led her to ask questions about the church. Her profession was one in which 'we as women had to do better, we had to get better grades than men to get in and we had to fight hard when we were there to maintain that. So I've always been used to that, I've always been used to being surrounded by men and having to make my mark.' Another woman felt that she owed her personal development to her work, in stark contrast to the church: 'The person I am today is very much attributable to the opportunities that work has given me, not what the church has given me, and I think that is for me a very sad indictment on the church, that, you know, that we talk about the body, you know, Paul talks about it. We talk about everybody having gifts, and yet we fail to mobilise those, we fail to actually help people to utilise their gifts ... and the church is the poorer, and Christ is the poorer because the church isn't being effective in the way it could be because of all that.'

A number of interviewees commented on the different practices applied in missionary situations to those in home churches. Described by one woman as the 'missionary argument. We're quite happy to let women go to every other part of the world and do X, Y and Z, but just not on our own doorstep.' A male church leader called this 'a kind of hypocrisy in the Christian church which allows women to go into the mission field and be pioneering, church planting, you know, leaders – and then come back home and they're supposed to, you know, reside under male leadership'.

A similar contradiction was also noted in regard to headship in marriage. As one woman commented, 'The man is still traditionally seen as the head of the household. But in practice very often it's the women who takes the headship role because very often it's the women who look after the finances, the women who take the lead in the family life. A lot of women are working as well, some of them maybe earning more than their husbands and so on.' Another woman agreed: 'In most homes it is simply utter whitewash to say that the man makes the decisions because it actually is usually the women, especially in the area of, you know, children. I think women routinely make all the decisions and the man says, that's grand, dear. And that's, to me that is the norm and I think that whatever the Bible says it cannot mean that the male makes all the decisions because I think in most homes that's completely

the reverse.' For these interviewees such contradictions challenge the idea
of headship.

EXPERIENCE OF WOMEN IN LEADERSHIP

Some women had grown up in contexts that had provided good role
models of female leaders. For other women it was their experience as
adults of women in positions of church leadership that led them to
question a headship model that excluded women. One woman who felt
that women should not be ordained was questioning her own view
because of her experience of an ordained woman: 'She's doing amazing
things. She's fantastic ... She's doing so many things which I haven't seen
men do. You think that can't be wrong that she's in that position, you
know; she's there for a reason.' A woman involved in politics spoke of her
mother facing a similar challenge: '[She] would be very opposed to
women in the ministry. In saying that she now has a lady vicar who she
thinks is wonderful, so it's another one of those things where you're
challenged by a reality. You have a kind of a – I suppose a theoretical
belief, and then you find the reality and suddenly you think well actually
they're doing a very good job, and what exactly were the arguments
against it?'

A community worker also attributed her acceptance of women to her
contact with ordained women: 'Certainly my ideas of women would have
changed ... [now] I think they are as able as any man. Previously I
wouldn't have been particularly keen on women ministers ... that's
probably because the ministers in my home congregation when I was
growing up wouldn't have seen women [having] a role within the church
... [Now] I know lots of good women ministers ... [they] are just as able,
given the chance, you know, to actually prove themselves.'

These encounters are not necessarily the sole reason for women
changing their view on this matter. A community worker spoke of how
she 'got to know, for one reason or another, quite a number of women
ministers or women who were studying for ministry ... So I've had quite
a lot of friendships with people in those circumstances. So the kind of
experiential side of it, of these people who have a very strong sense of
calling and vision and rightness about what they're doing obviously has
certainly shaped [my view] ... Starting from [these] experiences led me
into looking at the Bible and saying right, okay, what is here about this

and what can I learn about this and how do I relate this experience of what I see to what's in the Bible; how do those fit together?'

Male church leaders also spoke of how experience of female leaders had led them to a theological and spiritual assessment of headship. As one said, 'Having seen women in action, both in the overseas mission set-up and also then here, I've been very much aware that the Lord's blessing was upon them, and the Lord's anointing was upon them, and they were in the pulpit, leading house groups, doing all sorts of things. And I felt well, if the Lord is blessing these people he's not doing so and contradicting himself at the same time.' Another spoke of a woman who preached in his church who in his opinion 'has a very good teaching gift ... that doesn't just benefit women, but benefits men ... So to me it seems incongruous that God could give [her] a teaching gift and yet in Scripture forbid her to teach men.'

For another man it was 'working with people who were women involved in ordained situations' that had made a difference to the way he viewed their participation: 'And like a lot of other issues in life, either *vis-a-vis* politics or all sorts of other things, living with people, having to work with people, having to come to terms with people often makes you think much more seriously about what you understand the Bible to teach ... I mean those things have been a significant issue for me in terms of having to face it and think about it and look at it and say, "Well, I really can't see any valid reason why this person shouldn't be doing what she's doing."' In each case, abstract ideas have been challenged by real encounters.

FAMILY BACKGROUND

A further factor influencing women's questioning of headship is an early foundation of personal value and worth received from their family: 'I was always brought up to believe I could do anything. You know, you can do anything with your life, there's nothing you can't do, there's no one you can't be and I believed that ... It was a case of in Christ you can do all things. It was always that simple.'

Some women identified their father as significant in this process: 'My father was a very non-sexist sort of person ... I always felt very valued and affirmed by him. And so I guess I grew up in a family where there was a great feeling of equality and just equal respect.' Such affirmation can be expansive for women: '[My dad] was equally chuffed that he had a daughter than as if he's had a son and there was that sense that, you know, anything is possible, if you want to go for it, go for it.'

For other women it was their mother who was the vital influence: 'She did really push me to be my own person, and that if eventually I went that road too, that I would have much more to my life as well. So without being an overt feminist, and probably without even wanting to have anything to do with feminism she was very strong that I would have my own education, my own career, my own means.' Women talked of mothers as decision-makers and occasionally breadwinners, giving them a sense of female strength: 'I have a very strong role model in my mother because I mean she's been the major breadwinner in my family since I can remember.'

This sense of equal value had left an impression on those women who contested the headship they encountered. A woman not brought up in a Christian home explained how her early sense of her own potential affected the way she approached the biblical material: 'It was when I became a Christian that I first faced issues like [headship] because I was brought up to think that I was completely equal to my brother, that I could do anything I wanted to do, that the money would be poured into me just as much as into [him]. So it was never an issue. I mean I grew up thinking I could go and do what I liked … I mean I did have to work out things from the Bible, but I think because I had such a healthy view of myself, I went to the Bible thinking, you know, that what people have been telling just cannot be right – that women are meant to take second place or they're meant to be inferior or they're meant not to make any decisions because my personality isn't like that.'

In these instances the sense of equality, personal self-worth and inherent value which the women imbibed as children, led to a questioning of a headship idea that gave authority and sometimes a notion of greater importance to a man.

EXPLORING THE BIBLE

Mixed in with their other reflections, women and men spoke of their explorations of the Bible in their questioning of headship. Many of their descriptions of how they approached this issue in the Bible and of detailed arguments of particular Scripture passages are among the elements outlined earlier in this chapter. Taking the overall sense of biblical revelation, and coming to individual passages in the light of a biblical understanding of women's equal humanity and value, many had sought to make sense of what the text has to say. And while this process was not necessarily without struggle and for some not all issues had been resolved, for those who questioned forms of headship there was a belief that their view was consistent with and endorsed by Scripture.

In addition to discussing what the Bible actually says, there was some reflection on *why* and *how* the Bible is used in considering this question. Several spoke of the authoritative role of Scripture within evangelicalism and for themselves personally. As one male church leader put it, 'What I do feel very strongly about, that if women are to be involved in the life of the church and leadership it must come through Bible teaching. Because if we're a conservative church here, believing the Bible to be the word of God, then that's the deal. We've got to come from there. We've got to persuade people's minds. There will be those who will never be persuaded because of their antagonism or because of whatever. But I am convinced that if we are to get women as part of the leadership in the church ... it must come through Bible teaching.' As another man commented, in dealing with parts of Scripture most frequently used to support headship, 'For someone who would have a high view of the Bible, one can't walk away and say well I'll just ignore that.'

For both of these men, the emphasis on Scripture comes in a context that had a tendency towards pragmatism: 'My fear sometimes is, for people like me, that we're pragmatic evangelicals and we go back to Scripture on the things that suit us to go back to Scripture on.' This does not necessarily imply that the Bible is simply being manipulated by personal agendas. It is rather a desire that Christians come to an understanding of 'male and femaleness together. Not as a tokenism, not as pragmatism ... but ideally it would be good if churches came to that theologically, academically and spiritually, that this is right. Not just this is convenient.'

Following on from the importance of having a biblical understanding of the way women and men relate, is the matter of how such understanding is reached. This is the area of hermeneutics. While theories of hermeneutics are frequently left to theologians, the act of interpretation is something everyone engages in when they read the Bible. One aspect of hermeneutics concerns how we as readers come to the text and the ideas and often unconscious assumptions that we bring with us. As one man reflected: 'I'm sure it would be lovely – and this is an idealism – if we could just come to the Bible without our presuppositions and without our baggage and without our ethos, but that's not [possible]. Our life is born out of community and culture and ethos.' Hence, there are 'people who are committed to the Bible, you know, and committed to the church, committed to God' who hold diverse views. Not everyone sees it this way, however. This male church leader wondered if it was 'just the secular society around in your face ... that's causing those who are very conservative to feel that we are very compromising, while others of us are thinking no, we're trying to think this through and get a proper hermeneutic as to the role and function of women leaders'.

In questioning headship, while some see compromise with a secular society, others see a conversation between their own experience and Scripture. As one female church leader commented on headship: 'It looks very straightforward, you know, when you read it in the Bible. And then the rubber hits the road in the real world and kind of throws you back to the Bible to look and see, you know, could – could God really have meant that because it's just not working! So I suppose there I'm talking about being prepared to go back to Scripture with questions which I think particularly those who take a hard line on headship are not prepared to do. I mean they are prepared to read the Scripture, see what it says right in their face, and leave it at that, and everything else just has to fall in line with that ... In raising the headship thing you're actually raising for me a question about how you interpret Scripture, and how you manage and deal with Scripture. So there may well have been much more going on there in Scripture, and there certainly is much more going on in the world.'

A concern was expressed that personal experience will take precedence over Scripture and even eclipse it. One male church leader spoke of this: 'I think as long as people don't set aside the Scriptures because of experience ... that somebody who really feels that Paul says, and God says because Paul says, in Ephesians chapter five, that men should be in the lead, and yet here's this woman and she's a wonderful leader, I'll go with what experience tells me and forget the Scriptures. I think if that's the way we address it, and I think that very often is, we're in big trouble about a whole load of other issues. But as long as the Scripture is being addressed and wrestled with to some extent alongside the experience, and not being ignored, I think women in roles doing the business actually changes attitudes.'

Biblical hermeneutics, the 'addressing and wrestling with' Scripture, is the task of understanding how we may come from our own particularities in history, society and culture to a text originating in very different times, in order to discover its meaning – or even many meanings – both for when it was written and first used, and for ourselves today. R.T. France comments that without hermeneutics 'all our talk about the authority of the Bible has very limited cash-value. To claim to live and think under that authority is, whether we like it or not, to be committed to responsible hermeneutics, and it would do a lot for the mutual respect and understanding of Christians if that fact were more widely recognised.'[75] Certainly the question of headship is one area that focuses around competing claims of biblical meaning. Because of this, one man suggested that it is not simply contemporary society, or women themselves who are creating the conflict by questioning headship, but actually Scripture itself. Rather than seeing a questioning of headship as a 'sex war kind of scenario' he viewed it as 'a matter of biblical exegesis ... If women hadn't been pushing, even in a gentle way for the right to preach the word of God and the right to celebrate the sacraments, if women hadn't been pushing for that men should have been, because I think there's a scriptural mandate somewhere along the line there. So I don't think women are the cause of conflict. I think some women make it worse, but maybe it's the Scriptures themselves that are the cause of the conflict, which is not an unusual kind of scenario, and maybe it is the discovery of scriptural truth, or the re-discovery of scriptural truth that because of the times we live in is relevant.'

As important as *how* the Bible is interpreted for the 'discovery or re-discovery of scriptural truth' is *who* does the interpreting. Frequently as far as the question of headship is concerned, those who have done the interpreting and thereby provided the authoritative reading are men. For one woman this was a means of men perpetuating their own self-interest: 'The only people who've done the teaching are the men because they've needed it to justify their own control. It's like history is written by the winners, "Oh look, the Scripture's written to justify the fact that [we're in charge] ... and after all man was made first and Eve was the one who was tempted, she sins so there's no way you can possibly put her in charge of anything."'

What appears ironic to many women is that in many if not most cases when women's inclusion in an area traditionally inhabited only by men, such as ordination, is being considered women are excluded from the debate itself: 'A lot of what goes on inside the church about the ordination of women – it's like the women aren't part of the discussion. This is all going on about us, you know, as if we don't really – well again it's not taking us seriously. Let's take me seriously here, at least let me be part of the conflict I'm, you know, crucially involved in.' A male church leader observed the same dynamic: 'And so if you've men in leadership who then have to pronounce on men's roles and women's roles, you know, you inevitably only get one side of the picture, and so that produces tensions ... that was when I was working with a group which ... had very strong views on men's and women's roles, and they felt that eldership was for men, not for women. And so the discussion and development of that became contentious in itself, because it was only the men who were allowed to discuss the thing.' These comments illustrate the point that Carol Becker makes when she suggests that 'the debate about Paul will never be resolved in favour of the leadership of women in the church so long as the denominations remain so masculine ... Only when the paradigm changes can we engage in fruitful discussion about Paul's wisdom on the leadership of women, in both the home and the church.'[76]

What is clear is that for evangelicals in Northern Ireland, the Bible is as much a part of the process for those who question headship as it is for those who continue to advocate male authority over women.

Given the different views, the detail of the biblical arguments, and the variety of practical application of headship, it is perhaps not surprising that for some women and men the question of authority is still one of confusion and some puzzlement. For women, however, it is hardly an abstract or mere theoretical concept and it therefore evokes much deep feeling. While for some headship is incorporated in ways with which they clearly are comfortable, for others the notion of male authority impacts on their lives in a restrictive and even diminishing manner. It may be, however, that even when issues of authority are resolved in ways that facilitate women's gifting and ability in all areas of life, and when issues of participation, inclusion and difference are addressed, it is the domestic context of many women's lives, explored in the following chapter, that determines the extent of their church, community and political participation.

6

The Domestic Question

Speaking of her congregation's practice of having coffee together after a Sunday service, one woman commented about the teasing that goes on when men serve the coffee, something they do on a regular basis: 'There's still banter goes on, you know. Even in a place like this, where mostly men do the coffee on a Sunday morning actually. You know, people come in and see a man doing the coffee, [it's] still bantered about, it's not taken for granted.' In this congregation, which has women in leadership and consciously aims to support their inclusion, a man making and serving coffee is still a source of fun. However good-natured such banter is, it speaks of the issues involved in the domestic question, namely the sexual division of domestic labour that exists not only in reality, but also ideologically. Supported by a myth and often resulting in a trap for women, the domestic question is an integral part of women's church, community and political participation.

The Reality

The reality is that women are the main domestic carers. They are the primary carers for children and also cater for the domestic needs of husbands. They sustain homes through the many tasks involved in housework and invest time and energy in the personal development of family members. At times, they may also care for other relatives who through age, illness or particular circumstances, need specific care and attention. Among the women interviewed, over one quarter either currently or in the past had care responsibilities for family members other than husbands and children, and given the age range of those interviewed, this percentage is likely to increase over the course of their lifetimes. These responsibilities ranged from providing total physical care for someone or sharing care needs with other family members, to offering ongoing emotional and regular practical support, or liaising with service providers, organising and making household and care decisions.

The nature of much of the care for children and other family members is that it is both inflexible and repetitive in nature. Put simply, children need to be picked up from school, a meal has to be on the table, a dependent relative cannot be left alone. And this situation often pertains from one day to the next. A community worker spoke of her experience of 'the nature of home life and children and to a lesser extent husband' as one in which 'you have to be there for them, you have to get up, you have to cook, you have to clean ... there's just something that says, you know, I have to be home now, I have to leave my work now and go home ... I can't do that tonight because he's not well, or whatever.' As one woman commented about her shared care of a dependent relative over a number of years: 'There was no way we could not turn up when we were on the rota because she couldn't be on her own. And so therefore there was an enormous pressure at times. I mean there was many a day I was [at work] and I knew I had to be with [her] by half past five and it was a nightmare to get away ... but I couldn't not get myself out of here to be there ... it was absolutely imperative that you turned up and you couldn't afford to forget.'

While the operation of a sexual division of labour within families means a husband/father may take responsibility for certain tasks, such as gardening, washing the car, and painting and decorating, such jobs are both qualitatively and quantitatively different to the responsibilities that women assume in such a division. If the lawn does not get mown or the car washed or the door painted, no one goes to bed feeling hungry or forgotten. Aside from the sheer monotony of some domestic tasks, it is this lack of room to manoeuvre inherent in 'a sexual division of labour and time'[1] that is particularly restrictive on women's activities.

Caring work involves not only practical tasks in servicing material needs, but also input into the emotional development of others. Women spoke of the time and attention that their growing children needed: 'As the children grew older then, you know, they tend to think they need you less physically and you suddenly realise they actually do still need me to be there emotionally.' Another woman said the needs of older children can be 'more time-consuming in some ways, but you don't sort of have to be there for the four o'clock feed any more or whatever or the three o'clock pick-up from school. So I think it's more manageable when they're older, but more demanding emotionally when they're older and they always have a crisis at midnight.' As a community worker was finding out, 'they don't want to talk to you until eleven o'clock at night these days, which is a new experience for me'.

For many women, therefore, their participation in their churches, in the community, or in the public world, either in a paid or voluntary capacity, and in other areas of paid employment, is something that occurs alongside rather than replacing these domestic, caring responsibilities. Frequently for women '"having it all" simply turns out to mean doing it all'.[2] As one woman commented of her ongoing work in church-related ministries and of her family life: 'It has been slog, truthfully. I can get to the end of my life and say, I mean even if my life was to finish now, I have packed two lifetimes in. I really have. I've worked very hard.' Frequently it is a question of, in the words of one woman, 'juggling, real juggling'. For some women it was a matter of making choices: 'I mean people talk about women juggling balls. I mean what I have done in certain periods of my life is dropped several of them, deliberately. I mean I had to, oh very deliberately, put them down.'

A number of factors are involved in their handling of domestic realities for those women involved in church, community or politics. For some women in paid situations, a major component that facilitated their participation was working on a part-time basis, especially if the hours involved coincided with the school or nursery/playgroup times of children. As one woman heavily involved in her church expressed it:

'I've always worked part-time. I think it would have been difficult to work full-time.' Part-time working enabled them to have some church, community or political involvement but still be the main 'hands-on' carer of their children, and continue to maintain the home environment. Although to do so was not necessarily easy, it is one option that has enabled women with children also to have involvement outside of the home.

It is above all having some flexibility in their work sphere that enables women to combine their wider participation with their domestic responsibilities. Again, part-time employment, wherein women put in extra hours during school weeks in order to enable them to take time off in holidays or if a child is ill or has some other need, worked well for a number of women. Clearly, for this to be possible employers' co-operation is required and only certain occupations and organisations facilitate this. However, it can suit both parties. As one woman active in the community sector put it, 'If I'm flexible during ten months of the year, my employers can be flexible two months of the year.' Such flexibility is not without the tendency for women to overwork in these situations. In the words of another community worker, 'It's one thing having that time to take, it's another thing having time to take it.'

For other women flexibility in working patterns facilitated them working at home if a child was ill, taking unpaid maternity leave to have extra time with a child before returning to work, or reducing hours to look after children or other dependants. Some women were able to take their children with them into their church or community endeavours when appropriate, given the nature of the projects with which they were involved. However, it is not only women who need such flexibility and facilitative structures. One woman spoke of how both she and her husband having part-time work meant they could fully share parenting. If a husband is employed in a job that gives him flexibility in working hours then clearly he is more available for those immovable and non-negotiable child needs like school pick-ups.

Having help from others for domestic responsibilities was also a vital means of enabling women in their church, community and political participation. Some women spoke warmly of their husbands' practical support of their involvement, and they also spoke of the invaluable help with childcare from parents, friends and members of their churches, and the use of childminders, day care and nursery places. Some women had outside help not only in looking after children, but also with household chores. While some women employed household help outside the family, others shared household tasks among family members. As one woman said, 'I tried to share the load a bit, well in terms of pure mechanics of running the home, you know. One's responsibility is the dusting, one's responsibility is cleaning the bathrooms, I do the shopping and the cooking, [my husband] does the hoovering, though I did it last night. So we try to share the load a bit, recognising that each of us has significance and therefore one should not have all the domestic tasks to do ... But it's usually me who's battling for that it has to be said. I mean no kid's going to say, "ah mum, can I do the dusting today?", and [my husband's] too busy really.'

A community worker explained how she had come to new domestic arrangements with her husband when she took on her current post: 'I said to [my husband], "look, you know, if I go for this we're going to have to do something about home. I can't continue to do everything that I'm doing at home and do this as well." And, I mean, he has always been very, very supportive. He said, "well, you know, what are you suggesting?" I said, "well, I think we've got to carve some of the work." He said, "well, what is the work?" I said, "well, there's cooking, cleaning, ironing, washing, shopping, blah blah blah blah." So I said, "supposing we decide, you know, who's going to do what." We'd never been this organised before, and he said, "okay"... So I said to him, you know, "is there any part of this sort of load of tasks that you'd like to do?", and he said he'd like to try the cooking, so I thought "well, wonderful." Of course then it transpired that whoever did the cooking would have to do the shopping really, because you have to shop for what you're going to cook, and for the last two and a half years I haven't cooked a dinner. So I mean that's one of the ways we manage.'

For a few women, shared household responsibility was the normal pattern. One woman active in the church was aware that this practice was counter to most homes: 'You see [my husband] and I, we run our lives completely, I mean, alien to most people, to my family; they can't believe. We do everything, I mean [he] cooks the dinner, we just share everything. There are no roles in our house, we don't have roles and we just do everything. If something needs to be done, one of us does it. And when people come in, they can't cope with [my husband] running in with the coffee tray. Or, you know, me ... using the electric drill.'

For most women, however, although their husbands did more in the house than men have done in the past, sharing household chores was not on an equal basis. A full-time community worker uses the language of sharing to describe her domestic arrangements, but this is clearly far from equal: 'My husband can't cook, full stop, cannot cook. It's disastrous even to let him near anything remotely like cooking. So I do all the cooking. We probably would share things like ironing although I probably do more of it. And we'd share things like, I mean, he would be pretty helpful round the house although I would probably end up doing the bulk of it.'

Aware of the difficulty of the idea of equality as far as housework was concerned, one woman who was active in the church in a voluntary capacity and also worked full-time expressed her frustration: 'I think that's the saddest thing about it, that here we are in the twenty-first century discussing, you know, women's vital participation in the community. And the thing that's stressing me the most isn't that, and isn't how I'm received by men in my [work] and my congregation, because I can cope with that. But it's the fact that I still have to come home and think about taking food out of the freezer, and keeping my toilet clean ... I think there's something wrong there still. I have a husband who, who is really, he really genuinely tries to do his fair share, you know, and gets really upset, really hurt if I suggest that there's more that he could do.'

For some women there was a recognition that households simply could not be maintained in the same way now they were engaged outside the home. As one woman put it, 'I've become less house-proud.' Several spoke of reducing the amount of housework done. Unfortunately this can be a cause of friction in some homes: '[Housework is] the bit that has suffered most. I mean I would always tend to do things with children rather than do the house and that sometimes then caused a lot of tensions at home, you know. And [my husband] sort of, because of his upbringing, you know, was more inclined to think a tidy house was something that had to be and so there were a few tensions around that from time to time.'

Whether women reduce the amount of housework done, or try and redistribute the load among other family members, or even employ outside help, one constant usually remains. This is that household and care arrangements remain the responsibility of the woman. She may get others to help, but it is she who does the organising, the one who takes ownership of domestic needs and sees that they are addressed by whatever means.

In the context of her husband's practical support and his belief in her involvement outside the home, one woman said, 'I could say that, with hand on heart, he has totally supported me. But I do notice for both of us when we have decisions to make about our involvement in various things, family life and home responsibilities weigh much more heavily on me and will affect the decision that I make much more than it does him ... And even now ... while if I said to [him] ... will you arrange this aspect of domestic life for me, he will happily do it, if you give him a task to do, he will happily do it, but he rarely would take the initiative. He would not say, you know, this needs to be done and I will do it ... In practice it's the woman who carries the weight of it.' Once a source of tension for her, this woman had adapted to this pattern: 'Part of having a slightly easier domestic environment is the fact that now I don't get frustrated with that ... We used to come to a head because I felt, you know, he wasn't taking the initiative, he didn't see the things that needed to be done and he didn't do them. Whereas now I will quite clearly say to him, a, b, c, d needs to be done, will you do this and I'll do this and we can get ourselves organised and we can do whatever it is. So we've come to an accommodation on that. But I definitely carry the weight of it. And it often strikes me for women, you know, who are either at work or who would work a lot in the church, that that's an aspect of life that men, that they just don't take – it's not that they're being bad people – they just don't take it into consideration.'

Speaking of a time of caring for dependent relatives when 'you manage because you have to ... it never occurred to me not to manage', one woman reflected on the way men's lack of ownership of household chores can manifest itself: 'Women have always had to do three things at once. They've all got very used to it. And it doesn't matter whether it's your own home, whether you share it with a husband or whether you don't, in nearly all cases a husband who helps with the dishes and does the occasional hoovering the stairs really thinks he ought to be thanked for it. And he forgets they're his dishes and his stairs and his shopping and his children. In a sense he thinks he ought to be congratulated because he throws in a helping hand occasionally. I say, who organises the childcare, who decides what meals we're going to have, who does the shopping to get all those things in? The answer's usually the same.'

Even if household tasks are shared equally, the responsibility for domestic and care needs rarely is: 'We're both working. We're both busy. We're in different evenings at times, so just whichever one of us is here, you know, whichever one [is] around in the evening does the dishes after the dinner's over, or whoever's in first starts the dinner. It's just very much – get things done as you can. I still think that ... I see the things that need to be done. [My husband's] quite happy to do them. But I don't feel he's as responsible for kind of keeping things rolling on a weekly basis and getting things done as I would be. I would tend to be the one who – who sees the things that need to be done, plans what needs to be done, but we would probably share fairly evenly I would say the actual doing of them.'

Another woman expressed what ownership of domestic responsibilities meant in terms of childcare: 'I'm even thinking here of my own personal life here, in that I'm in a marriage that is very, very equal, but if [my husband] was working say on Tuesday night and I was working on Tuesday night, I would always have to find the childcare. It would never, it would never occur to [him], "okay, [we need] childcare." Or, do you know, if someone phones up and says [to him], "meeting next Thursday night," he'd say, "yep, fine," whereas next Thursday night I go, "okay, children, now ... you know, [who] can look after them?" ... whereas [he] would just go "yes, fine." And [even] if I'm [already booked for that night], I'll have to find [the childcare], even though he's said, "fine." And that is coming from I would say a fairly equal partnership ... He's not carrying it, the responsibility. The ownership of it is not there ... it's definitely not there. And again, I have to say I'm coming from this sort of equal partnership. You think of so many women [who] are in partnerships that are just not – he won't do it. If the dinner's not made the children will starve. It's as plain as that.'

It is this ownership of domestic responsibilities, 'the kind of things that you carry in your mind all the time ... just even carrying the weight of it at times', that mean women frequently have additional demands on their time and energy. The fact that men, even those who are fairly active at home and with children, have this domestic back-up upon which they rely, gives them one less thing to factor in to their time management and commitments, and fulfilment of any sense of calling or vocation. Further, work environments, churches and forms of public participation often assume this domestic support for the men who participate. This is illustrated in the church sector where women are becoming ordained ministers. In these instances, their congregations effectively lose the practical support of a clergy wife – not only in caring for the minister's domestic needs but acting in many ways that help in the functioning of a manse and local congregation, from secretarial tasks to hospitality.

The same dynamic applies for those in other demanding contexts. Speaking of one situation 'that maybe has been the place that I have found it hardest to be a woman', one woman spoke of being 'resentful of men ... because I knew that they were going home and a meal would be set in front of them.' A community worker reflected on her position compared with her male counterparts: 'Whilst I see my husband and my male peers, they've got children as well but ... at the end of the day they are able to put [their work] first because they've got, on the whole they've got wives or mothers at home who won't. My husband, and he's completely brilliant with the family, and not, this is not a criticism at all, but he – he doesn't just leave work at [a certain time], or, he stays on because ... his work's really important. But I have to [leave work on time] because I have to. Because if I don't do it nobody will [be there for the children]. But if he doesn't do [something at home] because he really believes that something needs done [at work] I'll do it. So there's a fundamental difference. At the end of the day we try to have equality and try to share out tasks and everything, but he basically can put what he believes to be his calling first. He can do that still, and I can't.'

Part of the reason that this situation still exists, with women maintaining ownership of domestic and caring responsibilities, also frequently carrying them out, is that it is perpetuated by a mindset that endorses this arrangement. It is not simply a matter of custom and practice, but is underpinned by a domestic ideology.

The Ideology

The ideology that underpins the reality that women are the main domestic carers is that women *should* carry domestic responsibilities, and further, especially in regard to children, that they should prioritise these over other aspects of their lives. While household chores are often viewed as being something women can do alongside their involvement outside of the home, childcare is seen as incompatible with too much outside engagement.

The Northern Ireland Life and Times Survey[3] conducted in 1998 provides a picture of current social attitudes towards women in regard to home, paid work and family. One third (34 per cent) of respondents agreed[4] with the premise that a job is all right, but what most women really want is a home and children. There is no difference in attitudes between Protestants and Catholics and negligible difference between women and men. Responses do vary with age, however, with agreement to the suggestion that women really want home and family increasing from nearly one fifth (19 per cent) of 18–24 year olds to over one half (55 per cent) of 65 years of age and over. Overall, 44 per cent disagree with this statement while a fifth of respondents reject its premise by neither agreeing nor disagreeing with the statement.

A similar pattern emerges when considering traditional sex roles through the statement that a man's job is to earn money and a woman's job is to look after the home and family. Among the 28 per cent in agreement there is little difference in the results for women and men (at 27 and 28 per cent respectively) and only 4 per cent between Catholics (at 27 per cent agreement) and Protestants (at 31 per cent). However, belief in these traditional roles increases with age from 15 per cent of 18–34 year olds up to over one half (54 per cent) of those 65 and over. Over half (53 per cent) of all respondents disagree with these traditional roles and, as with the previous statement, one fifth neither agree nor disagree.

When exploring traditional roles through a different question, namely that it is not good if the man stays at home and cares for the children and the woman goes out to work, the same pattern is evident. There is 28 per cent agreement, varying only slightly among women and men (27 and 31 per cent) and Catholics and Protestants (28 and 31 per cent), but a trend to greater agreement for those 65 and over (at 48 per cent) with one fifth of 18–24 year olds in agreement and 17 per cent of those aged 25–34. Over half (51 per cent) of those questioned disagree that this traditional role reversal is a bad thing.

The attitudinal picture these three sets of findings suggest is one of a generational shift in views about traditional roles for women and men, with more younger people rejecting the sex roles supported by many older respondents. The picture changes, however, when considering specific details of women's role in regard to the care of children. While 82 per cent of respondents considered that before they had children married women should work full-time outside of the home, this reduces to 68 per cent for women whose children have all left home, 22 per cent where the children are all at school, and down to only 6 per cent if there is a child under school age. Nearly half (47 per cent) believed women should stay at home if there is a child under school age, and a further 39 per cent that a woman should work part-time in these circumstances. Once the youngest child begins school, 59 per cent considered part-time work for women suitable. These figures are similar to the Northern Ireland Social Attitudes (NISA) 1991 survey. Half of the NISA respondents believed women should stay at home if a child was under school age, 36 per cent believing in part-time work (a total of 86 per cent, the same for the Life and Times Survey combined figures). The figures for supporting full-time work when there is a pre-school child and when all children are at school are slightly higher at 8 and 26 per cent respectively.[5]

In reality, despite these attitudinal findings, in the autumn of 1998, figures for women with from one to four dependent children show that at least 45 per cent worked full-time (the figure for those with three dependent children), and 68 per cent of women with one child worked full-time.[6] As a number of those interviewed for this book stated, out of economic necessity some women have always worked outside the home. However, the attitudes outlined above indicate that childcare is still considered a priority for women. As one woman observed, 'It's interesting, a friend of mine had a baby, and everybody's asking her is she going back to work, and nobody's asked her husband is he leaving! And I find it really weird, because you know, there's no reason why they both couldn't work part-time for that matter if that's what they wanted to do. But there's this kind of natural assumption ... '

This domestic priority is not only about the practicalities of care, but also arises from a belief in the orientation of women to care. Hence, for example, while a supportive partner can be a vital factor in facilitating women's political participation, a survey of women councillors found that

> many of the respondents believe that women not only put their families first, but that they *should* do so, postponing any public aspirations until their children are of school age, if not older. So while a common complaint across the parties was the dearth of pre-school provision in Northern Ireland ... the view that husband and children should come first was widely held.[7]

The authors of the report comment that the internalised traditional expectations about motherhood mean that even with childcare facilities women would defer public ambition.[8]

In speaking to the women active in the church, community or politics, it is clear that this ideology of prioritising children over other endeavours impacts on their lives. It is acquired not only through religious channels, but also from social norms. As one woman commented, not coming from a Christian home, ideas about women came to her 'from secular assumptions about women. Growing up in the fifties and early sixties, women stayed at home.' Such societal and religious expectations about women are summed up in the words of one male church leader, 'What higher vocation can a woman have than to look after her children?'

Certainly some endorse this domestic world as women's priority. As a woman active in the church said, 'I would tend to think that when children are smaller it's important for the mother to be around, and only every individual mother knows when their child is ready to be allowed a longer bit of rope.' A woman whose children were no longer pre-schoolers commented, 'When you have children you have a responsi-bility to them, and I mean I would feel ... if it ever came to a toss-up where I had to decide [what to do in my outside involvement], the children would be the deciding factor.' Another woman, while very much aware of social changes, endorsed this view: 'While there have been great strides in emancipation made, do you know, and my husband is very good, and does a lot, I still think it would be important for me to be at home.'

Some endorsed the role of a mother at home with her children because of the neglect of children that they had witnessed through their work. While recognising that lone parent mothers do not necessarily have the choice to stay at home, one woman commented: 'I think our society has suffered because ... more and more women have gone into careers and work out full-time ... Their children are suffering because we've too many latch-key kids coming home whose needs are not being met because mum is too tired to meet them and it has awful repercussions. I mean we see it day by day in the education scene.' As a community worker put it, while she had 'moved beyond the sort of thinking ... that I used to have about a mother has to be the primary carer for her children', nevertheless her experience working with families meant 'I have to say that if a woman doesn't put her children first I quake for the next generation.'

For one woman involved in politics, her belief that 'the most vital years you have with your children is from birth till they start school' meant that 'if it was possible to make it law, I would give women an allowance to stay at home'. While, where necessary for a family, proper childcare should be provided, 'we should think about, you know, doing something to encourage women to stay at home. This government I think is encouraging women to go back to work. I think I would encourage women to stay at home.'

A female church leader viewed women's responsibilities as moving in 'seasons. I'm becoming more and more convinced that there are seasons in our lives, where things are different, just like there are seasons whenever you're very responsible up-ways and down-ways, down-ways towards children and up-ways towards parents, ageing parents.' Given the changing needs in a family she spoke of how 'sometimes somebody has to probably give way and ultimately it's usually the woman in that season of small children'.

A number of women felt that the decision to work outside of the home when there were children was a matter of individual choice, and not something that could be predetermined for everyone. One woman involved in the church spoke of it being important for her 'really to support my husband and care and look after and whatever the children. I feel that's important. But I think every woman has to work that one out for herself. And I don't think you can lay down hard and fast rules. I think in all these issues like that you've got to be very flexible really.' Another woman who had given up her career for a time because of the demands of her husband's job said, 'I think for each [woman] it's going to be different and I would never, ever, ever say to somebody the way I did is the right way. It was right for me.' As a community worker put it, 'I've met women who would say it was their calling to stay at home and look after the children, and that's – that's great. I think you have to know what's right for you to do, and if you're, if you're comfortable, and if you feel that you're happiest staying at home looking after the children then that's perfectly right … But personally I think if you choose to go outside the home and work, you should be given encouragement, you know, to be able to do that.'

In taking this stance, these interviewees are, in the words of one woman active in her church in a voluntary capacity, 'acknowledging that all women are different, I think that's, you know, very important too. For me I don't view it as a sacrifice to give up a career to look after a child. But for another woman it would be a major sacrifice, and therefore she … shouldn't be forced to do it. But I shouldn't therefore judge her and say, "oh you should be at home with your child."

Likewise she shouldn't judge me ... It's recognising that we do have different attitudes to it.'

The sense of judgement to which this woman refers comes partly when women make choices that challenge the domestic ideology. While, as discussed below, some of those who stay at home express a sense of their choice being undervalued, it is guilt that may be induced in women who are active outside of the home. As one woman observed, 'every working mum I know feels an element of guilt'. A community worker spoke of her first year of working when 'I was riddled with guilt.' While knowing that her children were well-adjusted and happy, a woman employed by her church said this was something that 'I probably in my worst moments torture myself [about]'. Similar self-criticism was reflected by a community worker, despite her grown children articulating no sense of deprivation: 'I would look back at my early years in community work, and think there was times when I definitely should have given my children more attention than I did ... Now they would say no, they would say they'd have actually managed very well, but there's times ... and maybe it's just because any kind of working mother who's trying to build a life for herself outside the home I think is always consumed with guilt. You're always torn in this kind of conflict, you know, and particularly if something happened to the children, you're always in this kind of conflict ... you know, should I be at home with the children, or should I be in [work]?'

In particular this guilt is something women experience, rather than men, and that both women and men perpetuate. A community worker noted, 'I know that sometimes women can be hard on women, because as a married woman you should do, you should this, and, you know, this is where you fall in. And it's hard to get the balance right because ... as a woman you'll always feel guilty if one of your children is sick and you're out at work. And you think, right, you know, the husband, it'll not take a fizzle out of him, you know, so what. But we always will have this. And I think sometimes we put this on other women.' One woman spoke of being aware not to pass on to her own daughters the guilt that she herself had experienced from parents and parents-in-law about care issues, which were not similarly passed to sons in the family: 'I don't want them to feel, probably the guilt ... that I would have felt, that probably my mother and [my husband's] mum would put on to us. And I know my mum would do it and I know [my husband's] mum does it to [his] sister, but not to [him] and I can see that she does. But yet she doesn't do it to him and equally my mum wouldn't do it to my brother. It's a daughter [thing], you know. And I just want to make sure ... I don't do it to them.'

Some women wanted to challenge assumptions about female responsibility to care, not on the basis that women don't have such responsibility, but that this does not mean necessarily that they cannot have other involvement, and further, that it should be matched by their husbands taking responsibility for childcare. A community worker said, 'I would have thought that for a husband ... the thing that matters most to him is his family, but he still works and nobody questions that, you know. I think the husband and children can be more important than anything else, but that doesn't say that work is not something that's also important.' For one woman, she did not consider that prioritising her children in her life meant that she had to be their full-time carer: 'At the end of the day family does come first, but if I can have them looked after by someone I trust I would do that.' A woman active in para-church said that, 'in terms of the upbringing of children and so on ... that should be equally shared, there should be a partnership between husband and wife, and career aspirations, you know, need to be looked at from both perspectives.' A politically involved woman reflected: 'I hear a lot about women's issues. I'm not quite sure there are women's issues as such. To me family is a parent issue, and both parents have to sit down and discuss what they're going to do, what's best for the family, what's best for the parents.'

In raising the issue of prioritising children in the life of men, women are not suggesting necessarily that fathers do not consider themselves responsible for their children. Rather, they are challenging assumptions about what that responsibility means in actual practice. Even if there is an attitudinal change in regard to some traditional sex roles, as survey findings suggest, the ongoing reality that in the main women carry domestic responsibilities not only in practice but in terms of ownership, points to the difficulty of transposing abstract attitudes into changed mindsets and appropriate actions.

One woman reflected on the difference in practice that seeing family as their primary responsibility means for a husband and wife: 'I suppose in all that I do, I still see myself as a wife and mother before anything else. And if you ask [my husband] ... he would say the same thing, about himself, that he sees himself as a husband and a father before anything else ... But I think while he says that, by how he acts and lives that is not reflected in the decisions that he makes. I mean and I think he says it with the best heart and he is, I mean in terms of what I have seen other husbands, his involvement at home, his involvement with the children has been terrific. But I am very conscious, as a woman, that when it comes to making decisions about what I do and the activities that I'll be involved in, the weight of being a wife and a mother weighs much more heavily with me and the decisions that I make as a result of that, than it would with [my husband as a husband and father]. Now I think he's politically correct and he knows the right things to say if you asked him ... And I'm not saying that to, you know, to make him look bad, but I think that is true of many men, who see themselves as very liberated and very pro-women and very supportive, which he has been all of those things.'

A male church leader expressed this difference in his own family situation. His wife's commitments outside of the home means he makes a family meal twice a week. Of this contribution he reflected: 'I think this is wonderful ... She's not overly impressed with that in that I don't do it any of the other five days in the week unless I really, really have to. I really don't do any ironing. Very little hoovering. If there's decorating or whatever to be done okay I do that, and wash the car, blah blah blah, so I suppose there's some kind of, kind of sharing of role in a sense, but in the end of the day paying lip service to some form of equality between us doesn't necessarily work itself out as actually equality in terms of doing the roles ... I have probably had more involvement with our children than would have been the case in my home when I was growing up, but not nearly as much involvement with them as I suppose my wife would like me to have had. So again there is, okay, maybe a willingness to admit on the intellectual level and on the spiritual level that things as they are are not right, but whether even personally being honest about it has really made a difference to the way I live and function is again another question ... It's a bit like a church that says that women [can participate] on the same basis as men. It's a wonderful statement to make. But in actual fact it doesn't mean anything. And it can equally be so in – at any level of those relationships I suppose.'

Put simply, in terms of a move to an attitude of equality or, in the words of a community worker, 'the equity thing – we should both be responsible to think about the family, but it doesn't work out that way, does it?' With the demands of many occupations in which men are employed, with long working hours and lack of flexibility, challenging the existing domestic ideology, for those who believe this is necessary, involves not only individual choices and changes, but a need to confront structures and the mindsets that sustain them. This is no minor task. As one woman said, 'I think we each have a responsibility, both male and female, but again you're swimming against a cultural tide if you demand a level of commitment to home and family that [men] are not culturally adjusted or mentally adjusted to giving.'

Without a change in ideology, domestic responsibilities will continue to be seen as a woman's issue or problem. So while one man saw a biblical argument for women's greater involvement not only in church, but in wider society, he nevertheless thought that 'they've just got to juggle about their whole family commitments then'. For him it becomes 'a very practical thing. How best can [women] manage their time.' There is no sense of change of the domestic ideology in his thinking at this point. And without a different ideology, there is no incentive to make structural changes. For example, Yvonne Galligan and Rick Wilford comment that the 'UUP and DUP provide clear evidence of a preference for the perpetuation of traditional gender roles within their organisations and in terms of public policy'.[9]

As one woman said, 'When are we going to change structures so that women don't have to do this? So that men take more responsibility for what's going on at home? You know, it's always these working women, but that's because the structures are male and you have to fit in with them. When is society going to change, that somehow things develop that men can take more responsibility at home, you know? That's the way it should be addressed, instead of women all the time being made to take all, bear all the burden. And I think it's possible to do both and to do both well, if structures change.' Aware that her circumstances enabled her to fight for change and get structural arrangements that enabled shared parenting, she knew that if 'I was working [in certain places] and had babies, you know, and my husband worked in [a factory] and had to do overtime six nights a week, my thing is I have to give up my job to look after these kids. So they don't have the same choices. But I think then that comes down to people like me and people in councils, the women in councils and all, to campaign for the thing. Things have to change you know, there has to be job shares, there has to be flexible working hours. There has to be times when men can have job shares, men can work flexible hours. I think that whole thing, I mean that's hundreds of years work, it really is.'

In addition to the need for 'family-friendly policies' in places of employment and social institutions that benefit men as well as women, there is a need for attention to the gender pay gap, wherein women still are paid less than men for the same kind of work. After all, as one man noted, 'insofar as usually the man's wage is probably more than the woman's then it's going to be easier for the woman to [stay at home] than the man'. Yet, as good as these developments are for facilitating greater participation of women in the world of work and men in caring roles in the home, Bonnie Miller-McLemore argues 'they are partial' and do not speak to the 'moral and spiritual quandaries about how to live life'.[10] These quandaries are about how to encompass in the way we live the human need of both women and men for creativity in both their work and their relationships. What she talks about is more than the idea of the work–life balance, which 'aims to create a closer fit between employment practices and people's needs, especially for those with parenting and caring responsibilities'.[11] For it is not simply a case of managing a better balance between different aspects of our lives, as helpful as that may be, but about envisioning 'adequate models of loving and working'.[12] As one woman said, in speaking about how 'it's really hard to be an activist and be a mummy' the question is not just 'who does the hoovering, who does the cleaning, who does the shopping?' but 'who gets to fulfil their calling most, and who gets to invest in relationships most, and who gets to express themselves most? I just don't really hear debate about that.'

A common point raised with this kind of discussion is the fact that it is women who bear children. Both those who support a traditional domestic ideology and those who are in favour of women's greater participation in the work place, see this as a major point of difference between women and men that inhibits women, for a time at least, in terms of their involvement outside the home. As one male church leader said of women's domestic caring responsibilities, 'Should they put them first? The answer's yes. Should that mean they haven't any career, gifting or calling? The answer's no. Do they have more difficulty balancing that than men do? The answer's yes. But there are ways and means. But I don't think you can argue – I don't – wouldn't even want to try to argue against physiology and biology.' Citing the example of a woman he knew who was severely physically debilitated during her pregnancy, he observed, 'at the minute her career's on the back burner, but there's absolutely nothing [you can do about that], the men can't bear the children, so practically speaking there are problems for women there that men don't have. Likewise nursing the child ... I think practically speaking there are problems for women.' The difficulty women have through their maternity, even without complications, negotiating work in church, community, or politics, is due to their having to negotiate a system not designed to accommodate their particular needs. One way of beginning to construct an adequate model of working and loving, of envisioning ways for people to encompass work and relationships in their lives, is to ask, why should the world of work be organised around the bodies of those who do not have children, that is, men? What would it look like for church, community and political participation to be organised so that both those who do and those who do not bear children can be included in those spheres and also be involved with the care of children? Such questions challenge the existing public/private divide and the sexual division of domestic labour and the domestic myth that accompanies these dichotomies.

The Myth

The myth that accompanies the domestic ideology is that all women love domesticity and childcare. For example, in a survey of male electoral voters, in response to the statement that women are by nature happiest when making a home and caring for children, half of all men agreed and, with the exception of APNI supporters, 'a majority of men aligned to each of the other parties believe that women are naturally disposed to find happiness within the private realm, a view that is especially pronounced among DUP and Sinn Féin supporters'.[13]

Some women do indeed find the domestic realm one of enjoyment and fulfilment. A number of women spoke deeply and warmly about their experiences in the world of home and family. A woman now working part-time in the community sector expressed her feelings: 'Family are very special to me ... I suppose I have never been a very career-minded person. I have never been the sort of person who's wanted to get to the top of any ladders. That's just not me ... I actually [feel] very privileged to be at home. I enjoyed my years at home with the kids. And I know there are many women who feel ... career's important to them ... but for me, I just love being at home with my children, and the times, the relationships with other people that I was able to build up through the children, I found very special years. In fact I struggled going back to work. It was probably finances more than anything pushed me out initially, which is often the case.'

For women who view family matters in this way, it is not a question of feeling under any kind of obligation or social pressure to be the full-time carer for their children. One woman who had left her job when her children were born, returning to work part-time when they were at school, commented, 'I felt that it was my desire – I'll not even use the word responsibility – it was my desire then to be with my children, our children, until they're in a situation where they will be up and away from the home. And if at that time I want to come into full-time work or full-time committee or full-time voluntary work, that's my choice. And God willing, with good health, I can do whatever I want when they're up and away. But for the time that God has given us to have them, which is maybe only eighteen years and that means I have only another four years with our older daughter. Four years isn't long to enjoy her, so I'd better keep enjoying it.' Even among women who were considerably active outside the home throughout their children's lives expressed delight in their domestic lives: 'I do see myself as a wife and mum before everything else and embrace that and enjoy it.' Other women, while not being as effusive in their comments, nevertheless expressed contentment in their domestic role.

However, while some women relish the domestic world of home and children, there are those who do not. A community worker put it graphically, 'I personally would have died if I'd stayed at home. I couldn't have – it just wasn't in me to stay at home and be a full-time mother, you know … I think you need to build a life for yourself outside the home as well. But that's very difficult to do without … without the proper kind of support. But I think it's almost essential for a woman if she, if she can manage it, to have some kind of life and a calling of her own as well.' A woman employed by her church expressed something similar: 'I think if I had to have sat at home with the kids for five or six years doing nothing else, I think I would have cracked up, I really would have. Now I love my kids, I love being with them and the first year of [my first child's] life I was at home because I had no job, you know. But I mean I spent my life wandering round [the shops] just to get out of the house and see people.

Men would be killing themselves! They would be running away, [saying], "I'll do overtime the night", you know!' Another woman spoke of how difficult she found her maternity leave, finding herself getting 'into a rut ... I don't think I could be an un-busy person. I think if I wasn't busy I wouldn't – and this is going to sound really trite – but I wouldn't be fulfilled. I genuinely feel that ... and I think [my child] would probably suffer if I wasn't busy.'

Women without children reflected on the choices they might have made or would make if they had children: 'I'm not sure of what I'd have done if I was married and had children. Would I have given up work to look after children or not? Having seen how important a stimulating job has been to me, in retrospect I would say no I wouldn't have.' One community worker said, 'I have to be honest, I don't know if I could cope with being a full-time housewife and mother. I think it would probably drive me mad, you know.' Another community worker expressed the same feelings: 'I don't see that I would be a very good mother if I was at home all the time, because I think I'd go round the twist and [I] think everybody would go with me, you know!' A married woman simply said, 'As far as giving up work to look after children and things like that, I don't think I would want to do that.'

Even some women who had chosen to spend more of their time as hands-on carers for children spoke of needing some form of activity outside of the domestic world. While she had spent time with her children when they were young, and believed this was important for mothers to do, a woman active in her church spoke of how she returned to work because, 'I did want to get out of the house, you know, I'd had enough time doing housework and making meals, and the usual. I wanted to be involved with people outside, and even before I did work, I was involved in other voluntary things.' Another woman who was a lay leader in her church alongside caring for her family said, 'I have a real vision and calling for the church here, which was more important than trying to continue my own individual career, but I think I would have found it very frustrating if [giving up work] had meant baking buns all the time – if that was the limit ... I don't know what I would have done in that situation.' Put succinctly by another woman: 'I find part-time to be a good balance because it was helping me to have time with my son and also interaction with other adults.'

Those who hold to a domestic ideology that sees it as a woman's place to be the full-time carer of her children and home and to prioritise these responsibilities over other activities, in the main endorse outside activity and contact for women, accepting the validity of this. In this sense it is a difference in the amount of outside engagement envisaged that separates those who hold to a domestic ideology and those who do not. However, the expression of the desire and need for greater involvement outside of the home speaks to the reality of the childcare experience as one that can be isolating and lacking in personal fulfilment, and is not necessarily the idyll that the ideology can suggest.

Ironically, those women who choose to stay at home, very much wanting to be the main carer for their children, sometimes feel a denigration of their chosen role. While some women who work outside the home talk about the guilt involved in their decision, those who stay at home speak of the lack of value of what they do, epitomised in the phrase 'I'm *just* a housewife'.

A community worker spoke of how 'in society in general there is that sense of "just a housewife or a mother" or whatever ... I think we've almost swung to the extent where there's almost a stigma, you know, to being a full-time mother or whatever, which I feel is sad.' Another woman contrasted her sense of personal affirmation as a 'stay-at-home' mum with the experience of her friends, '[My husband] would even say continually to the kids, you know, even things like "isn't it wonderful Mummy has stayed home to look after you?" You know, and he would reaffirm me in that, whereas ... going on experience from talking with my friends and that, they don't get that at home. And so they need – they all need to get their self-worth from somewhere. And so many find it in the workplace because they don't – they're not valued at home. And that's tragic, because there's no greater calling. There really isn't, because you are rearing the next generation ... I feel the woman is so pivotal there and yet so often she feels so degraded in the role that she can't give it her best.' While she did not necessarily believe that a woman 'would have to expect to completely deny herself and slave for the rest of her life for her family and husband, and have the slippers ready when he comes home and, you know, newspaper and pipe', a young woman active in the community also felt that 'women shouldn't be made to feel bad if they do do that, because I think there can be that extreme, like, "what do you mean, you stayed home to look after your children, you're being exploited", and sometimes it's like no, family is a priority.'

Often talk about the lack of value of women at home in comparison with the worth associated with the world of paid employment is posed in terms of value-judgements being made of the women in each sphere. In other words, the talk is about how women are judged by the choices they make. In a way, this is another expression of the domestic ideology that sees women as those who are responsible for domestic caring because it focuses on the women involved rather than a society that undervalues caring tasks and those who carry them out. The sexual division of domestic labour and the resulting disvaluing of caring is another instance of those activities associated with women having lesser value than those associated with men. As Germaine Greer has said, 'Running a house is a complex task requiring high levels of management skills; if men did it, the domestic sphere would be invested with prestige and value.'[14]

Perpetuating the notion of private and public worlds to which women and men belong respectively is the idea that domesticity is the natural domain for women. This applies to both childcare and household tasks. As one woman put it: 'I do feel that bringing up children is one of the most important things anybody can do and I do think women are more innately carers than men are.' A male church leader commented, 'When it comes to child-rearing issues, because at the end of the day biologically men can't have children, women ... perhaps have more of a maternal instinct and a desire to stay at home and look after the child.' He added, 'It's hard to sift out I think a very natural cultural order that comes simply because of the – the differences between the sexes, and a way in which the church has assumed therefore a role for women.' Another man also linked the fact that women are the ones who carry and give birth to children to their domestic role: 'Maybe [it's] to do with the fact that it's the women who bear the children and who bring them into the world, that they have traditionally been the homemakers. I think women have gifts in homemaking that – that probably many men don't have ... Certainly the men I know, and I'm looking at myself as well, if I had to ... there are certain things that I could do in the home, I could, I could provide a meal for the family. It would be very, very basic. Now maybe if I had practice I could become good at it, but I'm uncomfortable in those situations. Now maybe that's because I've not been in them that I'm uncomfortable in them but, and maybe it's because of the, what we are as men and women that men have traditionally been the kind of, you know, the hunters, the fighters, the kind of, physically stronger and doing the physical things, whereas generally speaking the things in the home are not the things that take brawn, but that take those other gifts.'

The idea that the domestic world does not involve hard work or is not physically demanding was spoken of by a full-time community worker. At a time when her older brother left school and first started working while still living at home, her mother had care responsibilities for an ill parent and so, while still at school, she carried many of the domestic responsibilities in the home, with 'never an awful lot of expectation of him in terms of what was happening in the house'. She spoke of 'my mum's kind of underlying idea that, you know, he's a man, he's out working hard. And even now ... my mum would have that, oh don't be making him do any work, he's out working all day. And I'm thinking and what do I do, you know, do I not work as well? And there is that kind of mentality. And I think my brother inherited that to some degree.' She spoke of how her brother had come to appreciate the demands of her job and hence been far 'more willing to pitch in. But I think as well as that he shows a lot more appreciation for the fact that I do a lot of the stuff.' The idea is that 'real work', work of value, is done outside of domestic life, the latter being more suited to women physically. It is hence more natural, and therefore more likely to lead to women's happiness.

As some women pointed out, domestic life can be very demanding: 'In a way it's the most stressful job of the whole lot, because you're, you know, with young children twenty-four hours a day, very tied down and it's certainly undervalued.' One woman spoke of how she had changed the way she asked women about their lives: 'Very often I say to women, what do you work at and invariably in the early days, women would say, och I'm just at home, I'm only a housewife. And I caught myself saying, you are not only a housewife, you work very hard. So I now say, do you have paid employment outside of the home? Now that's maybe being politically too correct, but I think it is giving people, giving women a place that if they are in the home, that's as honourable and important a role as getting paid employment somewhere else.'

Drawing attention to the myth that all women love domesticity and childcare is not to suggest that women should not enjoy their home and family immensely, or choose to spend most of their time in that domain. Rather, it is to recognise that not all women want to do this, just because they are women. Rejecting a full-time domestic role is not the same as rejecting motherhood for those women who do not find the former fulfilling in and of itself. As one woman put it, 'I just couldn't stay at home every day, twenty-four hours, with two children. You know, I'm their mother. I am definitely their mother twenty-four hours a day, but I'm just not their – their childcare person. I just couldn't do it. And it is not good for me nor them to be with them all the time. It just doesn't work.'

What this woman and others want is not to have their identity as a mother eclipse all other aspects of their lives, which is the trap that the domestic ideology can often lead to.

The Trap

The potential trap involved in the domestic question is that all women come to be viewed through the domestic lens of family life, and a particular type of family life. However, not all women have children. While one woman involved in her church recognised this, even as she spoke of women with and without children, women are first presented as those who give birth to and rear children: 'I think God has a purpose in life for women. I think ... he has created them to bear children and to be a parent to children. But we've many women who are not mothers and God has a role for them.' Of course, there is truth in what she says. However, the domestic trap in which this truth is enmeshed becomes apparent if the same is said of men, that God has created them to procreate and be a parent to children, but that there are many men who are not fathers and God has a role for them.

Viewing women first and foremost as those who should be wives and mothers can make Christian communities uncomfortable for single women. A para-church worker commented: 'I do feel that being a single person in my church is a difficult place to be. It's a very family-oriented church, and a very family-oriented community.' As a community worker pointed out, 'I feel much more accepted as an individual in the community sector. In church I felt very much that I didn't fit in because I didn't have a husband and children and the usual things that you have, you know, apparently to be the norm. I felt a great deal of loneliness and sadness within the church and anger because I didn't feel accepted as a single person ... There's more diversity in the community than there is in the church. It's easier to kind of fit.'

The sense of dis-ease that some may feel when a woman is not in an established family arrangement was encountered by a woman now involved in politics. At one time a man asked her if she had been out with her boyfriend at the weekend. 'And I said "no." He said, "why not?" I said, "I've no boyfriend." And he said, "are you a lesbian?"... He was serious, it was a serious question. I thought how does one lead on from the other? How does that happen? ... How are those questions related? They're not, that's a complete tangent – where did that come from? I thought it said an awful lot about him.'

The way society is comfortable with identifying women primarily by their marital status is seen in attitudes towards the title 'Ms' as an alternative to 'Miss' or 'Mrs'. Unsuccessful as a single replacement for the two latter terms, 'Ms' has become associated with women whose marital status is not known, or those who do not fit neatly into single or married categories (those who are separated, divorced or cohabiting). It frequently carries negative associations. As one married woman said: 'I don't like this "Ms" that we're called ... I don't like it in the general sense because I am "Mrs" and I suppose it's just a personal thing. I remember a [woman] at [work] who was married and preferred to be called by her maiden name and be called "Ms" and I thought, well what's the problem? I mean, why aren't you willing to be called "Mrs" to show that you're married and why aren't you willing to take your husband's name? I found it strange, but maybe it was feminism at the end of the day.'

However, for other women, 'Ms' is a title that 'gives them the privacy men take for granted'.[15] As another married woman pointed out, 'I think ["Ms" is] a good idea ... because people don't particularly want their status to be public, or to be known ... it seems to me that if they use "Ms" they don't really want their status to be involved in how people perceive them.' It is not that women who choose "Ms" necessarily wish to hide their marital status, although some may. But it is an objection to the inability of society to relate to them without their status being known. Perhaps only by men being asked to establish if they should be called 'Mr' or 'Master' every time they give their name, or to give their marital status, could they experience something of the impact of having one's status relative to men established as the defining characteristic for women. As Margaret Gibbon argues, 'The desire to mark women's status relative to men (as unmarried, married, divorced) only makes sense in a patriarchal society where women are not accorded independent status on a par with men and need to have their sexual un/availability signalled.'[16]

It was not only single women, but women raising children on their own who voiced the difficulty in matching up to the domestic ideal. One woman spoke of how, out of her situation, she challenged other Christians in her church about the evangelical practice of headship: 'What about widows? If a widow has children then you're the head of the family, and there's no alternative, you have to get on with it and make all the decisions. So what's the difference between doing it as a widow and doing it as a wife? Along with your husband, you know, making the decisions together, and I couldn't get a satisfactory answer from them.' A male church leader referred to headship in the situation when a woman's husband is not a Christian: 'I think it devolves to the woman simply because a man cannot lead in spiritual things if he is not a spiritual man himself, so if you like I suppose that's ... a second – a second-best, but yet better than not having any kind of spiritual leadership.' His understanding of headship relies upon a particular nuclear family model; family arrangements outside of this are left in a situation of 'second best'.

Even for women who do have children, often less than half their adult working life is taken up in the direct care of offspring. Yet still the dominant lens through which they are viewed is that of domesticity. This is a difficult area to raise because for many women being a wife and mother is their primary understanding of themselves and any talk about other identities can be viewed as devaluing women and these roles. As one woman said in talking about the options presented to women of *either* being a career woman *or* having a family, 'I think the danger is that one of those has to be the norm.' That is not the intention here, nor is it to pose only alternative identities from which women must choose. Rather, the point is that there is a danger in any reductionism of a woman to one aspect of her life if it eclipses other contributions she may wish to make. In other words, while some women may focus on being a wife and mother, for other women, other aspects of their lives are also integral to how they see themselves, and to who they are.

One woman remembered how she had deliberately sought to maintain other aspects of her life when her first child was born: 'I always had this thing, you know, I don't want to be kind of somehow domesticated in the wrong sense. I mean I saw so many even in my generation, saw so many young couples, getting married, having children and they just sort of became so interested in their domestic situation that their involvement outside of that, whether it was in church or other things, became very limited. So I suppose there was always a drive in me not to let that happen ... You do have to work around [children] and your life does change and differences do occur. But we always kept on being involved and were determined to do that and I was too.' Maintaining this mix of motherhood with civic involvement is not always easy, for reasons already outlined. One young mother whose community involvement was very much an expression of her faith, spoke of the difficulty in discovering 'how to be a really good mummy, and still hold really tightly to the principles that you believe in and be active in living out your response to those principles that you really believe.'

A number of women talked of how, when they become mothers, some women actually lose their identity, and do not experience the contentment that the domestic myth suggests: 'Women have lost their identity when they have got married. And I often say, why if it's the most natural thing to have children ... why do so many women lose their identity, suffer from terrible loss of self-confidence, self-esteem, and their identity, if something is so natural?... And it's because our culture says that women have to stay in the house all the time, look after children, be happy, be ... yes, appear to be happy... And so many women aren't. They are not. I hear constantly about the mask that they're having to wear. You know, and they have lost themselves ... They feel they have to give everything up for the sake of their children, for the sake of their husband.'

After years of caring for others, one woman said, 'I thought, who is [this person], she's [her] daughter and she's [his] wife and she's [their] mum and she's the Sunday school this, and who is she? Who am I, because I didn't literally have a life and that's why I'm determined to make the best of this end of it. You know, I think I've been released to do this ... I mean my [children] are at an age when ... they're independent enough to know that mum has a life as well. I think it's good for them. I think it's good for your children too, for them to realise that you're a person. So often you're just mummy, but you actually are a person, you have things that you like to do and that you want to do and that you can do on your own. I think sometimes you need to re-evaluate your own identity.' Because of her experience she believed, 'There are times that women need away from their kids, they need to be individuals, they need to be reminded.'

The domestic trap wherein women are viewed only as wives and mothers has an effect on their church, community and political participation. Only an ideology that views women primarily as child-bearers could produce the comments to the Northern Ireland Women's

Coalition elected representatives that they should 'stand behind the loyal men of Ulster' and 'that women must start breeding for Ulster'.[17] Commenting on one woman's unsuccessful attempt to be selected as a party electoral candidate, Steven King notes that the chatter was not so much about her political opinion as 'the fact that she is a young mother'.[18] A male church leader spoke of how viewing women through the domestic lens prevents them being seen as church leaders: 'I've often commented on how many [male lay church leaders] ... whose wives would be far better [leaders] than their husbands. And again I think it's a cultural thing that the congregations tend to vote for the man because they assume the woman is at home maybe looking after the family or whatever, and they see the man as being more proactive and out and about, and working, and I think that's a pity. I think it's down to culture ... I feel there's still a sense in which the church presses women down. If not even theologically, [then] culturally and naturally, because it seems to still be a kind of natural order thing in some people's lives, that the husband is the one who's quite active in the church.' For a woman active in her church, attitudes to women at home were connected to attitudes to women in the church: 'Our men need to be taught how to understand their women in their home scene ... To respect them for the minds that they have and the abilities that they have ... If they respect them in their homes, they will respect them in their church.'

There is another aspect to the domestic trap that has a very negative effect on women, namely, the belief that women's domestic role, and not the parenting role of the father, is key to family and, hence, social stability. Built on the idea that it is innate for women to care for children, there is a much harsher social and moral judgement made on absent mothers than there is on absent fathers. One woman expressed this view in talking about women who leave their children. While she did not believe she had the right to make judgements on others and knew she was not aware of their particular circumstances, she realised, 'If I'm really, really honest, deep down inside I still, you know ... can't understand a woman that puts herself before her children.' One male church leader said, 'Generally speaking, women are tenderer than men, although some men are too. They're created in many ways for motherhood, and for, dare I say, for the home. I don't mean by that necessarily a woman is tied into the home, but I have watched in my experience that women who have been prepared to stay at home with their children when their children were small have tended to have better integrated children, and also I have seen some of them profoundly Christian through that.' Another man thought that 'to some degree families can almost survive better with an absent or partially absent father than an absent or partially absent mother'.

Against such public opinion it is perhaps not surprising that women internalise this responsibility: 'I would have the usual woman guilt thing, you know, anything that is ever wrong is my fault, the way I do it is wrong, you know, no quality time; that's why they are the way they are.' For some, women's responsibility extends further than their children. One woman remembered the comment of a man in a community group setting discussing issues of society conflict: 'I'll never forget it, he said that he blamed the partners – the wives – the women of prisoners for the crimes that they had done ... Women were to take all the guilt, all the burden of what the men had done!'

It is not, of course, that mothers do not have a valuable role to play in raising children. But blaming women for social ills leaves other causal factors, whether social or individual, uninvestigated. It is always easier to blame others than to take responsibility oneself.

For one woman, critical of the domestic ideology, the view of a mother as invaluable in a child's life is undermined by one aspect of Christian theology and practice. Speaking of a course about 'bringing up kids in the faith' she pointed out how 'This man went on and on and on, ramming on about how the first two years of a child's life, it's the mother has to be there, the mother should be there. The mother should not be out, the mother should be with it, it needs its mother, mother, mother, mother, mother ... [But] it's very strange ... for the first two years of a child's life, the mother is the all-important figure and then suddenly the image is absolutely wiped off the face of the earth, it's now Father God. Suddenly because two years you've got your mother, but after two years, totally discard any image of mother, totally discard who was the most important thing for the first two years and then just say father. Why is it not continued on, you know?' For her, and others, such omission is indicative that in reality the domestic ideology does not actually value the women that it claims to eulogise.

Those women who challenge the domestic ideology and its accompanying myth and trap are not simply rejecting one model, but offering an alternative way to build healthy families and socially responsible and involved citizens. A number of women talked about their outside activity and the consequences it had for home life as an important part in their children's personal and social development. For these women, shared household tasks among family members was a means of teaching children independence and self-reliance, equipping them to look after themselves. As one community worker put it, after nearly a year of doing everything at home as well as her full-time job, 'I convinced myself I suppose, [the children] were fit and able, well able. They can clean their own shoes and iron their own shirts and I don't think it did them any harm either, it helped them to stand on their two feet.' For one teenage boy, his mother's lack of time for home baking had resulted in him learning to cook and thus gaining a new skill.

Clearly the amount children can do depends on their age. Speaking of her older children a community worker described how 'we've encouraged them to take on responsibilities for themselves ... I don't do their washing or ironing or clean their rooms. You know, they really do look after themselves very well in that respect. And I have friends who think I'm very hard. I have female friends who think I'm very hard doing that. I know why I'm doing it, and I know it's not a bad thing to do. In fact I see it as a good thing to do with the children. I see it as empowering them, and – and, you know, helping them to be independent ... I mean I've got lots of ... female friends who work full-time, who still make sandwiches for their secondary school-aged children for their lunches. You know, they get up in the morning and make the sandwiches ... I don't understand that.' This woman saw it as part of a child's development to learn these basic life skills as naturally and easily as possible: 'What I discovered when my children were small was, you know, when the kids, like, they pull the flex of the iron when you're trying to do the ironing. They actually want to do the ironing. You know, so we tend to stop them, you know, "oh go and play," you know, or whatever, because we think that they'd enjoy playing better. If we actually listen to what they're telling us, you know, they want to do what we're doing. And my primary school children make their own school lunches.'

To some, including many of this woman's friends, such involvement by children in the practical day-to-day domestic tasks appears harsh. However, Bonnie Miller-McLemore believes children are more resilient than social mores suggest and that 'given love, children also need daily exercise at the practice of loving others as they love themselves, and this means a family system in which their pitching in is also essential to the family's functioning'.[19] And from such participation in the family, as a number of women interviewed recognised, children also learn how to be responsible within the wider community. One woman saw how her daughter had a wider social experience than many of her middle-class friends: 'She's probably been exposed to totally different lifestyles, more so than probably a lot of her friends would have been. And I think that's been really good, you know... And the kids would come out with me to visit people and some of the folk come and visit our house, so I think it's given them an exposure to a greater range of people and I think that's really good. Because I think they appreciate what they've got a lot more and hopefully accept people as people and wouldn't have the barriers that maybe some other people have just because of lack of exposure, lack of opportunity to meet different people. So I think it has affected them, I hope for the better in the end of the day.'

Other women spoke of how they talked over with their children their decision to become active in either the church or community sectors. A community worker had discussed the impact of her work with a friend, 'and she said she thought it was good for the children to know that ... there were things other than them to be involved in. And I suppose I kind of saw it as that, you know, setting a kind of example, that there were other people outside of this family that needed help and that there were other things that you could do. And they all know that the reason why I'm doing it is because I believe God has called me to it.' As another woman said, 'I also believe that as well as loving my children I have a duty, a responsibility to love my neighbours in the broader sense, that I have to also find ways of doing that too, and that [my children] have got to learn that that is part of me, and part of what ... part of being a mummy, and part of being a person is ... that I have other responsibilities to other people.'

For these women, church, community or political participation is not excluded by 'being a mummy'. While church and charitable endeavours have usually been accepted as extensions of women's domestic role, these women are talking about something more than this. They are challenging the ideology of a division between the private world of family and the public world outside the home to which women and men respectively belong. This challenge requires a re-evaluation of both spheres in order to create 'a world in which women and men can work in fulfilling ways *and* participate in families'.[20] For other women (and men) who in many ways adhere to a domestic ideology, finding it fulfilling rather than confining, such changes may appear as socially undesirable and personally threatening. However, whether any changes are forthcoming or not will depend, as with the other questions so far considered, on the extent to which the whole question of women is made a matter of priority by individuals, churches and society.

7

The Question of Priority

'The difficulty [is], having got to a position where there is such a disparity [between women and men], whether you can therefore simply ignore the gender issue altogether and just let natural development take its course.' This dilemma posed by a male church leader is about the amount of specific attention that should be given to questions around women's participation in church and society. For while it was few of those interviewed who thought that such gender issues were not deserving of consideration, the vast majority who believe the subject is important differ in terms of how much of a priority it should be.

A Matter of Importance

How important is the question of women? There are always other matters that need attention in church and society and for many people these are of more immediate concern. This is perhaps most obvious in politics where constitutional matters have dominated the political scene over the past thirty years. Resolving the constitutional question has been the focus of electoral politics in which the candidates' or parties' stance on the national question has been the overriding issue. This single issue[1] has meant that other political matters, including that of gender, whether in terms of getting women involved in the political process or policy issues pertaining to women in society, have had a low priority in mainstream politics. As Gerry Adams once said, 'When the national question is resolved, then we can all have our diversity of attitudes, religions, hang-ups.'[2] This prioritising is echoed in Unionism, and to some extent 'the majority of women share these preoccupations'.[3] The formation of the Northern Ireland Women's Coalition was an attempt to break this monopoly of focus without ignoring constitutional issues. However, the absence of a position on the national question by the NIWC is one reason given by Sinn Féin women – sympathetic to the Coalition's desire to have more women in politics – for not supporting a woman's party.[4]

One community worker recognised this dearth of attention to the question of women, which she considered to be 'maybe the biggest problem we've got in our churches actually. And I think in Northern Ireland we're distracted by – rightly so – the Catholic–Protestant relation-ships, and so have to ... deal with that. But I think the women issue is ... is as big as this, and it's been neglected because, you know, we've other problems, and I think if the Protestant–Catholic issue maybe gets a bit more sorted, women will be the next big issue.'

Certainly, most of the women interviewees involved in politics were more concerned about additional people, whether female or male, becoming active for their particular political persuasion rather than specifically in women's inclusion, although some were also keen that women should play a fuller part in politics. In part their stance is indicative of the difficulty of getting *anyone* politically involved. One male church leader commented, 'Our problem is, not only do we not say to women, we don't say to men either, that you have a public responsibility and you should be involved in political parties, you know ... again the more evangelical you are the more likely you are to dodge it unless it's a certain kind of politics.'

This lack of civic engagement was also commented on by women in the community sector. As one woman put it, among churches there is 'a failure to engage in the sort of real issues that are affecting people'.

Depicted by one community worker as the church being 'too busy gazing at its own navel', Glenn Jordan speaks of a 'legacy of introversion where the focus of church life was on serving the membership and preaching to the lost'.[5] As a woman engaged in community development said, 'Too many Christians I think see their involvement inside their own church and that's their little world, and that's where they want to stay.' The desire to get anyone breaking out of what a male church leader described as an 'evangelical cocoon' and into an engagement with the wider society, let alone the public world, has for some placed the question of women far down on the list of priorities facing the church and evangelicalism.

A similar pattern is evident in the way people view the needs facing the church in general and individual congregations. Put simply, in the words of one woman, 'I think the lost around us are much more important than what women are doing.' A male church leader spoke of how 'the greater issue for us today is the decline of our denomination. You know, that's a bigger issue, and I suppose there are people who say to me, "look, the women's issue is not a big issue."' In the context of having experienced conflict in churches around other matters and her wish to avoid encountering such trauma again, one woman said, 'There are bigger issues, much bigger issues, I think, to fight for. A church that is New Testament is a much more significant issue to fight for within the church context, for instance, than whether a woman gets to be a [church leader] or not. I mean it's really, okay it's symbolically significant, but it doesn't, it's not the key issue for me right now.' A male church leader stated, 'I kind of took a conscious decision ... that I would try and not influence people on issues which I regarded as secondary in the sense they're not essential or fundamental issues as far as the gospel is concerned.'

The kind of thinking that produces this type of discussion about priorities is one that views the question of women as an additional and secondary matter to the more important concerns of political activism, social responsibility and the mission of the church. In other words, it does not see the question of women as an integral part of the form and ethos of government, the nature and structure of society, or the kind of faith community that Christians envisage the church to be. Regarding the question of women as an additional concern puts it in competition with other interests. It becomes yet another factor taking up the limited amount of energy and resources available in the church, community and political domain. If, however, the question of women is an intrinsic part of church and civic life, rather than an optional extra, ignoring it furnishes an impoverished vision of church and society.

For example, what happens if, even as part of their contribution, women bring a different focus and perspective that would otherwise be lacking, but women are not involved in political processes? Once a political settlement is arrived at, the form of government is established and it is too late for women's contribution to shape the process. As one politically active woman said, 'I think it's very important that there are women who influence decisions. I think it's very, very important … Because if you look at any major decision it's being decided by men, and I mean our lives are run by men, and I think, you know, if we're ever going to make any real difference then we have to find a way of being influential.'

Rather than being irrelevant to concerns over denominational decline, a number of interviewees saw the question of women as vital to the church's future. One female church leader believed that the church's failure to consider gender matters was 'one of the big reasons a lot of people rejected the church. People just see something that they don't see is right and isn't balanced. And the fact is we've more women in churches than men, far more women, and they actually do the bulk of the work with very little recognition. And that's a really bad witness.' As another woman commented, the 'male-dominated elderly world of the church is not going anywhere very fast … It's not living out gospel values, it isn't being a good example of anything to people outside of the church, it's not making us effective and it isn't cutting ice at local level.' A male church leader believed that, 'the reality is, and I don't see any scriptural hindrance to this, that if we do not come to terms in the church with the role of women and allow them to be the people God calls them to be and to do what God has gifted them to do, then the church that doesn't recognise that will only go into retrenchment and decay and decline.'

A female lay church leader saw the question of women as central to the mission to which the church is called: 'I must admit, it drives me round the bend to hear people talking about the whole women thing as if it is some sort of peripheral issue. "Yes it would be addressed if we had the time to address it, but let's face it, it's not what we're really all about, we're about evangelising the worlds and the nations", et cetera, et cetera. Well that will never happen unless you address the whole women issue ... The point about the church is that they've been following their mission to a certain extent with a hand tied behind their back, because they haven't released women in the way they ought to. So to me it is not a peripheral issue, it is an absolutely central issue and needs to constantly be brought central stage in all that we're doing. Otherwise we will fail to be about the mission that God has called us to.'

A number of interviewees voiced how, far from being a secondary matter, the question of women was intrinsic to the gospel: 'If you believe in the kingdom it means you really have to think about how you relate to other people and how you treat other people and therefore I am concerned about how we as a church treat other people, particularly women – because I'm starting to want to know how I've been treated and how I've let other people treat me as a woman.' A community worker felt that the question of women 'has a much greater significance because I think it speaks about respect for people, respect for individuals and the inherent kind of value on people'. In the words of another community worker: 'It's to do with human beings relating to each other and us needing to find other ways of doing that where we're not causing damage in every direction ... In a sense we're only at the starting block as regards women in things like politics and powerful positions ... I kind of feel women's development issues in church and community are so basic and long-term that, you know, we're only starting on a lot of it. And we're still dabbling at the edges really in terms of what's there, compared with the structural things that need to be changed.' Put simply by another female interviewee: 'I think in Christ we are one and we are equal and it should be the church that's giving the lead in this and yet that's not the case at all.'

To talk of the question of women as integral to church and society is not to suggest that this eclipses all other matters. Indeed, it can be a combination of factors that affect women's participation in church, community and politics. A number of women spoke of how it was the mix of them being young and female that was problematic for them in their particular sphere of activity.[6] For some women their lay status as well as their sex meant they had additional prejudices to overcome. For a number of women in the community sector, it was their involvement with Catholic and nationalist communities that contributed to the conflict they encountered in their home churches. One woman spoke of how her political viewpoint impacted on the way she was treated. There were also class barriers that created difficulties in other ways. These factors do not operate in isolation of gender, rather they can mesh together to produce particular difficulties for each woman, depending on her situation. This variety points to the fact that all women are not the same, which is not to say that women do not have much in common as women. This book has concentrated on the common questions facing evangelical women in their church, community and political participation. However, different social locations in terms of education, economic opportunities, age, and for evangelical women, church environment, can produce diverse experiences for women.

Whether or not the question of women is seen as a priority depends on the extent to which gender is believed to be an ongoing issue in society. In other words, whether or not there are unresolved matters about the way women and men relate and function in church and society, particularly the continuing discrimination women experience *because of their gender*. If, for example, you consider that there is no systemic prejudice against women in religious and social institutions and that a meritocracy exists whereby women can generally participate without hindrance, then you are unlikely to consider that special attention to gender issues is required. As one woman laughingly put it, 'I personally tend to see people as people other than as just men or just women. Bar ballroom dancing and sex, really the gender's not that important, you know! The rest of it [is] person to person. Maybe we talk too much about gender, maybe.'

This emphasis on viewing people as people, rather than as women and men, was expressed by several interviewees in regard to their participation in church and society. A male church leader wanted to pose a different question to one about women: 'How important is ... the ministry of all believers in the church? I would have thought crucial and core. Therefore how important is the ministry of women who are believers in the church? Crucial and important and to the core ... I picture the church as the body of Christ, ministering within itself towards itself and then ministering out into the world. Now that's what the church is, and that's core. That's crucial and women are part of that just as men are. And that's I think the tragedy of the church, that it's not functioning as the body of Christ, and it's not functioning with the ministry of all believers, and it needs to. And if it does then women will be to the fore as much as men will be ... So I don't think I'd say anything different about men and women in that area, just that everybody who's a believer should be doing something in terms of witnessing and service for the Lord, if not for the church. But women don't, women don't feature any more than men in that, I don't think.'

An emphasis on the ministry of all believers, while valid in and of itself, implies that there are not, at the present time, particular issues facing women that are different to those facing men. It does not take into account the sexual division of labour inherent in the participation question, the realities experienced by women in the question of inclusion, the nuances of the difference question, the influence of the question of authority, or the practicalities and ideology of the domestic question. All of these affect women's participation in the 'body of Christ', particularly as the social organisation of that body has largely been formed and directed by male leadership over the years. Put simply, while there are of course matters in common for women and men in their participation in church and society, there also are issues that are different and frequently more difficult to negotiate for women than there are for men. Treating everyone the same, without a consideration of gender, is in effect to the disadvantage of women because it does not take into account the variety of questions around women's participation that this book has attempted to raise.

Hence, while some are a little uncomfortable with an emphasis on women's participation *as women*, wanting rather to live in a world where gender was not an issue, they nevertheless expressed the need in the current reality to give attention to the question of women. As one woman remarked, 'I don't think women's participation is more vital than a man's participation, it's just that at the minute it's a big issue, because women are having to fight for that basic right to be involved, and to be accepted and to be heard.' Another woman commented that 'because women have been in the back seat for so long, it's important for them you know to be seen to be embraced and encouraged and involved and not kept in the back seat.' A female church leader felt that women's participation in church and society was not 'much more important than men's, except that it's important that it should be equally heard and given ... equal opportunity with the provision for input or for pushing ahead with whatever they want. It's just about making it possible.' If you accept that, to some extent, women's involvement needs to be 'made possible', then you are likely to support some attention to gender and to endorse some equal opportunity measures to safeguard women in their endeavours.

For others who view the discrimination against women as more systemic and deeply rooted in attitudes and institutions, and who have experienced sexist treatment themselves or witnessed it towards others, there is a more overt identification with a focus on gender and the question of women. One woman spoke of the 'incredible discrimination in the church, which I really believe is there and people are trying to push under the carpet all the time. Because I don't think people realise the pain that is involved in that discrimination. And I have first-hand experience of it and watched other people experience it. I know it's much wider than [the church] and it's to do with [society].' A community worker agreed: 'I think women are discriminated against in many ways in society, and I think that is changing but it's changing slowly.' Speaking of the experience women received in a particular religious institution, a female interviewee stated: 'I mean the treatment of women [there] has been absolutely appalling. I mean it's a scandal and it should have been exposed. And, you know, it's just a total and utter disgrace that it should go on within a church context.'

For women who echo these thoughts, attention to the question of women is of paramount importance and can only be dealt with by a direct focus: 'In terms of practice I think we need to identify what the problem is and ... where women are at, and young women are at, and actively work towards changing that, and then that should in turn change the structures. There's probably a meeting of minds required on both levels, but I would say ... this isn't on the agenda or recognised in the majority of places or churches, so probably the first step is taking notice that there is a problem.'

Those who view the discrimination against women as systemic are aware of mindsets and practices that impact on the lives of women. Hence, for example, while one woman can say about the use of inclusive language, 'I've never really been bothered by it myself so it's not really an issue for me', other women consider that the continued use of exclusive language undermines all women because it perpetuates the notion that normative humanity is male and not female.[7] As one woman asked, '*Rise up o men of God*, right, what are the women supposed to do?'

Similarly, two women interviewed who had successful professional lives and civic engagement outside of the religious sector, belonged to church congregations where women were not involved in leadership. Having no sense of calling or desire in the area of church leadership, let alone time to give in that direction, these women existed happily with the male status quo of their congregations. Given their own fruitful endeavours in other spheres, they did not see a connection between the attitude towards women in their particular congregations and the story of women in church and society throughout Northern Ireland. In contrast, Jane Shaw argues:

> The participation of women in leadership ... tells us something about how, and whether, women are valued in the rest of the church ... Whenever any who have been traditionally and historically excluded from leadership roles in the churches ... begin to take up those roles and occupy those spaces, then we show that all of us are made in the image and likeness of God, and matter to and are loved by God equally.[8]

Not all who want a focus on women necessarily believe that this should result in a new social order. Some thought that the question of women was important because of the need to affirm women in their traditional roles, viewing these and the women who fulfil them as undervalued in church and society. One woman commented, 'I think women are the central pin of it all but ... you don't have to be upfront all [the] time to run things either in society in general or in the church ... I think we are made by the same God. We've got the same mental capacities. We've the same abilities to do things and we need to have respect, men do need to respect that in us and they don't need to look at us and say, we're only a woman.' As a male church leader put it, 'I think [women] need to be allowed to make an equal contribution to the men. I think their contribution is subtly different, and there needs to be the room for those subtle differences to be appreciated and to be valued. I think they currently are under-represented in Northern Ireland, their contribution is neither invited nor adequately respected when it comes. But I think, I think that they do need to be viewed as equals.'

The current status quo within evangelicalism towards the question of women is, in the words of one woman involved in the community, 'almost a hush-hush thing, and women are very much still in the background'. One woman noted that 'the question tends not to arise until there's a need within the church, and then they start to sort of look at women and possibly maybe using women then, which is I think abusive to some extent. If we're to be treated, you know, if women are to have a role it's got to be sort of a constant thing.'

Addressing the question of women is no simple task. As one community worker reflected, 'the whole issue of how to be a woman with equal status ... needs to be, really be debated and discussed, because there's lots of ideals floating about, but, you know, how it actually happens, how people can feel that they have equal value alongside men in reality, is still, is really complex ... And how to do it within the context of, you know, a faith and a belief in trying to live out your faith and all, that's really, [it] still needs to be worked out, or struggled with.'

Perpetuating the status quo of non-attention to the question of women may seem to many to be the least contentious route. There are, however, consequences to failing to address this question, consequences that weigh more heavily on women than on men.

A Matter of Consequence

There are many contexts where it appears that there is no need to give attention to the question of women. In the absence of overt conflict around or even any discussion about women's participation, the impression usually is that gender is not an issue in these situations. While it is possible that this is an accurate impression, that indeed all involved are satisfied with the current participation, representation and working relationship of women and men, it cannot automatically be assumed. For silence on the question of women does not necessarily infer contentment with the status quo.

Because of the numerous difficulties that arise in women's church, community and political participation, women often diffuse actual or potentially contentious situations by their behaviour. As one woman said, 'I think probably I haven't encountered as much conflict because of my own way of dealing with it.' She commented that, anticipating that difficulties will arise over their involvement, women themselves often 'actually circumvent' conflict either before it arises or by acting to resolve it once it first emerges.

One way of doing this is to physically withdraw from certain contexts. A few women spoke of absenting themselves from situations where they knew their presence *as women* was causing difficulties or division. In one instance, where her presence would be 'almost a red rag to a bull', a woman delegated her leadership role to a man, both in order not to cause others offence and to protect herself from the discomfort of the hostility she would encounter.

On other occasions women simply do not raise the issue of gender. Speaking of a few opportunities denied to her in church because she was female, one woman 'would just carry that myself' and not discuss the matter with anyone in her congregation. Another woman did not suggest that women's participation in her church should be part of its review of congregational leadership because she knew it would prevent other beneficial changes that otherwise would be made. In this environment of existing dispute and division, as far as the question of women is concerned, 'what I believe in my head is not acted out perhaps in how I handle it in church life'. A woman involved in church leadership spoke of how, 'on the woman thing, I would have tended to want to keep my head down' so as not to 'cause any more trouble than there already is'.

Women also spoke of how they worked to establish good working relationships with others. By not focusing on gender issues even though they were relevant to various situations, one woman maintained an amenable work environment with her colleagues and those to whom she was responsible: 'I think I am the one who works at the relationship. If I was to become much more aggressive ... you know, and challenge a lot more, I think I'd have a lot tougher time.' In some instances women actually work to resolve the discomfort of male peers who find themselves working with women. Sensing an envy of her ability from her male colleagues, one woman spoke of playing down her role and doing the 'meek little thing' so that the men involved did not have to confront and deal with the issues of identity, status and power raised for them by her participation. In effect this means she took on a responsibility that was actually the men's in that situation: 'I've had to work alongside men who've been quite threatened and would try to make it my problem and at times I've embraced it as mine and I'm not so soft now.'

While usually unnoticed by others, such activity means women are carrying the burden of silence on the question of women. In other words, not discussing the kind of issues explored in this book does not make them go away. Rather, women continue to handle the consequences of their participation, largely because they have to. One woman reflected on her response to the conflict she encountered in a religious setting because of her gender: 'I suppose at some level I feel that everything is my responsibility. It's my responsibility to forgive people. It's my responsibility to live with the hurt that I have. It's my responsibility for the fact that I'm not recognised. It's my responsibility to make sure [I do my job]. And at no level does the church have any responsibility for me, nor do they see it. I am just there – I am somebody they use.'

Put another way, many women do not have the option to ignore the question of women because they live the question. In this sense, women and men are differently situated in relationship to gender issues: 'I mean it's like people saying, well really, you know, we're agreed on the essentials, [but] things like women, that's like peripheral. Well it's not peripheral if you're a woman. You know, it's totally vital to who you are and what you are and all the rest of it.' In contrast, in the words of a male church leader, 'The role of women, you see, it's easy for a man to say, "oh it's no big deal, it's no problem".'

Another man illustrated this difference for women and men when talking about his view that women should not teach and preach to men. His experience of listening to 'a woman who has a preaching, a teaching ministry that I appreciated and benefited from' led him to ask the question 'well then, how come the Scripture says that a woman has not to teach a man?' While he held to his original view by accepting what he believed to be the scriptural revelation, and 'the mind of God on these things', he observed that his wife, in facing the same question, 'would struggle more with that'. The implications of the same viewpoint are clearly different for this man's wife than for him.

It is not that men are not involved in the question of women. Clearly they are. But their general position of dominance and advantage in church and society often makes it both harder for them to appreciate women's situation and less inclined to work towards change. As a community worker noted, 'I just think so many men are very blind as to how they have made women feel second class.' The comment of one woman that 'It worries me sometimes that it is always women only asking, you know. Why is it mainly women asking these questions?' is answered by another community worker: 'I don't think it's particularly [good] for men, that they get away with, you know, treating other people as less than equal because of their sex ... I think that it's better for everybody if we have a more even balance in some respects, but I do think that men will pay a price for that in some ways, because I think that men have for so long held the, you know, the sort of lead role, the dominant role in society that as that changes I think it might be quite difficult for men to adjust. But I wonder whether men are ready for, you know, changes almost being forced on them by legislation and things like that when they're not necessarily perhaps ready to relinquish some of the power and authority that they've had, and even in very small ways, you know, even within … family life.'

In practical terms there are consequences for men in women's participation across the sexual division of labour, which is not simply about crossing this traditional divide but also about dismantling it. In the words of one female church leader, 'I think men and women should be equal in every area, but … until we have equal numbers of men in the children's work then we're not equal … You could have equal numbers of men and women as ministers but unless you have equal numbers of men and women teaching the children on a Sunday morning, you know, unless you have equal men and women serving the coffee and doing those things, well then we're not [equal]. So it has to go right across the board, so it's not just about [leadership], it's about everything.'

While there are implications for men in considering the question of women, to not do so creates less disturbance in their lives than to give it attention. Hence in the church, one woman observed, 'I think it has been sidelined and there have been a few brave men who've been wanting to get involved and wanting to think it through and wanting to encourage women to be released in the church. But for the most part most men can get on with their lives and, you know, it doesn't really affect them one way or the other, so there's no pressure on them really to be made to think about it. I think we need to make it more main stage. [And in] so many places, if we're talking about this issue, [the men] say, but it's not a problem for our women. But nobody has ever asked them, you know. And of course it's not a problem, you know, it's not a problem for the [men] because they're just happy to carry on as it is.'

While men may happily 'carry on as it is', this is not so for women. Living the question of women, particularly in contexts that produce conflict of various kinds, can take a personal toll on women. While not all women encounter prolonged antagonism or ongoing difficulties, others do. Sometimes this is specific against them as individuals and at other times women are affected more generally by forms of exclusion or attitudes and assumptions about sex roles. A number of women spoke of mental or emotional health issues faced by themselves, by other women they knew, and sometimes by their mothers, because of the restrictions they faced as women.

The personal toll that may be exacted on women in living the question of women is articulated by one interviewee who from an early age felt her calling to be in church ministry despite, at that time, being in a context that excluded women from leadership: 'I just think that for my journey and what I've had to come through to reach this point, the emotional pain of it all has been vastly underestimated. Not [by] myself, by others; they don't realise the emotional pain that can be involved in the demeaning of a human being on the basis of their gender. It's not a trivial issue, it really isn't. It caused me more pain ... and it still leaves the effect today. And it all stems back from the fact that as a young teenage girl with a feeling on the inside that she wanted to be something, that I was made to feel that my life wasn't worth as much as somebody else's life and that permeated me. It just permeated me and I think I paid a high emotional price to get here today, you know... But I think the church as a whole underplays the emotional damage it can do.'

As another woman makes clear, the effect of contention over women's participation and inclusion may be profoundly personal: 'When men, after opposing the ordination of women in whatever scenario ... when they come to you afterwards and say, "it's nothing against you personally," they haven't got a clue. Because of course it's something against you personally. You're a woman. And there's little you can do about that ... This is the way you were born, they're talking about the way you were born. And they're talking about the way you were born not being acceptable in their eyes, and they don't get that, they don't get that that is therefore about you personally.'

Another consequence of living the question of women is women's felt need in some way to prove themselves as capable for the task or position in question. An ordained woman expressed this in regard to her preaching: 'As a woman, I particularly feel that there's always that sense – there are some real conservative types in the congregation who wouldn't particularly be keen on a woman teaching – so therefore if I'm going to do it, I've got to do it well and that's my pressure.' Speaking of a previous employment situation one interviewee observed, 'I had to do twice the work to prove I was half as good. And it was quite true ... I was just simply a woman in a man's world. And that used to annoy me because I used to think you had to do so much to be accepted.'

Another woman recognised this same dynamic with the female students taking on a traditionally male subject at university: 'I would say most of the girls who went in when I went in would have been really pushing hard to get the best degree they could get to prove that they could do it. I don't think the girls now feel the need to do that. I think it's a good thing. But I always thought when we got to the point when we had sort of pass degrees being handed out to the girls as well as the boys, then there would be equality.' Her comments indicate that it is not simply women proving themselves to their own satisfaction or for their own sense of achievement or integrity, but doing so in relation to men. Put succinctly by a woman in church leadership, 'I do sort of think that it's true still that women have to be better [than men], to do the same things.'

A woman in politics supported this idea: 'I know ... women who have gone for selection within the party who ... feel that we have to be better than the man to have a chance of succeeding in selections.' Speaking of a variety of ways that women engage in church and society another female interviewee stated: 'It's almost as if whenever a woman comes into a role she's immediately being judged with much stricter standards than a man and that is not just by any stretch of the imagination.' Speaking of an ordained woman in her congregation another interviewee observed, 'Now she's a very capable woman. And, you know, because she is capable and is good at what she's doing, people don't have an issue. But if she failed ... if she wasn't so good at her job, I wonder would they tolerate her? They would tolerate a man quicker.'

A community worker who had experienced this disparity no longer considered that in her situation it was possible to live up to what was expected of her: 'Part of me would have said prove by your works that you can do it and eventually surely they'll see a woman can do the job. Now I think ... I have proved that women can do the job ... But it'll never be enough.' Another community worker echoed this sentiment in regard to not being given the same recognition or respect as a male colleague: 'I tried to fight it for years, to try and get accepted, worked maybe ten times as hard doing things to be accepted, you know, that I'm doing the work. But in my mind now I say that I know I've done the work, and somebody up there knows, and they're my boss.'

A further consequence of the unresolved questions around women's participation is the pressure women may feel not only in regard to their own performance, but how other women will be judged because of them.

Women in church leadership particularly expressed this sense of responsibility: '[In most cases] where a female minister is going, they are the first female to have been in that situation. And that has an impact on you ... I'm aware anyway that some of the things I do may well reflect on other female ministers ... It's necessary to keep it in your mind and to realise that, you know, accountability is too strong a word, but responsibility, that you need to be responsible in your actions, because I think sometimes people haven't been. And that has had a negative impact, and that makes it more difficult, and there are others who have had to forge the path, and make it – and because they have done that it has made it a lot easier for us.'

Another woman spoke of how she feared her decision to change the nature of her involvement in church leadership 'might be misinterpreted as, well, you see, women can't do it'. While men may make decisions about particular positions, the difference is that, as another woman noted, 'they won't be feeling, oh well I'll be letting the men down if I do this'.

One woman encapsulates the sense of burden that follows being one of the relatively few female church leaders whose 'performance' may impinge on other women: 'It's very hard to think of yourself, you know, in this whole woman thing, it's very hard to think of yourself as being some kind of example or role model. I mean that's just awful. That's a terrible burden for anybody to have to bear ... There's also the weight of the people who are coming after you, like you don't just look to your ancestral tradition or your denominational tradition, you don't just look to your peers, but you look to the women coming after you and you have to think, is this furrow I'm ploughing going to be useful to them?'

These women are not commenting on the notion of modelling good leadership *per se*. Rather their remarks relate to the sense that the validity of all women as church leaders is made to be dependent on them as particular individuals.

Given the variety of aspects of participation to be negotiated, it is perhaps not surprising that some women take a cautious approach to church or civic involvement. Thinking about difficulties encountered, a woman spoke of her work among other women in churches: 'I have found that I have been extremely careful about what I have done. By that I mean, I made a rule that I never went anywhere unless I was asked.' Another woman who wanted to organise a woman's Bible study in her congregation hesitated because 'I worry, you know, that I'm going to cause trouble', in case it was taken as an implicit criticism of the provision of Bible teaching in the church.

Thinking of developing her teaching gift, one woman talked of feeling 'to some extent caution. Because while I know this enthusiasm is here I'm also very strongly aware that people whom I most respect in terms of their Christian faith and their Christian commitment, the people who are really strong evangelicals are the people who would be more likely to be against women taking that kind of role, and there's always somewhere at the back of my mind, am I really doing the right thing in even contemplating this? Maybe I'm wrong and they're right, and there's also a reservation too about – if I go on and sort of speak in the church and so forth – about hurting those people. People who have supported me through my Christian life, who have supported me when I've needed prayer, could possibly be very hurt if I go on and do this.' While she was concerned about the effect her participation may have on others, she also was aware of the implications for herself in how others would relate to her: 'They would actually feel that this person – she can't really be a Christian if she's going to do that. I mean there is that element within the group that I intermingle with, and having your commitment questioned is one of the most hurtful things that can happen.'

A woman involved in politics attributed women's reticence to take risks to their expectation of negative consequences. While she did not consider this to have been her own experience, she observed it about women in general: 'I think women are more afraid to take risks, because they'll be hit harder if it goes wrong ... because they're women probably. Although I just hate to say that. But ... it's nearly expected that you'll do things wrong, so ... I mean we have to work harder, I suppose. We have to work harder to merit anything. Fair or not, that's how it is. And it's horrible ... But I think that then makes women more concerned that if they take a risk and it goes wrong, what the consequences will be for them. Men take a risk – if it goes wrong, oh well deal with it, you know. But women are more concerned with the consequences.' If she is correct in her understanding that women are 'hit harder' if their endeavours are not successful, it is little wonder that women are more hesitant to take risks.

Even a young woman in her twenties had modified her contributions to discussions because of repeated ridicule and disdain: 'I used to be more vocal about [inclusive language] ... I think at times, oh that does matter, you know ... and [so] you make comments, and people are just like, "oh, don't be so stupid."' An older woman voiced the continuing internal questioning she went through in her various endeavours: 'The next thing I have to say to myself, "how easy am I going to be put off here? How difficult is it?" If someone gets up and says something very embarrassing and you're the only woman in the room, how do you deal with it? Do you let it go and let it get the next time a bit more outrageous? Or do you say from day one, hang on, I'm not going to put up with that behaviour ... That's a very difficult thing to deal with.' She went on to say that 'I've known the bravest of women who have walked away from it and said "forget it. I'm not going to be doing that."'

Such negative experiences can affect a woman's confidence. As a church leader put it: 'It's very easy to do yourself down. It's also very easy to dismiss anything that anybody says that's good about you, because you're really not used to that, you know.' The subtleties of this influence were articulated by a woman involved in politics: 'When you're in a room it's not so much what's explicit, it's what's implicit, and, you know, if you're sitting in a room, and you're particularly a bit nervous about being there anyway, and to be frozen ... can drain you of your confidence.'

Such treatment can also drain women of their energy. As one interviewee put it, 'you get tired of always being that extra bit assertive, you know, you do get tired of always having to push, push.' Given the duration of the difficulties she had encountered, one community worker acknowledged she had ceased some of her striving and rather now, 'I have to admit that ... I almost get to just accept quite a lot, and I don't know if that's a good thing, you know, I don't know if that's a good thing or what, now accepting this is the way it is, I can't change it ... Am I giving up too easy on that? But I think ... for my own health and strength and that, and my own energy, I mean there's a lot of it I do need to give up, and say "right, okay, it's their problem now." I mean I can't change it. I can't change the way a lot of people think and that, but I can change my own way that I think, and how to handle [it all].' Speaking of other women in community sector leadership roles she observed that they 'have that skill there to – to push themselves, you know. But I've also seen what it's done to them ... I mean it took me a while to realise that part of that was because they were the woman, and that's why they were having so many problems, you know, in their work as a leadership role ... because they're having to work nearly ten times as hard in a leadership role than what a man would have to do to get that respect, or to get recognised.'

From the stance of living the question of women, women frequently make choices about whether or not to raise issues of women's participation and inclusion. They try and assess the various factors involved in such a decision: the need to maintain good working relationships; their own self-respect; the extent to which pursuing the question of women will be seen as a hindrance to the task at hand; their past experiences in talking about gender; their hopes for the future; the situation of other women; the implications for men; the concern to do what is right in any instance. Frequently there is no one right way to handle the situations that emerge. And often too, there is a sense that no matter how they respond they cannot please everyone involved.

Women's participation in church, community and politics is not only a story of struggle. It is also a narrative of women's personal satisfaction and a considerable contribution to church and society. A number of women, either because of the particular activities in which they are engaged, or because of the people they work with, do not have to negotiate much of the conflict experienced by others. And for those who do encounter hostile environments and practices, the difficulties of their involvement are not what these women would wish necessarily to emphasise. However, it is the fact of the more negative experiences that demonstrates the need for more attention to the question of women. For the question is not only about the stories of individuals, but about the overall identity, status and position of women in church and society. Exploring the question of women, therefore, is not simply focused on overcoming the more negative aspects of women's experience. It is also about constructive, honest and just Christian ways of relating between women and men in church, community and political arenas. In other words, it is about the kind of Christian community and civic society we wish to envision and bring into being.

A Matter of Culture and Theology

A major reason why women and men choose not to prioritise the question of women is its association with feminism, which for so many has negative connotations. Hence, those who spoke in favour of women's increased participation in church and society were keen to find ways of accomplishing this that were not stereotypically feminist, that is, strident, aggressive and anti-male. A politically active woman was keen to further women's advancement and influence 'without being seen as feminist in that sense, you know, [of] "here they go again".' A female church leader thought women's participation was important, 'but I wouldn't be strident about it, you know. I'm always a wee bit nervous of making a big issue or speaking out a lot about it, for the simple reason that I don't want to be seen as someone who's campaigning for women's rights or whatever.' Another woman who was involved in a church context that did not bar women from any sphere of participation explained, 'I don't beat a drum, you know, to liberate my sisters who are in [other denominations].'

Again, because of stereotypical perceptions of feminism, a male church leader spoke of preferring 'evolution rather than revolution' in regard to women's inclusion in his denomination, even while he acknowledged this meant 'a lot of women have been very patient, maybe some of them too patient, in what they've been willing to put up with'. Similarly, a woman spoke of how campaigning for women was counter-productive. She was opposed to 'us starting to fight for things before it's the right time. I think there has to be a right time. I think if we're prepared to wait for the right time, and go at the right pace, we can achieve more.'

Some women expressed a concern for how men would perceive the attention to the question of women: 'It needs to be addressed in a sensitive way, because I think men are beginning to get – well I don't know what you'd call it, feminist fatigue, where there's, "here we go, we've heard this so often … and we all know that women are special, and why are they still harping on about their needs?"… [So] I think it needs to be handled sensitively and the way it is presented I guess would need to be done in a – in a way that doesn't seem to be divisive or mud-flinging or negative or critical.' So often in comments like these the emphasis is on ensuring that the manner in which the question is raised does not become a barrier to its content being heard.[9]

Yet despite this aversion to being identified as a 'militant fighting woman', or being 'feminist in a bad way',[10] it is the impact of social changes of which feminism is a significant part that is continuing to influence evangelicalism today, albeit not directly. For women's increasing participation in the labour force and in social and public arenas inevitably influences evangelical women, even if it has less immediate bearing on the organisation and mindset of the religious institutions and faith communities to which they belong. From a personal viewpoint, for some women the often stark contrast of their church experience to that of their sphere of employment or activism leads them to examine the situation of women in their churches. A community worker observed how women 'have no role within the leadership of the church or a very limited role within the leadership of the church. And yet, within their job, they are, you know, involved in decision-making, policy setting, management, leadership, whatever, and it's as if the church doesn't recognise that as being valid within the church setting.' Such disparity of experience between church and non-church contexts resulted in one woman stating: 'It's much easier to be a woman in the community than it is to be a woman in the church.'

For some, any challenge suggested by this incongruity is resolved by isolating churches from outside influence. Hence one male church leader considered that 'when you go outside of the church I would feel that the principles that I feel govern how we operate, they don't apply to the world. They apply to the church.' For another man, however, there was a need 'to be thinking what is God saying, what's happening in the world, what are the swirls out there, and the swirls at the moment are the identity of male and female, inspiration of Scripture, things like that, and we need to be thoughtfully dealing with these things in the life of the church.'

However, whichever stance is taken – a model of separation from the rest of society, or a model of conversation with the rest of society – cultural mores are making an impact on evangelicalism. For despite the hostility to the common negative perception of feminism, the notion of gender equality that is very much a part of public discourse is embraced by nearly all the women interviewed. Their concern for women's increased participation in church, community and politics echoes the public rhetoric of equality for women. That there is endorsement of equal opportunity measures and even some acknowledgement, albeit reluctant, of the necessity for affirmative action indicates that women wish this rhetoric to become reality. But while welcoming appropriate structures and good practices, many evangelical women also are aware that women's inclusion involves more than legislation and proper procedures. Through their experiences of conflict and difficulty, they know that the question of women is about identity, power and theology. Here too contemporary culture has conversed with evangelical faith and practice.

The influence of the public discourse of gender equality has infused evangelical notions of male authority so that even those who maintain an understanding of the prerogative of a husband in decision-making do so in the context of the marriage relationship viewed as a partnership. This in itself has the potential to put traditional, gendered, domestic roles under scrutiny. Women's personal empowerment through employment situations, and their discovery and development of their gifts and abilities through service in church and civic engagement, has led many to challenge the notion of an ultimate male authority within the church, and others to question whether the existence of such authority should prevent women from full participation. So despite the fact that many evangelical women still live and work in churches which by and large continue to operate male headship, many women reject it. They do not reject Scripture, however. Rather, they find affirmation in the Bible for their beliefs and activities. This is perhaps one of the most crucial implications for evangelicalism – the growing articulation of theology and faith that facilitates women's fuller participation within church and society than traditional gender roles permitted. And this is not only in terms of issues of male authority, but also in terms of a spirituality that concerns the service of individual believers on the basis of their gifting and not of their gender.

While those interviewed for this book give evidence of this emerging articulation of evangelical faith and practice, much of evangelicalism, probably the larger part, and certainly the public voice, contests it. Sometimes it does this directly, it frequently does it by continuing to enact exclusive models of participation, and it does it by neglect of the question of women. However, even within an argument for a traditional male headship, there are traces of the influence of the public rhetoric of gender equality. Most of the contemporary explication of this position involves stating a spiritual equality while asserting a difference in role and/or nature for women. Women's spiritual equality, which in previous generations did not need to be affirmed, and was often denied, is now a part of the spiritually equal yet materially differentiated argument that maintains male authority. And perhaps, too, what is thought to be a change from 'aggressive, excessive, anti-male, over-the-top' feminists to those speaking on the question of women with 'much more measured, wise and accessible tones'[11] is not so much a change in the messengers but a change in the context of those who receive the message. It may be that those advancing the cause of women do not need to be as forceful in their viewpoint because of the current climate. Or it may be that some of those listening are now able to hear what is being said because they have become accustomed to ideas that thirty years ago were simply too alien.

While recognising the impact of the current social climate on evangelicalism and on some evangelical women in particular, it is also observable that less attention has been given to the fuller implications of embracing the notion of women's equality and inclusion in church and society. After all, if women's participation is not simply no longer prohibited but rather viewed as an integral part of the outworking of our involvement in human society and faith communities, then there are inferences around the question of women for how we think and function in church and society. Perhaps in part this lack of more detailed attention is because, as one woman commented, evangelicals lack the language to discuss these matters, which for so long have been veiled in silence and assumption. Perhaps as well, the implications are too enormous for evangelicalism to contemplate.

It may be also that hostility and defensiveness towards feminism has prevented evangelicalism from engaging in fruitful dialogue with the considerable contribution of feminist thinking. For in the past thirty years feminism has grown as a movement, developing the basic idea of equality to consider issues of difference, female embodiment and experience, and matters of identity, all of which could help evangelicalism explore the implications of the question of women.

What this research shows is a picture of a part of evangelicalism in Northern Ireland that is currently negotiating with the times in which it lives in regard to women. Its response is fractured, not unified. It is certainly confused in places, and hostile in others. It is not a revolution; it is not conscious or self-aware enough for that. It has the potential to be disruptive of evangelical norms and practices, but due to its fractured nature and hesitant demeanour, it is highly doubtful that it will be. For some this will be poor relief to the unwelcome infiltration of secular standards. For others, who prefer small, gentle steps in addressing women's participation, it will be a good thing. And for those who envision a community of women and men in the church and society that is both a critique and positive alternative to the current state of affairs, it will not be enough.

Appendix One
The Interview Process

In order to identify women to be approached in regard to an interview for the project, a list was drawn up of evangelical women known to be active in church, community or politics. A number of other individuals with knowledge of women's activism in these areas were consulted in compiling this list. The women interviewed were also asked, at the end of the interview, for the names of other women active in these sectors that it would be useful for the project to know about. (This continued up to the final few weeks of the interview process.) In addition, notices were placed in two evangelical Christian news sheets (with a combined circulation of almost 4,000), explaining the project and inviting interested women to take part. From this accumulation of names, women were identified to reflect a variety of forms of participation, ages, marital and maternal status, geographical location, and denominational affiliation. The primary identification was of the different sectors and it was not always possible to know, for example, about the denominational affiliation of a para-church worker, community worker or political activist before meeting that person. Out of 78 women with whom there was direct contact requesting an interview, 70 interviews were completed.

The denominational profile of these 70 women was as follows: the Presbyterian Church in Ireland, 25; the Church of Ireland, 14; the Methodist Church in Ireland, 9; the Life Link network, 9; Baptist churches, 8; and 5 from among Pentecostal, Evangelical Presbyterian and independent fellowships. (Because of the women's past involvement in different denominations, the experience and influence of denominations not listed here was also included in the research.) With a few exceptions there were women from each denomination, each age group, from throughout Belfast and Northern Ireland, both married and single, with and without children, who were active in each of the three sectors being examined, that is, church, community and politics. In terms of educational profile, the majority of women (47) had university degrees, 14 of the women had professional or vocational qualifications (as indeed did some of the women who also had degrees), and 11 women had school and/or secretarial qualifications.

The male interviewees were chosen not only as those who would have experience of congregational church life and knowledge of their denomination, but also because among them they held a range of views on women's church participation. Of 11 men approached, 10 interviews were completed. The denominational profile of 8 of the men was determined bearing in mind the institutional size of the three main Protestant denominations, and for 2, to reflect the percentages of women from smaller Protestant churches who were interviewed. Hence, there were 3 men each from the Presbyterian Church in Ireland and the Church of Ireland, 2 from the Methodist Church in Ireland, and 1 Baptist and 1 from the Life Link network.

All the interviews were conducted between March and December 2000. Three pilot interviews were held with women from the list of known activists after each of which there was opportunity for the interviewee to comment on the process. As no changes were made in the interview schedules after this point, these three interviews were included in the project findings. The interviews were held mainly in homes, places of work, or location of church, community or political activity. The interviews were taped and then transcribed. The actual taped interviews lasted in total for 120 hours. However, visits with the 80 interviewees lasted 166 hours in total.

Appendix Two
Interview Schedules

WOMEN IN CHURCH

I'd like to begin by asking you about your responsibilities in the church.

Tell me about your involvement in the church (para-church organisation) and how you came to be doing this.

Can you tell me both the good things about what you do and the things you don't like?

How have you been received by other people as a woman doing what you do?

Do you experience conflict because you are a woman?
– And if so, where does this conflict come from and how do you handle it?

What would you like to do in the future; where do you see yourself going next?

For women in para-church organisations, I'd like now to ask you about your church.

Does your church know about/support what you do?

How are you involved in your church; what kind of things do you do?

Is your experience in working in the para-church organisation different to your experience in the church?
– If so, how?

I'd like now to think about how you understand your church/para-church involvement.

Do you consider that you hold a position of authority?
– If so/If not, how do you understand authority?

Do you think there is a difference between authority and leadership?

Do you hold any view on 'headship'?
– in church/home/work places?

How far does what you believe now about women come from your own working out of the Bible and how much from what others have taught you?

I'd like to ask you about your domestic situation.

What domestic/caring responsibilities do you have?

How have you managed to carry these out and do what you do in the church?

Do you think women *should* put their husband and children first before fulfilling their own careers, gifting or calling?

Has your involvement in the church affected the way you see your home life and vice versa?
– If so, how?

For women who are not full-time in the church/para-church and are also in employment.

> Tell me about your job and what it involves.

> How do the issues we've been talking about come up in relationship to your job?

This project is about women's involvement in the church and community.

> Would you like more women to be involved in the kind of things you do?
> – Why/Why not?

> What changes would there need to be to help more women be involved?

> How important is the whole issue of women's status or role in church and society?

In the next set of questions, I'd like to ask you about some other areas that we are dealing with in this project.

> First of all, the label evangelical. What does evangelical mean to you?

> What do you think feminism is?
> – How do you feel about it?

> What do you think about gender-inclusive language?

> Are you involved in politics in any way?

> Are there ways in which you are active in the community apart from your role as...?

I've come to my last two questions.

> Firstly, is there anything else you would like to say?

> Finally, are there any other women from the evangelical community you think it would be good for me to know about for the purpose of this project?

WOMEN IN COMMUNITY

I'd like to begin by asking you about your responsibilities in the community.

> Tell me about your involvement in the community and how you came to be doing this.

> Can you tell me both the good things about what you do and the things you don't like?

> How have you been received by other people as a woman doing what you do?

> Do you experience conflict because you are a woman?
> – And if so, where does this conflict come from and how do you handle it?

> What would you like to do in the future; where do you see yourself going next?

I'd like now to ask you about your faith.

> What part does being a Christian play in what you do in the community?

> Does your church know about/support what you do?

> How are you involved in your church; what kind of things do you do?

> Is your experience in working in the community different to your experience in the church?
> – If so, how?

I'd like now to think about how you understand your church and community involvement.

> Do you consider that you hold a position of authority (either in the community or your church)?
> – If so/If not, how do you understand authority?

Do you think there is a difference between authority and leadership?

Do you hold any view on 'headship'?
– In home/in church/in work places

How far does what you believe now about women come from your own working out of the Bible and how much from what others have taught you?

I'd like to ask you about your domestic situation.

What domestic/caring responsibilities do you have?

How have you managed to carry these out and do what you do in the community?

Do you think women *should* put their husband and children first before fulfilling their own careers, gifting or calling?

Has your involvement in the community affected the way you see your home life or vice versa?
– If so, how?

For women who are not full-time in the community and are also in employment.

Tell me about your job and what it involves.

How do the issues we've been talking about come up in relationship to your job?

This project is about women's involvement in the church and community.

Would you like more women to be involved in the kind of things you do?
– Why/Why not?

What changes would there need to be to help more women be involved?

How important is the whole issue of women's status or role in society and church?

In the next set of questions, I'd like to ask you about some other areas that we are dealing with in this project.

First of all, the label evangelical. What does evangelical mean to you?

What is your understanding of feminism?
– How do you feel about it?

What do you think about gender-inclusive language?

Are there ways in which you are active in the community apart from your role as...?

Are you involved in politics in any way?

I've come to my last two questions.

Firstly, is there anything else you would like to say?

Finally, are there any other women from the evangelical community you think it would be good for me to know about for the purpose of this project?

WOMEN IN POLITICS

I'd like to begin by asking you about your political involvement.

Tell me about your involvement in politics and how you came to be doing this.

Can you tell me both the good things about what you do and the things you don't like?

How have you been received by other people as a woman doing what you do?

Do you experience conflict because you are a woman?
– And if so, where does this conflict come from and how do you handle it?

What would you like to do in the future in politics?

I'd like now to ask you about your faith.

> What part does being a Christian play in what you do in politics?
>
> Does your church know about/support what you do?
>
> How are you involved in your church; what kind of things do you do?
>
> Is your experience working in the political world different to your experience in the church?
> – If so, how?

I'd like now to think about how you understand your church and political involvement.

> Do you consider that you hold a position of authority (either in politics or in your church)?
> – If so/If not, how do you understand authority?
>
> Do you think there a difference between authority and leadership?
>
> Do you hold any view on 'headship'?
> – In home/in church/in work places
>
> How far does what you believe now about women come from your own working out of the Bible and how much from what others have taught you?

I'd like to ask you about your domestic situation.

> What domestic/caring responsibilities do you have?
>
> How have you managed to carry these out and engage in political activity?
>
> Do you think women *should* put their husband and children first before fulfilling their own careers, gifting or calling?
>
> Has your involvement in politics affected the way you see your home life or vice versa?
> – If so, how?

For women who are not full-time in politics and are also in employment.

Tell me about your job and what it involves.

How do the issues we've been talking about come up in relationship to your job?

This project is about women's involvement in the church and community.

Would you like more women to be involved in politics/the kind of things you do?
– Why/Why not?

What changes would there need to be to help more women be involved?

How important is the whole issue of women's status or role in society and church?

In the next set of questions, I'd like to ask you about some other areas that we are dealing with in this project.

First of all, the label evangelical. What does evangelical mean to you?

What is your understanding of feminism?
– How do you feel about it?

What do you think about gender-inclusive language?

Are you involved in any other community activism?

I've come to my last two questions.

Firstly, is there anything else you would like to say?

Finally, are there any other women from the evangelical community you think it would be good for me to know about for the purpose of this project?

MALE CHURCH LEADERS

Can you tell me first of all about the participation of women in your own congregation and in the denomination as a whole. How would you describe it?

Thinking of yourself, do you have (other) experience of working with women?

What are your reflections on your experience of working with women?
– Are you aware of differences or challenges or changes that resulted either for yourself personally or the church/others involved?

Would you say that women's participation in the church has ever caused conflict and if so, how was that handled?

How do you understand the church's interaction with the wider community and public world?

What is your attitude to cross-community involvement by your church and/or individual members of your congregation?

Would you like to see more women involved in the church, community and political sectors? Why/why not?

What changes would there need to be to bring this about?

How can the church support women who take an active role in the church, community and politics?

How important is the whole question of women's position and participation in church and society?

Do you hold any view on headship?

What have been the main influences on you in reaching this understanding?

Do you think a woman should put her husband and children, her domestic and caring responsibilities first before fulfilling her own career, gifting or calling?

What is your understanding of feminism?

What do you think about gender-inclusive language?

Is there anything else you would like to say?

Notes

CHAPTER 1

1 Words of one man to a woman interviewed for this project when he learned she was involved in education specifically designed to foster women's personal growth and development and employment opportunities.

2 Mary Stewart Van Leeuwen (ed), *After Eden: Facing the Challenge of Gender Reconciliation* (Eerdmans, Grand Rapids, Michigan), 1993, p. 22.

3 For example, while it is correct to assert in terms of different denominational traditions that evangelicals 'are not particularly concerned with the details of church order' and that 'the evangelical emphasis is always primarily on the Church as the body of Christ' [Alwyn Thomson, 'Evangelicalism and Fundamentalism' in Norman Richardson (ed), *A Tapestry of Beliefs: Christian Traditions in Northern Ireland* (Blackstaff, Belfast), 1998, p. 258], attention to a proper gender order is very much part of evangelical ecclesiology, whether openly acknowledged or not.

4 Stanley J. Grenz, *Revisioning Evangelical Theology: A Fresh Agenda for the 21st century* (InterVarsity Press, Illinois, PA), 1993, p. 11.

5 The subject of feminism is considered below. Here feminism should be understood as that contribution which seeks to redress injustice against women.

6 David W. Smith, *Transforming the World? The Social Impact of British Evangelicalism* (Paternoster, Cumbria), 1998.

7 Kenneth S. Kantzer and Carl F.H. Henry (eds), *Evangelical Affirmations* (Academie/ Zondervan, Grand Rapids, Michigan), 1990. This consultation held in May 1989 was co-sponsored by The National Association of Evangelicals and Trinity Evangelical Divinity School.

8 John Stott, *Evangelical Truth: A Personal Plea for Unity* (IVP, Leicester), 1999, p. 141.

9 Timothy George, cited in Alister McGrath, *Evangelicalism and the Future of Christianity* (Hodder and Stoughton, London), 1994, p. 155.

10 Derek J. Tidball, 'Facing Contentious

Issues', in Steve Brady and Harold Rowdon (eds), *For Such a Time as This: Perspectives on Evangelicalism, Past, Present and Future* (Scripture Union, Milton Keynes), 1996, pp. 256–67.

11 Rob Warner, 'Fracture Points', in Clive Calver and Rob Warner, *Together We Stand: Evangelical Convictions, Unity and Visions* (Hodder and Stoughton, London, Sydney, Auckland), 1996, pp. 60–93.

12 McGrath, p. 147. While it is dogmatism which is part of the 'dark side' and Alister McGrath also uses other examples (namely, the holy spirit, the authority of Scripture and denominational affiliation), nevertheless the only place in which women are discussed is in this negative context.

13 E. Margaret Howe, 'Women, Ordination of', in Walter E. Elwell (ed), *The Concise Evangelical Dictionary of Theology* (Marshall Pickering, London), 1991, pp. 557–8.

14 Hermeneutics is concerned with how we interpret and use the Bible.

15 David Bebbington, *Evangelicalism in Modern Britain. A History from the 1730s to the 1980s* (Baker/Routledge, London), 1992, p. 269.

16 Oliver Barclay, *Evangelicalism in Britain 1935–1995. A Personal Sketch* (InterVarsity Press, Leicester), 1997, p. 103.

17 Warner, p. 78. This book, as a popular Christian paperback, is not a detailed studied contribution on the subject. However, it is more likely to be read than some of the more detailed volumes on evangelicalism and is therefore important for its influence.

18 The need for this can be further illustrated in Walter E. Elwell (ed), *The Concise Evangelical Dictionary of Theology* (Marshall Pickering, London), 1991, which includes several pages on women under the entries of 'Biblical Concept of Woman', 'Ordination of Women', and 'Women in the Church'. It also has an entry under 'Man', understood generically (but confusingly also used in the text for a male person), entitled 'Doctrine of Man', 'Natural Man', 'Old and New Man', and 'Origin of Man'. None of these makes reference to the sexual duality of humanity or femaleness

although there are a number of references to Adam as a male person. However, dealing with sexual differentiation in the context of a theology of humanity (that is, doctrine of Man) would offer the possibility of examining women's status/role/personhood in a far more positive light and indeed would challenge assumptions about maleness as normative humanity.

19 John Stott, *New Issues Facing Christians Today*, 3rd edition (Marshall Pickering, London), 1999.

20 Jocelyn Murray, 'Gender Attitudes and the Contribution of Women to Evangelism and Ministry in the Nineteenth Century', in John Wolffe (ed), *Evangelical Faith and Public Zeal. Evangelicals and Society in Britain 1780–1980* (SPCK, London), 1995, p. 112. One study of the explanations behind clerical attitudes to women's ordination in the Church of England concluded that scriptural and theological beliefs alone were unable to account for the opposition to ordaining women. Rather such arguments are used to support an opposition deriving from a more pervasive sex role ideology. See Nancy Nasonclark, 'Ordaining Women as Priests, Religious Versus Sexist Explanations for Clerical Attitudes', *Sociological Analysis*, Vol. 48, No. 3, pp. 259–73.

21 Wilard Swartley, *Slavery, Sabbath, War and Women* (Herald Press, Scottdale, PA), 1983.

22 There are those, as I indicate below in regard to Northern Ireland, who view beliefs regarding women (among other issues) as a defining factor in their Christian identity.

23 Stott, *Evangelical Truth*, p. 143.

24 Tidball, p. 267.

25 McGrath, p. 155.

26 Warner, p. 79.

27 Stott, *Evangelical Truth*, p. 142.

28 For example, John Benton, *Gender Questions: Biblical Manhood and Womanhood in the Contemporary World* (Evangelical Press, Darlington, England and Auburn, MA), 2000; Stott, *New Issues Facing Christians Today*; Nigel Wright, *The Radical Evangelical. Seeking a Place to Stand* (SPCK, London), 1996; Warner.

29 In quotations from the interviewees,

non-italicised text in square brackets indicates editing of the person's words for the purposes of clarification, abbreviation or confidentiality.

30 Mark Chaves, *Ordaining Women: Culture and Conflict in Religious Organizations* (Harvard University Press, Cambridge, MA), 1999.

31 The apparent contradiction between ordination as an association with the norm of gender equality and the absence of equality in reality for women in churches is not so strange. The principle of gender equality is far from realised in society in general despite legislation and the widespread acceptance of the idea of gender equality. The difference between norm and practice and the reasons for this are explored in the coming chapters.

32 Chaves, p. 83.

33 Ian R.K. Paisley, 'The Free Presbyterian Church of Ulster', in Richardson, p. 128; R.C. Beckett, 'The Evangelical Presbyterian Church in Ireland', in Richardson, p. 190.

34 For more on the relationship between fundamentalism and evangelicalism see: Alwyn Thomson, *The Fractured Family* (ECONI, Belfast), 1994.

35 Margaret Lamberts Bendroth, *Fundamentalism and Gender, 1875 to the Present* (Yale University Press, New Haven and London), 1993, p. 6.

36 This is consistent with the contention made earlier that gender is more commonly raised when related to women because it is women who become invisible when attention is not given to gender. In this instance, male hegemony and power in these areas was being threatened and hence the response was to reassert this dominance by a focus on men.

37 Bendroth, p. 30.

38 Ibid., p. 8.

39 Callum G. Brown, *The Death of Christian Britain* (Routledge, London and New York), 2001, p. 9.

40 Ibid., p. 96.

41 For example, militarised youth movements like the Boys' Brigade.

42 Brown, p. 87.

43 Ibid., p. 192.

44 Brown's contention is that, contrary to the majority of social science scholarship on secularisation that sees the latter as an inevitable process following industrialisation in which Britain has been increasingly declining in Christian influence for the last two centuries, secularisation really properly began only in the 1960s. Further, key to this process is women's religiosity.

45 Freda Donoghue, Rick Wilford and Robert Miller, 'Feminist or Womanist? Feminism, the Women's Movement and Age Difference in Northern Ireland', *Irish Journal of Feminist Studies*, 1997, Vol. 2, No. 1, pp. 86–105.

46 This refers to the Belfast Agreement that came out of the multi-party negotiations and was finally reached on 10 April 1998 which was Good Friday and hence is popularly known as the Good Friday Agreement. It was endorsed by referendum vote in May 1998 by 71 per cent overall, with a small pro-Agreement majority among the unionist voters.

47 *Newsletter*, 24 April 1998.

48 Cited in Kari Jo Verhulst, 'Gathering in Power and Hope', *Sojourners*, Sept/Oct 1995, p. 12. Focus on the Family is a religiously conservative American organisation (of whom James Dobson is the founder and president) which runs publishing, film-making and counselling services for families in America and around the world.

49 David J. Ayres, 'The Inevitability of Failure: The Assumptions and Implementations of Modern Feminism' in John Piper and Wayne Grudem (eds), *Recovering Biblical Manhood and Womanhood. A Response to Evangelical Feminism* (Crossway, Wheaton, IL), 1991, pp. 330–1.

50 See, for example, Carol Percy, 'Finding Feminism: Difficulties for Women in Northern Ireland', *Irish Journal of Feminist Studies*, 1998, Vol. 3, No. 1, pp. 32–3.

51 Chaves, p. 187.

52 Martyn Percy argues that the framework within which fundamentalism and revivalism (which may be viewed as part of an evangelical spectrum) operate is one of competing powers and that Scripture is used as an agent to ensure divine power is in control. Martyn Percy, *Words, Wonders and Power: Understanding Contemporary Christian Fundamentalism and Revivalism* (SPCK, London), 1996.

53 For examples of both co-operation and

difficulties encountered see: Eileen Evason, *Against The Grain: The Contemporary Women's Movement in Northern Ireland* (Attic, Dublin), 1991; Monica McWilliams, 'Struggling for Peace and Justice: Reflections on Women's Activism in Northern Ireland', *Journal of Women's History*, 1995, Vol. 6, No. 4, pp. 13–39; and Catherine. B. Shannon, 'Women in Northern Ireland' in M. O'Dowd and S. Wichert (eds), *Chattel, Servant or Citizen. Women's Status in Church, State and Society* (Institute of Irish Studies, Queen's University, Belfast), 1995, pp. 238–53.

54   Elisabeth Porter, 'Diversity and Commonality: Women, Politics and Northern Ireland', *The European Journal of Women's Studies*, 1997, Vol. 4, No. 1, pp. 85–6.

55   An account of the formation of the Coalition and its early experiences is found in Kate Fearon, *Women's Work: The Story of the Northern Ireland Women's Coalition* (Blackstaff, Belfast), 1999. A shorter version of their story is in Kate Fearon and Monica McWilliams, 'Swimming Against the Mainstream: the Northern Ireland Women's Coalition', in Carmel Roulston and Celia Davies (eds), *Gender, Democracy and Inclusion in Northern Ireland* (Palgrave, Basingstoke), 2000.

56   This simple equating of nationalism with Catholicism or unionism with Protestantism reflects common parlance and perception rather than an unproblematic acceptance of these equations in this book.

57   Rosemary Ridd, 'Powers of the Powerless', in Rosemary Ridd and Helen Callaway (eds), *Caught Up in Conflict: Women's Responses to Political Strife* (Macmillan Education, Basingstoke and London), 1986, p. 3.

58   Donoghue, Wilford and Miller, p. 101.

59   Monica McWilliams, 'Women in Northern Ireland: An Overview', in E. Hughes (ed), *Culture and Politics in Northern Ireland 1960–1990* (Open University Press, Milton Keynes), 1991, p. 93; Donoghue, Wilford and Miller, p. 89. Roisin McDonough states that the coining of this phrase is attributed to the late Belfast community worker, Joyce McCartan. Roisin McDonough, 'Independence or Integration?', in Kate

Fearon (ed), *Power, Politics, Positionings – Women in Northern Ireland* (Democratic Dialogue, Belfast), 1996, http://cain.ulst.ac.uk/dd/report4/report4e.htm.

60   McDonough. In this article she attributes this negative image primarily to hostile media influence.

61   Feminism can be defined as an ideology and practice of women's liberation (not just of equality) based on the notion that women suffer injustice because of their sex. There are differences in the understanding of why this liberation is necessary and how it is to be achieved. Hence, feminism is frequently referred to in the plural 'feminisms'. For an outline of feminist thought and a Christian engagement with it see: Elaine Storkey, *What's Right with Feminism* (SPCK, London), 1985; and Van Leeuwen.

62   While second-wave feminism was chiefly a secular movement, many Christians, including evangelicals, were involved in the endeavours of first-wave feminism.

63   Van Leeuwen, p. 20.

64   Ibid., p. 21.

65   A variety of evangelical theological positions and manifestations of evangelical sub-culture is provided in Glenn Jordan, *Not of this World? Evangelical Protestants in Northern Ireland* (Blackstaff and Centre for Contemporary Christianity in Ireland, Belfast), 2001, although gender is not a major analytical component in this contribution on evangelicalism.

66   This included over 2,000 Protestant respondents.

67   Together these three denominations account for 84 per cent of Protestant churchgoers throughout Northern Ireland according to figures taken from the 1991 Census of Population. HMSO, *The Northern Ireland Census 1991 Summary Report* (HMSO, Belfast), 1992.

68   Frederick W. Boal, Margaret C. Keane, and David N. Livingstone, *Them and Us? Attitudinal Variation Among Churchgoers in Belfast* (Textflow Services Ltd, Belfast), 1997, pp. 95–6.

69   Ibid., p. 69.

70   Research suggests a possible female evangelical population of between 109,000 and 124,000. Based on figures supplied in Patrick Johnstone, *Operation*

World (OM Publishing, Carlisle), 1993; Boal, Keane, and Livingstone; Steve Bruce and Fiona Alderdice, 'Religious Belief and Behaviour' in Peter Stringer and Gillian Robinson (eds), *Social Attitudes in Northern Ireland. The Third Report* (Blackstaff Press, Belfast), 1993. See note four in chapter two.

71 Throughout this book the term lay leader is used for those persons involved in church leadership but not ordained as minister, pastor, rector, vicar, and so on. Hence, for example, lay leader includes elders in the Presbyterian Church who, while ordained, are not ministers. Lay leaders may be those who serve on Methodist leaders boards, Church of Ireland select vestries, Baptist elders and deacons, and various leadership teams in churches.

72 For information on the Belfast Agreement see note 46. Given the political circumstances at the time of researching for this book, identifying women's self-assessed attitude to this Agreement is a better indication of political difference than party membership. It is important to note that support for the Agreement does not automatically imply wholehearted assent to all it contains, anymore than opposition to the Agreement necessarily infers a rejection of everything it proposes. However, these positions do indicate whether the women concerned have consented to support its implementation or focus on alternatives.

73 Life Link is a small but growing network of new churches in Northern Ireland.

CHAPTER 2

1 Rosemary Sales, *Women Divided: Gender, Religion and Politics in Northern Ireland* (Routledge, London), 1997, p. 5.

2 Following on from the discussion of the terms 'sex' and 'gender' at the beginning of chapter one, the phrase sexual division of labour is used here descriptively of the way labour is generally divided on the basis of male and female. There is a sense in which this sexual division is imbued with gendered value, for those areas occupied mainly by women are generally held in less regard and frequently receive lower financial remuneration than many predominantly occupied by men. Further, men and women operating in non-traditional areas for their sex, to some extent, also are subject to the gendered value of the sector. In this sense it is possible to talk of a gendered division of labour. This is a theme that is explored in various ways throughout this book. For clarity and the purposes of this particular chapter it is appropriate here to use the term sexual division of labour.

3 Figures are for autumn 1998. Equal Opportunities Commission for Northern Ireland, *Where Do Women Figure?* (ECONI, Belfast), 1999.

4 In the 1991 Northern Ireland Social Attitudes Survey women make up the majority of those with conservative Protestant (67 per cent), mainstream Protestant (57 per cent), and Catholic (55 per cent) religious affiliation. Sixty-one per cent of women (compared to 39 per cent of men) are frequent church attenders. Steve Bruce and Fiona Alderdice, 'Religious Belief and Behaviour' in Peter Stringer and Gillian Robinson (eds), *Social Attitudes in Northern Ireland. The Third Report* (Blackstaff Press, Belfast), 1993. The 1993 Belfast Churchgoers Survey also found a majority church attendance by both Protestant and Catholic women (each at 59 per cent). Further, 'in virtually every age cohort females predominate in similar proportions to the overall gender ratio'. Frederick W. Boal, Margaret C. Keane, and David N. Livingstone, *Them and Us? Attitudinal Variation Among Churchgoers in Belfast* (Textflow Services Ltd, Belfast), 1997, p. 144.

5 These three churches organise on an all-Ireland basis and the statistics, therefore, relate to the whole of the island of Ireland. Twenty out of the fifty-one ordained Church of Ireland women are auxiliary ministers. Auxiliary ministers are ordained but have no stipend and traditionally have acted only as assistants to an incumbent (the minister in charge of a parish), and not been in sole charge themselves.

6 The figure for the Republic of Ireland was 25 per cent.

7 No statistics are kept centrally on the gender composition of Presbyterian Church in Ireland elders.

8 Methodist Church in Ireland, *The Role of Women in the Church*, 1998, p. 7.

9 There were three women prior to 1975 who held Westminster seats.

10 In the 1996 elections to the Northern Ireland Forum for Political Dialogue (initially the Northern Ireland Forum for Political Understanding and Dialogue) less than 10 per cent (7 out of 72) of members were women.

11 The statistics for this and the preceding paragraph are from: Equal Opportunities Commission for Northern Ireland, *Where Do Women Figure?*; Yvonne Galligan and Rick Wilford, 'Women's Political Representation in Ireland', in Yvonne Galligan, Eilís Ward and Rick Wilford (eds), *Contesting Politics: Women in Ireland, North and South* (Westview Press, Oxford), 1999, pp. 130–48; Becky Gill, *Losing Out Locally: Women and Local Government* (Fawcett, London), 2000, p. 5.

12 The four SDLP and three Sinn Féin candidates were not selected for winnable constituencies, and the UUP had no women candidates. Galligan and Wilford, pp. 130–48.

13 The APNI party had the highest proportion at 27.3 per cent.

14 Galligan and Wilford, pp. 130–48.

15 APNI: 50 per cent female membership; UUP: 42 per cent; SDLP 47 per cent; Sinn Féin: 33 per cent.

16 Yvonne Galligan and Rick Wilford, 'Gender and Party Politics in Northern Ireland', in Galligan, Ward and Wilford, pp. 169–84.

17 Galligan and Wilford, 'Women's Political Representation in Ireland', p. 138.

18 Equal Opportunities Commission for Northern Ireland, *Where Do Women Figure?*

19 Deirdre Heenan and Anne Marie Gray, 'Women and Nominated Boards in Ireland', in Galligan, Ward and Wilford, p. 191.

20 The Civic Forum is a 60-member body, two places remaining vacant at its inception.

21 This body is made up of 10 MLAs (all of whom are male) and 9 other appointees among which are the 2 women nominated.

22 Galligan and Wilford, 'Women's Political Representation in Ireland', p. 135.

23 Kate Fearon, 'Conclusion', in Kate Fearon (ed), *Power, Politics, Positionings – Women in Northern Ireland* (Democratic Dialogue, Belfast), 1996, http://cain.ulst.ac.uk/dd/report4/report4e.htm.

24 Women's Resource and Development Agency, *Women and Citizenship: Power, Participation and Choice* (WRDA, Belfast), 1995, p. 11.

25 In Great Britain in 1970 women working full-time earned 63 per cent of the average hourly earnings of men also working full-time. The equivalent figure for 1999 is 81 per cent. Equal Opportunities Commission, *Women and Men in Britain: At the Millennium* (EOC, Manchester), 1999. In Northern Ireland in 1998 women working full-time earned 84 per cent of men's average full-time hourly earnings compared to 75 per cent in 1984. Equal Opportunities Commission for Northern Ireland, *Where Do Women Figure?*

26 Equal Opportunities Commission, *Research Findings: Attitudes to Equal Pay* (EOC, Manchester), 2000.

27 Eilish Rooney, 'Framing the Future', in Fearon, *Power, Politics, Positionings*.

28 Women's Resource and Development Agency, p. 16.

29 Methodist Church in Ireland, *The Role of Women in the Church*, 1998.

30 Rick Wilford, 'Women's Candidacies and Electability in a Divided Society: The Northern Ireland Women's Coalition and the 1996 Forum Election', *Women and Politics*, 1999, 20 (1), p. 84.

31 These figures relate to the 47 respondents from the 70 candidates approached. Wilford, p. 82. A survey of women councillors in Northern Ireland also demonstrated that in 'both occupational and educational terms, the respondents are untypical of the region's female population'. Rick Wilford, Robert Miller, Yolanda Bell, and Freda Donoghue, 'In Their Own Voices: Women Councillors in Northern Ireland', *Public Administration*, 1993, 71 (3), p. 343.

32 Heenan and Gray, pp. 185–200.

33 In one survey, 42 per cent of women councillors attributed their political involvement to family background. Wilford, Miller, Bell, and Donoghue, pp. 341–55.

34 Kate Fearon, *Women's Work: The Story of the Northern Ireland Women's Coalition* (Blackstaff, Belfast), 1999, p. 74.

35 Launched in 1995 in association with the Women's Support Network and based at Downtown women's centre, 'Women into Politics' is open to women interested in any of Northern Ireland's parties. 'democra*She*' was launched in 2000 by a partnership of the Ulster People's College and the Northern Ireland Women's Initiative and offers training to women in all political parties.

36 APNI, SDLP and Sinn Féin. Galligan and Wilford, 'Gender and Party Politics in Northern Ireland', pp. 169–84.

37 Ruth Lister, *Citizenship: Feminist Perspectives* (Macmillan Press Ltd, Basingstoke), 1997, p. 137.

38 Ibid., p. 119.

39 They surveyed three local council districts in Belfast in which 47 per cent of women attended their local group for several days each week and 10 per cent every day.

40 Eilish Rooney and Margaret Woods, *Women, Community and Politics in Northern Ireland: A Belfast Study* (University of Ulster, Belfast), 1995, p. 33.

41 Eilish Rooney, 'Women in Party Politics and Local Groups: Findings from Belfast', in Anne Byrne and Madeleine Leonard (eds), *Women and Irish Society: A Sociological Reader* (Beyond the Pale Publications, Belfast), 1997, p. 535.

42 Day nursery places per 1,000 of the population for children up to and including four years of age was 34.8 in 1998 which is well below the UK average of 71.3. Equal Opportunities Commission for Northern Ireland, *Where Do Women Figure?*

43 Writing in 1996, Kate Fearon notes that the SDLP, Sinn Féin and PUP offer childcare provision at their annual conferences, the APNI having discontinued this due to lack of demand, and the UDP planning to introduce it. Kate Fearon, 'Painting the Picture' in Kate Fearon (ed), *Power, Politics, Positionings*.

44 In the run-up to the 1997 general election the Labour Party adopted a policy of all-women short-lists for a number of constituencies. A male party member challenged this practice by taking a case of sexual discrimination to an industrial tribunal. The tribunal upheld his case. The Equal Opportunities Commission took further legal advice and this concluded that the selection of candidates fell outside the terms of the Sex Discrimination Act. This and additional complications in Europe leave the legal situation in some confusion. It is, however, unlikely that any party will risk the measure of all-women short-lists again without changes in legislation. This same caution is not thought to apply to other measures such as twinning and zipping outlined below. For further details see Mary-Ann Stephenson, *The Glass Trapdoor: Women, Politics and the Media during the 1997 General Election* (Fawcett, London), 1998, pp. 52–8.

45 Twinning is used in single-member constituencies under a first-past-the-post voting system. Neighbouring seats are paired taking into account their 'winnability'. Each pair selects one man and one woman by the members of the two constituencies selecting the candidates together, each member voting for one man and one woman. The top man and the top woman are selected and decide between them who should have which seat.

46 Zipping is used where there are regional lists with a proportional voting system. In this case women and men are alternated on the lists of candidates.

47 Equal Opportunities Commission Press Release, 10 March 2001.

48 For more details on how this process was achieved and the elected members' experience of it see Becky Gill, *Winning Women: Lessons from Scotland and Wales* (Fawcett, London), 1999.

49 Galligan and Wilford, 'Gender and Party Politics in Northern Ireland', p. 183.

CHAPTER 3

1 Sexism is used here in its original sense of prejudice or discrimination against women on the grounds of their sex, that is, because they are women, rather than

in the way it is sometimes applied as prejudice or discrimination against a person (female or male) on the grounds of their sex.

2   Joyce Williams talks in terms of the church becoming inclusive of women rather than women being included in the church, in order to emphasise that women's inclusion is the responsibility of the whole church and not just of women. Further, the phrase indicates there are implications for the church in becoming gender inclusive that is about more than simply adding women into the existing status quo.

3   The importance or otherwise of focusing on gender is considered in chapter seven.

4   There are, of course, other reasons than lack of familiarity given for objecting to women in church leadership positions and these are considered in chapter five.

5   When women talk about their experiences in the church they are not necessarily referring to an evangelical context, although many of them are. The focus here is on women's experiences within the church (and civic society) rather than on the religious identity of those with whom there may be conflict. There are, of course, profound implications for evangelicals and evangelicalism in responding to this window into women's reality in church and society.

6   Disvalue refers to negating or removing value in contrast to the word devalue which indicates reducing value.

7   The perception of women as a threat to men is discussed in chapter four.

8   It may be interesting to compare the number of committee/board commitments of these women with male leaders, given that there may be a number of men with similar if not more demands on their time.

9   Another man speaking of the same institution and the involvement of lay and ordained women within the denominational structures commented, 'I mean even when one is trying to make a conscious effort to balance it out in some way it's exceedingly difficult to do it, because the denomination hasn't quite caught up with the aspiration.'

10   For example: how gender stereotypes are perpetuated through metaphorical uses of words; the association of negativity to words to do with women; in lexicography, the place of gender in the way words are defined and examples used to illustrate meaning; and how gender affects language use, such as the vocabularies of women and men and the nature of women and men's conversation.

11   Veronica Zundel, 'Women Have a Word for it', *Third Way*, May 1988, p. 21.

12   For men, of course, there is a different relationship to generic terms. For a man 'he' primarily means 'me', but can also mean 'not me'. For a woman, 'he' primarily means 'not me', but can also mean 'me'.

13   It is a matter of debate as to whether it is that language forms ideas or that ideas are reflected in language. However, what is clear is that language and ideas are bound up together.

14   These examples are taken from a discussion in Dale Spender, *Man Made Language* (Pandora, London), 1990, 2nd edition, pp. 151–57.

15   Mary Stewart Van Leeuwen (ed), *After Eden: Facing the Challenge of Gender Reconciliation* (Eerdmans, Grand Rapids, Michigan), 1993, p. 344.

16   A further group of women showed little interest in the subject, considering it did not affect them at all. A few felt it was silly, 'a load of old guff', and a very few were opposed to it altogether.

17   Margaret Gibbon, *Feminist Perspectives on Language* (Longman, London and New York), 1999, p. 43.

18   Ibid., p. 52.

19   Politically correct language avoids derogatory or exclusive terms not only in regard to gender but also race, ethnicity, and disability. Originally designed to help counteract secondary status and discrimination on the grounds of gender, race and so on, it frequently shares the derision often associated with gender-inclusive language.

20   'Member of the Legislative Assembly' or 'MLA' is the designation for those elected to the Northern Ireland Assembly.

21   Politically correct.

22   There are ramifications of this within the life of individual congregations. One woman commented on hearing of

the experience of a woman at a theological college who was not studying theology in order to become ordained. When she made this fact known to the male students, 'they started to talk to her. But before that they ostracised her. And I think that – that's chilling. The thought that you could have a minister who was ministering to a congregation who had behaved in that way.'

23   Four years after the first ordinations of women in the Church of England, a survey conducted among women priests in six Church of England dioceses by the clergy section of the Manufacturing, Science and Finance Union revealed 75 per cent of the interviewees (and therefore over one fifth of the women clergy in these areas) reporting some form of harassment or bullying (the majority from male colleagues but also some from parishioners). Forty per cent had experienced verbal abuse, 37 per cent had experienced exclusion in terms of being isolated or 'cold-shouldered', 23 per cent had been subject to harassment of various types and 10 per cent had suffered some form of physical abuse. (*Are Anglican Women Priests being Bullied and Harassed? A Survey by MSF Clergy and Church Workers, February 1998.*) One senior Synod member, having seen the results of the survey, commented: 'It is way beyond sexism or chauvinism, it is downright misogyny, women priests feeling hated and devalued by their own colleagues' (Martin Wroe, 'Women Priests Accuse Clergy of Harassment and Bullying', *The Observer Review*, 5 April 1998, p. 1).

24   On the other side of this experience, one woman spoke how she had left her church congregation in part because of their attitude towards women.

25   Chapter seven gives some indication of the effect such conflict can have on women.

26   Equal Opportunities Commission for Northern Ireland, *Sexual Harassment at Work: Guidance on Prevention and Procedures for Dealing with the Problem* (EOCNI, Belfast), 1993, p. 4. The guide cites a 1986 survey conducted in Northern Ireland in which 22 per cent of women reported sexual harassment at work, 45 per cent of these women

saying it occurred often (p. 5).

27   Ibid., p. 4. The guide comments that 'the Commission recognises that men may also be harassed, although in the vast majority of cases the recipients are women, and the law applies equally to men'. (p. 5).

28   Ranging from unnecessary touching to assault.

29   Including unwelcome sexual advances, suggestive remarks, innuendo or lewd comments.

30   For example, the display of sexually suggestive material, or leering, whistling or making sexually suggestive gestures.

31   Referring to conduct that denigrates or ridicules or is intimidatory or physically abusive of the person because of their sex, such as gender-related degrading abuse or insults or offensive comments about appearance or dress.

32   A vivid account of one woman's experience of double victimisation involving a religious institution is given at the beginning of Lesley Orr Macdonald, 'A Spirituality for Justice: The Enemy of Apathy', *Feminist Theology*, No. 23, pp. 13–21. Another example of institutional failure to respond is given by Kate Fearon who relates how the NIWC were unsuccessful in getting the Northern Ireland Forum for Political Dialogue to adopt a code of practice on sexual harassment in order to get 'some relief from the constant onslaught of verbal abuse'. Kate Fearon, *Women's Work: The Story of the Northern Ireland Women's Coalition*, (Blackstaff, Belfast), 1999, p. 65.

33   Carol E. Becker, *Leading Women. How Church Women Can Avoid Traps and Negotiate the Gender Maze* (Abingdon, Nashville), 1996, p. 119.

34   Ibid., p. 118.

35   Matthew 5:28. All biblical quotations are from the New Revised Standard Version (NRSV), unless otherwise stated.

36   Mary Evans, *Woman in the Bible* (Paternoster, Exeter), 1983, p. 45.

37   Ibid., p. 45.

CHAPTER 4

1   A discussion of this issue can be found in Mary Stewart Van Leeuwen, *Gender and Grace: Women and Men in a Changing*

World (IVP, Leicester), 1990 and Elaine Storkey, *Created or Constructed? The Great Gender Debate* (Paternoster Press, Cumbria), 2000. Both these authors propose alternative ways to address this subject. Mary Stewart Van Leeuwen suggests that separating sex and gender is a false way to investigate the subject because psychologically and biologically women and men are more alike than different; because sex and nurture are mutually influential; and because sex and gender identity are less important than the identity of being called to the office of the advancement of God's kingdom on earth (see especially chapter three). Elaine Storkey argues that relations between female and male are better understood in the context of four paradigms to be held simultaneously: difference, similarity, complementarity, and union (pp. 115–17).

2   Comment of a male church leader interviewed.

3   Comment of a male church leader interviewed.

4   Comment of woman para-church worker interviewed.

5   Comment of a political activist interviewed.

6   Comment of a male church leader interviewed.

7   See, for example, Rick Wilford, Robert Miller, Yolanda Bell, and Freda Donoghue, 'In Their Own Voices: Women Councillors in Northern Ireland', *Public Administration*, 1993, 71 (3), pp. 341–55.

8   Kate Fearon, *Women's Work: The Story of the Northern Ireland Women's Coalition* (Blackstaff, Belfast), 1999, pp. 106–7.

9   See, for example in relation to politics, Robert L. Miller, Rick Wilford, and Freda Donoghue, *Women and Political Participation in Northern Ireland* (Avebury, Aldershot), 1996, pp. 212–14.

10 On 20 June 2000 the Northern Ireland Assembly debated the motion 'That this Assembly is opposed to the extension of the Abortion Act 1967 to Northern Ireland.'

11 The NIWC put forward an amendment that the Assembly 'refers the question of the extension of the Abortion Act 1967 and related issues to the Health, Social Services and Public Safety

Committee and requests that the Committee make a report to the Assembly on the matter within six months', Northern Ireland Assembly Official Report (Hansard), 20 June 2000. Jane Morrice stated the NIWC had 'tabled this amendment today because we do not want a heated, emotional, disturbing debate for the next four hours. We want this discussion to take place with as much access to information and advice as possible' (Hansard), 20 June 2000.

12 Forty-three voted to oppose the extension of the Abortion Act 1967 to Northern Ireland and 15 voted against this opposition (Hansard), 20 June 2000.

13 Fearon, p. 63.

14 Eilish Rooney and Margaret Woods, *Women, Community and Politics in Northern Ireland: A Belfast Study* (University of Ulster, Belfast), 1995, p. vii.

15 Fearon, p. 148.

16 Ruth Lister, *Citizenship: Feminist Perspectives* (Macmillan Press Ltd, Basingstoke), 1997, p. 157.

17 Ibid., p. 157.

18 Women's Resource and Development Agency, *Women and Citizenship: Power, Participation and Choice* (WRDA, Belfast), 1995, p. 17.

19 Roisin McDonough, 'Independence or Integration?' in Kate Fearon (ed), *Power, Politics, Positionings – Women in Northern Ireland* (Democratic Dialogue, Belfast), 1996, http://cain.ulst.ac.uk/dd/report4/report4e.htm.

20 Becky Gill, *Winning Women: Lessons from Scotland and Wales* (Fawcett, London), 1999, p. 24.

21 Ibid., p. 24.

22 Ibid., p. 25.

23 Van Leeuwen, pp. 113–14. This example is taken from her own field work in West Africa.

24 Ibid., p. 115.

25 Further, the norm has also functioned on the assumption that women will be responsible for issues of care, nurture and other domestic needs. Hence, on the whole, the men who participate in this norm have done so without needing to occupy themselves to the same extent with such concerns.

26 Carmel Roulston, 'Democracy and the Challenge of Gender: New Visions, New Processes', in Carmel Roulston

and Celia Davies (eds), *Gender, Democracy and Inclusion in Northern Ireland* (Palgrave, Basingstoke), 2000, p. 30.

27 Carol E. Becker, *Leading Women. How Church Women Can Avoid Traps and Negotiate the Gender Maze* (Abingdon, Nashville), 1996, p. 94.

28 Known respectively as the dual cultures perspective or difference model, and the dominance approach. For a consideration of these two approaches see Margaret Gibbon, *Feminist Perspectives on Language* (Longman, London and New York), 1999, especially chapters six and seven; and Leonora Tubbs Tisdale, 'Women's Ways of Communicating: A New Blessing for Preaching', in Jane Dempsey Douglass and James F. Kay (eds) *Women, Gender and Christian Community* (Westminster John Knox Press, Louisville, Kentucky), 1997.

29 Certainly comments of the other interviewees about men presuming that women would follow their leadership would support the view that power relationships are involved.

30 Jean Baker Miller has argued that feminine intuition or (more negatively) feminine wiles results from women as subordinates being attuned to men as dominates in order to be able to predict their pleasure/displeasure. Intuition is therefore not a mysterious gift, but one of many skills 'developed through long practice, in reading small signals, both verbal and non-verbal'. Jean Baker Miller, *Towards a New Psychology of Women*, 2nd edition (Penguin, London), 1991, p. 10.

31 For example, differences between women and men may be celebrated as diversity within the unity of humanity: 'One humanity, one unified image of God, but two sexually distinct embodiments'. Van Leeuwen, p. 213. Think also of the difference Daphne Hampson's choice of the phrase 'neighbouring sex' rather than 'opposite sex' makes when considering the relationship between women and men. Daphne Hampson, *After Christianity* (SCM, London), 1996, p. 77. Miroslav Volf proposes that rather than either attempting to erase gender differences or synthesising them, women's and men's personal identities

should be unthinkable without each in some way including the other. See Miroslav Volf, *Exclusion and Embrace: A Theological Exploration of Identity, Otherness, and Reconciliation* (Abingdon, Nashville), 1996, chapter 4.

32 Becker, p. 132.

33 Ibid., p. 130.

34 This is a reference to a common form of head-covering used in churches that advocates women covering their heads in church as a sign of their submission to men. See chapter five.

35 For example, in regard to women participating in politics on the basis of the different contribution they bring arising out of their domestic concerns, 'women can make a difference by celebrating stereotypically modernist virtues which distinguish them from men and yet which are largely man-made'. Rick Wilford, Robert Miller, Yolanda Bell, and Freda Donoghue, 'In Their Own Voices: Women Councillors in Northern Ireland', *Public Administration*, 1993, 71 (3), p. 344.

CHAPTER 5

1 Andrew Perriman, *Speaking of Women: Interpreting Paul* (Leicester, Apollos), 1998, p. 13.

2 Elaine Storkey, *Created or Constructed? The Great Gender Debate* (Paternoster Press, Cumbria), 2000, pp. 88–9.

3 These are perhaps best represented by two North American organisations. Christians for Biblical Equality (CBE) was formed in 1986 and advocates theological and social equality. The Council on Biblical Manhood and Womanhood (CBMW) arose in response to the growing awareness of views expressed by CBE, stating one of their concerns as the 'increasing promotion given to feminist egalitarianism with accompanying distortions or neglect of the glad harmony portrayed in Scripture between the living, humble leadership of redeemed husbands and the intelligent, willing support of that leadership by redeemed wives'. CBMW's *1988 Danvers Statement* in John Piper and Wayne Grudem (eds), *Recovering Biblical Manhood and Womanhood. A Response to Evangelical Feminism* (Crossway, Wheaton, Illinois), 1991, p. 469.

4   Perriman, p. 12.

5   These are the terms used by Wilard Swartley, *Slavery, Sabbath, War and Women* (Herald Press, Scottdale, PA), 1983.

6   John Martin, *Gospel People? Evangelicals and the Future of Anglicanism* (SPCK, London), 1997, p. 112.

7   R.T. France, *Women in the Church's Ministry. A Test Case for Biblical Hermeneutics* (Paternoster, Carlisle), 1995, pp. 38–9.

8   John 3:3, 7.

9   See, for example, Merrill C. Tenney, 'The Gospel of John' in Frank E. Gaebelein (ed), *The Expositor's Bible Commentary* (Pickering and Inglis, London), 1981, p. 47; and C.K. Barrett, *The Gospel According to St John* (SPCK, London), 2nd edition, 1978, pp. 205–6.

10   While most evangelicals would be aware of the principal verse from which this phrase comes (John 3:3), they are probably more familiar with the idea of being born again than the concept of the kingdom of God which is also referred to in this verse and frequently throughout the gospels, and yet which usually receives far less attention.

11   France, p. 13.

12   A thorough presentation of the case for male authority is made in Piper and Grudem. A shorter presentation that its author acknowledges owes much to this publication can be found in John Benton's *Gender Questions. Biblical Manhood and Womanhood in the Contemporary World* (Evangelical Press, Darlington), 2000. Arguments against male authority are found in Mary Evans, *Woman in the Bible* (Paternoster, Exeter), 1983 and Alvera Mickelsen (ed), *Woman, Authority and the Bible* (Marshall Pickering, Basingstoke), 1987. A shorter discussion is available in France. See also, Marilyn B. (Lynn) Smith, *Gender or Giftedness: A challenge to rethink the basis for leadership within the Christian community*, A study on the Role of Women prepared for the Commission on Women's Concerns of the World Evangelical Fellowship, 2000.

13   This quotation is from the NIV. The NRSV used on other occasions in this book translates this 'the husband is the head of his wife'. See further below in the case against male authority.

14   Ephesians 5:21–33.

15   1 Corinthians 11:2–16.

16   1 Corinthians 11:10.

17   Thomas R. Schreiner, 'Head Coverings, Prophecies and the Trinity. 1 Corinthians 11:2–16', in Piper and Grudem, p. 125.

18   Schreiner, p. 138.

19   Particularly Ephesians 1:22; Colossians 2:10, but also Colossians 1:18; 2:19 and Ephesians 4:15.

20   1 Peter 3:1–7.

21   Genesis 1:26–8.

22   Benton, p. 38.

23   Raymond C. Ortlund, 'Male–Female Equality and Male Headship. Genesis 1–3', in Piper and Grudem, p. 98. John Benton comments that God describes himself 'almost exclusively' in male terms not because the male is more in God's image than the woman, but because 'God is so masculine in his work, his power, in his sacrifice', that is, in taking the initiative in creation and redemption. Benton, pp. 42–3.

24   Ortlund, p. 102.

25   Linda Ann McClaughlin, *A Critical Analysis of the Biblical Teaching on the Status and Role of Women*, MPhil Thesis, Queen's University, Belfast, 2001, p. 26.

26   1 Timothy 2:11–15.

27   1 Timothy 2:12.

28   1 Timothy 2:13–14.

29   1 Corinthians 14:34–5.

30   John Stott, *New Issues Facing Christians Today*, 3rd edition, (Marshall Pickering, London), 1999, p. 314.

31   Proponents are keen to underline this as a positive feature while opponents of this view see this as part of the problem.

32   J.I. Packer, 'Understanding the Differences', in Alvera Mickelsen (ed), *Women, Authority and The Bible* (Marshall Pickering, Basingstoke), 1987, p. 298.

33   Ibid., p. 299.

34   Ian R.K. Paisley, 'The Free Presbyterian Church of Ulster', in Norman Richardson (ed), *A Tapestry of Beliefs: Christian Traditions in Northern Ireland* (Blackstaff, Belfast), 1998, pp. 128–9.

35   It can be argued that while the view of spiritual inequality is not taught, the practical outworking in some parts of evangelicalism of a view of male headship communicates female inequality without the need for words,

and in some cases, despite the statement of spiritual equality.

36 Galatians 3:28.

37 Evans, p. 65.

38 Gretchen Gaebelein Hull, *Equal to Serve. Women and Men in the Church and Home* (Scripture Union, London), 1987, p. 195.

39 Perriman, p. 32.

40 Ibid., p. 31.

41 Ibid., p. 33.

42 See France.

43 Evans, p. 76. Mary Evans also argues that this is further supported by a strong 'but' that begins verse 24 (although obscured by most translations) that renders the text, 'The husband is the head of the wife... But just as the church is subject to Christ, so also wives ought to be ... to their husbands.' The 'but' makes little sense if 'head' denotes authority. In such a case 'therefore' rather than 'but' would be more applicable (p. 67).

44 Ephesians 5:21.

45 1 Corinthians 7:3–4.

46 Even some of those who support a view of male authority agree with this reading, although they do not believe it to detract from male authority over women.

47 1 Corinthians 7:3–4 and 11:10 use *exousia*. 1 Timothy 2:12 uses *authentein*.

48 France, p. 66.

49 1 Timothy 2:13–14.

50 1 Timothy 2:14.

51 Romans 5:12–21.

52 2 Corinthians 11:3.

53 Phyllis Trible, *God and the Rhetoric of Sexuality* (SCM, London), 1978, p. 19.

54 Genesis 2:19 offers a different order of creation, with the animals and birds depicted as made after the man. This would affirm male priority in an order of creation argument, but diminish women's personhood in that the woman was made after the animals and birds.

55 Trible, p. 90.

56 Andrew Kirk, 'Theology from a Feminist Perspective' in Kathy Keay (ed), *Men, Women and God* (Marshall Pickering, Basingstoke), 1987, p. 30.

57 Genesis 16:13.

58 1 Corinthians 11: 11–12.

59 Acts 2:1-4, 17–18.

60 Acts 1:14; 1 Corinthians 11:5; 1 Timothy 2:8–10.

61 Acts 21:9; 1 Corinthians 11:5.

62 Acts 6:5.

63 Priscilla, described as one of Paul's co-workers in Romans 16:34, is mentioned in particular as instructing Apollos (Acts 18:24–6). The tendency to put her name before her husband's when the two are mentioned (Acts 18:18, 26; Romans 16:3; 2 Timothy 4:19) suggests she was the more prominent, either because of her social standing or her ministry in the church.

64 Lydia in Acts 16:40; Prisca (Priscilla) in 1 Corinthians 16:19 and Romans 16:3–5; Nympha in Colossians 4:15.

65 Philippians 4:2–3. In the letter to the church at Philippi, a church that began in the home of Lydia, and of which Euodia and Syntyche were a part, there is no indication of any restriction on women's involvement.

66 Romans 16:7.

67 1 Timothy 3:11.

68 Perriman, p. 83.

69 This view has been criticised as being anti-Jewish and based on a failure to distinguish between official records and actual practice and the use of material post-dating the time of Jesus. Perhaps the most pertinent question is Jesus' treatment of women in comparison not to his own time, but to the practice of the contemporary church.

70 Matthew 27:55–6; Luke 8:1–3, 10:38–41, 24:10; John 4:28–9, 39; 20:17–18.

71 Male chauvinist pigs.

72 Christel Manning, *God Gave Us the Right: Conservative Catholic, Evangelical Protestant, and Orthodox Jewish Women Grapple with Feminism* (Rutgers University Press, New Brunswick, New Jersey and London), 1999, p. 125.

73 While this man did not have any objections with women teaching boys in Sunday school, another male church leader remarked that he knew of other ordained men who say that women should not even do this.

74 Mark Chaves, *Ordaining Women: Culture and Conflict in Religious Organizations* (Harvard University Press, Cambridge, MA), 1999, p. 25.

75 France, p. 27–8.

76 Carol E. Becker, *Leading Women. How Church Women Can Avoid Traps and Negotiate the Gender Maze* (Abingdon, Nashville), 1996, p. 85.

CHAPTER 6

1 Ruth Lister, *Citizenship: Feminist Perspectives* (Macmillan Press Ltd, Basingstoke), 1997, p. 119.
2 Gaby Wood, 'Call Me a Feminist', *The Observer Review*, 16 September 2001, p. 2.
3 Results obtained from the Northern Ireland Life and Times Survey website at www.qub.ac.uk/ss/crs/nilt.
4 This figure is a combination of the two responses of 'strongly agree' and 'agree'.
5 Celia Davies, and Aine Downey, 'Women's Rights or Responsibilities? Reconciling the demands of home and work', in Peter Stringer and Gillian Robinson (eds), *Social Attitudes in Northern Ireland: The Third Report* (Blackstaff, Belfast), 1993, pp. 49–64.
6 Equal Opportunities Commission for Northern Ireland, *Where Do Women Figure?* (EOCNI, Belfast), 1999.
7 Rick Wilford, Robert Miller, Yolanda Bell, and Freda Donoghue, 'In Their Own Voices: Women Councillors in Northern Ireland', *Public Administration*, 1993, 71 (3), p. 345.
8 Ibid., p. 346.
9 Yvonne Galligan and Rick Wilford, 'Gender and Party Politics in Northern Ireland', in Yvonne Galligan, Eilís Ward and Rick Wilford (eds), *Contesting Politics: Women in Ireland, North and South* (Westview Press, Oxford), 1999, p. 182.
10 Bonnie J. Miller-McLemore, *Also a Mother: Work and Family as Theological Dilemma* (Abingdon Press, Nashville), 1994, p. 39.
11 Equal Opportunities Commission, *Women and Men in Britain: The Work–Life Balance* (EOC, Manchester), 2000, p. 1.
12 Miller-McLemore, p. 82.
13 Robert L. Miller, Rick Wilford, and Freda Donoghue, *Women and Political Participation in Northern Ireland* (Avebury, Aldershot), 1996, p. 166.
14 Germaine Greer, *The Whole Woman* (Anchor, London), 1999, p. 79.
15 Margaret Gibbon, *Feminist Perspectives on Language* (Longman, London and New York), 1999, p. 62.

16 Ibid., p. 92.
17 Monica McWilliams and Avila Kilmurray, 'Athene on the Loose', *Irish Journal of Feminist Studies*, 1997, Vol. 2, No. 1, p. 19.
18 Steven King, 'What have we got against women in politics?' *Belfast Telegraph*, 13 March 2001.
19 Miller-McLemore, p. 126.
20 Ibid., p. 195.

CHAPTER 7

1 Kate Fearon comments on the irony of Seamus Mallon of the SDLP suggesting the NIWC was in danger of becoming a single-issue party which would grow in on itself rather than expand and kill itself off. See 'Painting the Picture' in Kate Fearon (ed), *Power, Politics, Positionings – Women in Northern Ireland* (Democratic Dialogue, Belfast), 1996, website: cain.ulst.ac.uk/dd/report4/report4e.htm.
2 Fionnuala O'Connor, *In Search of a State: Catholics in Northern Ireland* (Blackstaff, Belfast), 1993, p. 346.
3 Carmel Roulston, 'Women on the Margin: The Women's Movement in Northern Ireland, 1973–1995' in L.A. West (ed), *Feminist Nationalism* (Routledge, London), 1997, p. 57.
4 Kate Fearon, *Women's Work: The Story of the Northern Ireland Women's Coalition* (Blackstaff, Belfast), 1999, p. 18.
5 Glenn Jordan, *Not of this World? Evangelical Protestants in Northern Ireland* (Blackstaff and Centre for Contemporary Christianity in Ireland, Belfast), 2001, p. 78.
6 Sometimes it was simply that the woman was younger than those with whom she worked. Hence, one forty-year-old woman spoke of being described as 'the wee girl'.
7 See the discussion in chapter three.
8 Jane Shaw, 'How Unlike God', *Third Way*, November 2001, Vol. 24, No. 8, pp. 24–6, pp. 25, 26.
9 Supporting this approach is the belief, held by some and refuted by others, that a just cause will receive a fair hearing if presented in inoffensive ways.
10 Expressions from two women interviewed.
11 Expressions from a male church leader.

Index